TAUT LINES

EXTRAORDINARY TRUE FISHING STORIES

EDITED BY
CAMERON PIERCE

ROBINSON

ROBINSON

First published in Great Britain in 2016 by Robinson

1 3 5 7 9 10 8 6 4 2

Introduction and selection copyright © Cameron Pierce, 2016
Line drawings by Jim Agpalza

A CIP catalogue record for this book
is available from the British Library.

ISBN 978-1-47213-667-1 (paperback)

Typeset in Great Britain by SX Composing DTP, Rayleigh, Essex
Printed and bound in Great Britain by Clays Ltd, St Ives plc

Papers used by Robinson are from well-managed forests
and other responsible sources

MIX
Paper from
responsible sources
FSC® C104740

Robinson
is an imprint of
Little, Brown Book Group
Carmelite House
50 Victoria Embankment
London EC4Y 0DZ

An Hachette UK Company
www.hachette.co.uk

www.littlebrown.co.uk

TAUT LINES

EXTRAORDINARY TRUE FISHING STORIES

Contents

All the Great and Beautiful Fishes:

AN INTRODUCTION BY CAMERON PIERCE

HALLOWEEN PASSES AND the first heavy rains bring water to the basement. My north coast home sits atop a natural aquifer that feeds a seasonal creek down the hill. The creek is nameless, fishless. Naturally, so is the aquifer beneath my house, but when the basement floods, I can't help imagining subterranean fish lurking beneath the cracked concrete foundation.

Fishing is one of the earliest subjects of literature. Since the earliest writings of civilization, humans have been writing about fish and the pursuit of them. *Taut Lines* is a book of the present with regular forays into the past, reflecting not on where we're going, but where we've come from.

With winter steelhead season looming and most other fishing seasons either winding down or closed, autumn is the time when I reflect back on the months and days that have passed, and the fishing I have done. This year, my first living on the Oregon coast, I tussled with twenty-three different species of fish. White sturgeon, which I targeted and caught more frequently than any other fish while living in the city, are not among my catch this year. The fish that stand out most vividly include my first sea-run cutthroat, a two-hundred-pound ragged-tooth shark caught at the mouth of the Great Fish River in South Africa, and a freezer full of Chinook salmon, but smaller quarry leaves an equally powerful imprint: a peamouth chub taken from the pool beneath a waterfall, a fish streaked orange and red, its spawning colors, a sixteen-inch rainbow trout taken in January, turned into the best trout sandwiches in the world, and some of the brightest, most beautifully colored bass and panfish

1

I have ever caught, taken while kayak angling on a remote forest lake. And then there are the individual days that I still relive in my mind, going out on Puget Sound in a friend's boat and limiting out on enormous Dungeness crabs, then proceeding to catch a mess of flounder and other bottomfish; landing eight different species and over thirty fish in two hours on a quiet spring afternoon, no one else on the lake but me; catching and releasing various populations of wild cutthroats and rainbows from small streams.

As an enthusiast of all fish and all bodies of water, I have attempted to incorporate my love of variety into this book. But as all anglers know, the fish themselves are only half of fishing. Finding peace, spirituality, or a sense of belonging in nature; the meditative tranquility that settles into the mind and body as you cast into the waters for hours on end; the companionship or, alternately, the solitude: these are some of the things that hook anglers as much as the fish. They are all explored in this book. Some of them may even inspire your next great fishing adventure or, if you're presently between fishing seasons as I am, hopefully they'll tide you over until your next day on the water. In the name of variety, I have extended coverage to some fishes typically overlooked in fishing anthologies, up to the great white shark from *Jaws*, the most famous (and feared) fish in all of film and literature.

There are as many types of fishing literature as there are fishermen. Among the most beloved books of my childhood was an anthology of humorous stories about the follies that inevitably plague anglers. Several stories of this type are found in *Taut Lines*, including Rudyard Kipling's 'On Dry-Cow Fishing as a Fine Art' and Eric Witchey's 'Bats, Bushes, and Barbless Hooks.' Fishing is more than folly, however, and so many of the stories tackle more personal and profound subjects. Kevin Maloney's 'Soldiers By the Side of the Road,' Gretchen Legler's 'Border Water,' and Gabino Iglesias's 'Fourteen Pounds Against the World' are just three of many heartbreaking essays which prove that while fishing is an effective medicine for grief and loss, it can also lead to contemplations of death and mortality, both the fish's and our own. A passion for angling is most often passed down through families, and so many of the pieces in *Taut Lines* examine familial dynamics in relation to fishing, like 'Fish' by Judith Barrington and 'Unsound' by Nick Mamatas. There are great stories of big fish by angling legends such as Jeremy Wade, Bill Heavey, and Zane Grey, along with Tele Aadsen's daring story of rescue, 'The Man in the Fish Tote', and Weston Ochse's moving account of war and longing, 'I Used to Be a Fisherman'. This collection also features a modernized version of the first text written about sportfishing, 'Treatise of Fishing with an Angle' by Dame Juliana Berners and 'Fishing for a Cat' by Francis W. Mather, perhaps the earliest known essay devoted to catfish angling. There are also some long-lost classics, like former *Atlantic* editor Bliss Perry's 'Fishing with a Worm.' From trout fishing in Africa to salmon fishing in Ireland, *Taut Lines* contains a little of every type of angling experience.

Above all, *Taut Lines* is a book of extraordinary true fishing stories. Whether you're well-acquainted with Izaak Walton or this is your first time wading the waters of fishing literature, I hope you enjoy these stories as much as I do. All of them, to me, are classics in their own right. Strange, heartbreaking, whimsical, instructional, or whatever the case may be, they can all be read again and again.

Now the rain falls heavy and soon the steelhead will return from the ocean to their spawning grounds, some of them navigating small rocky creeks. I'll spend the next few months on these waters, occasionally catching fish, but mostly reveling in the frigid beauty of winter. And when the rivers and creeks are too blown out to fish, I'll be holed up inside, revisiting the stories in *Taut Lines*, dreaming of my return to the water, for after winter steelhead season comes the trout opener, and after the trout opener the bass and perch will come in shallow to spawn. After that, the opportunities in the rivers, lakes, and seas will be almost overwhelming, and new fishing stories will be born on the water, some of triumph, others of loss. Anglers' lives are lived by the stories they tell and tell again. Here's to the wealth of extraordinary fishing stories already told. May they be remembered forever, and may you make many of your own.

Taut lines,

Cameron Pierce
Astoria, Oregon

Why I Fish

KIM BARNES

I

IT'S NOT THE first time I've been fishing, I'm sure, although I'm only four. It's 1962, and I live in the Clearwater National Forest of Idaho, with my mother and father and younger brother, surrounded by my uncles and aunts and cousins, all of us in our one-room wooden trailers that are circled in a creek-threaded meadow we call Pole Camp – not as in fishing poles (it will be years before I hear them called 'rods'), but as in the cedar poles the men fell and skid to earn their daily wage. They are gyppos, from the word gypsy, and like the Roma people, we are nomads, itinerant, our self-built 8 x 20 shacks fitted with wheels and tires and a heavy tongue that allows them to be hitched from site to site. We set up our camps near springs and creeks and the North Fork of the Clearwater River – this, our only running water. No electricity, but in the communal wash shed is a wood stove that, when kindled, heats a high-hung tankful, enough for a quick shower. I love standing with my mother beneath the warm spray, the miracle of it raining down.

But, today, I am in the company of my uncle, the youngest of the four Barnes brothers who left the impoverishment of sharecropping in Oklahoma for the impoverishment of cutting poles in Idaho, where they make up the crew of their uncle's family operation. 'No man should go hungry here,' their uncle has told them, remembering the Dust Bowl, the Great Depression, and it is true, just as it is true that hunger itself is relative. In another few weeks, we will fill our town lockers with huckleberries, and, in another, the venison we take each fall. The fish we catch the women will fry for breakfast, for lunch, for dinner, or they will slip them into milk cartons, and all through the winter, I will study them there, caught in a frozen current of ice.

Today, my uncle and I stay close to home, fishing the narrow reaches of Deer Creek, which drains the meadow, parallels the narrow road. The day is hot, and we stop at a road-side spring to dip our hands in the water and drink. Sawbugs cut the quiet, their summer buzz a reminder that the woods are tinder-dry, that the men must rise in the dark and work with the dew lest the spark of their work set the forest aflame. 'Hoot-owling,' they call it, and it is why I have these afternoon hours with my uncle to fish.

But it is not the fishing itself that will remain with me - not the worm on the hook, the tug on the line – but how I work so hard to be silent, stay still, the feel of the sun on my shoulders, the powder-fine dust that sparkles the air, the smell of tarweed and pine. There is the fork of a willow branch strung with brookies, and I am proud that at least one of them is mine. None of them is over eight inches, but we keep all but the smallest because pan-size are the sweetest, my uncle says, just right for the skillet. Some part of me must know that food on the table isn't a given, that you take what you can get, and that, today, the getting is good.

My uncle teaches me that what I catch, I clean, and so we squat low at the bank, and I learn the sharpness of a knife from vent to gill, how to thumb-strip the blood from the spine. I throw the guts to the orange-mottled crawdads that skitter from beneath the rocks. When I rinse the fish clean, they smell like the water, like mineral and silt. When we carry them back into camp, I am showered with praise – I have added to our family's bounty. Dusted in flour, fried in lard, the brookies come to the table salty and crisp, and this is another lesson I learn early on: how to peel the delicate skin, separate the meat from the tiniest bones. Fried spuds on the side, a peach cobbler in the oven, a pitcher of sweet tea – I am blessed in that circle of family as the larch and fir cast their shadows across the creek and fish dimple the surface for stonefly, caddis, mosquito, and midge. Maybe, even then, there was something in me rising with them.

II

THE NORTH FORK drains into the main Clearwater and weaves its way through the arid canyon to Lewiston, Idaho, where it meets the Snake and continues on to the Columbia. Rainbow and cutthroat run these waters.

What salmon and steelhead remain beat their way past the dams to spawn, as do the last of the lamprey eels that once draped the Nez Perce drying racks, the oily meat one more stay against the deprivation of winter.

On this day, I am twenty-something, two years into my college degree, living on cases of Top Ramen and three-for-a-buck macaroni-and-cheese. I am in the first throes of what will become a life-long love: Bob, my new beau, fishes beside me. Since my family moved from the logging camps to Lewiston, I have chosen my boyfriends according to their affinity for hunting, fishing, and camping, judged them by their ability to rig a rod, pitch a tent, and build a campfire, attempting, perhaps, to reclaim some part of that childhood I have lost. I have fished the nearby creeks and rivers and lakes, wetting everything from night crawlers (pulled from the soaked lawn the night before) to Jolly Green Giant cans of corn (nothing but Niblets will do) to wedding-band spinners, Rooster Tails, Mr. Twisters, and Kastmasters the size of hubcaps (excellent for reaching the far current of a river as big as the Clearwater). I have learned that you know a fisherman by the tackle box he keeps (I am the only woman I know who keeps one), and I am housewife-proud of mine with its sharpened hooks and spinners shined with four-ought steel wool, just as I am proud of the steelhead eggs I have harvested and cured myself (an atomic red jar of Pautzke Balls o' Fire for backup). Somehow, all this gear, the care and preparation, make me feel worthy of the fish I keep, as though my ablutions purify my intent.

Bob and I stand in the blistering heat, choosing our spots – mine at the mouth of a stream that feeds into the river. Over the years, I have learned to read water like I first learned to read books – instinctively, as though the ability were innate, part of my chromosomal map – and I know that the trout will be feeding there. Bob fishes thirty yards upstream. An Illinois flatlander by birth, a mountain-loving Westerner by choice, he came to the relationship still lugging his Plano of bass plugs, jigs, and poppers. He has his Eagle Claw, I have my Fenwick, this is our first time fishing together, and although we don't say so, we both know the challenge is on.

I wade out as far as I dare, the bald tread of my tennis shoes no help, and take up my cast. A few ten-inchers hit my Red Devil, and I drag them in, thread them on the stringer – that night's dinner. But I know there are bigger fish to fry. I pull out my largest Kastmaster, spit on my line for luck, wind up, and pitch like I am throwing for home. The filament shoots out, and I love the steady pull, how far the lure will take me. When it drops, I let it sink to a count of five, set my bail, and begin reeling in.

You know the saying, don't you? Big water, big lure, big fish. A Rainbow the size of a steelhead hits hard, and I work hard to land it, the muscles of my arms aching until I can drag the fish ashore. My blood is singing in my ears and a fine sweat has broken out across my chest by the time Bob reaches me. I hold up the treble-hooked fish with both hands and wait for his praise.

'Nice fish,' Bob says, and then, 'Better throw it back.'

'What?'

'Throw it back. He's too nice to keep.'

I look down at my beautiful catch, his brilliant pattern of colors – the consummate keeper.

'He's three meals, at least,' I say, but what I am thinking is, *You're just jealous.*

'He's good stock,' Bob reasons. 'He needs to stay in the gene pool.'

I stare at Bob as though he has taken leave of his senses. To turn the fish loose would be like throwing a meaty T-bone to the dogs. Who knows when such food might be on the table again?

And here is the thing: I don't remember what I did with that fish, if I kept him and ate him or released him back into the waters I have known since birth. What I know for sure is that it wasn't the last time I would be hungry, but that the hungry times would themselves grow leaner, become fewer and farther between.

When, two years later, Bob and I married, our honeymoon was a road trip to the Izaak Walton Inn in Essex, Montana. I remember how cold it was, even in July, and I remember bundling in my coat and crossing the road to the Middle Fork of the Flathead River, how I was mesmerized by its color – as though a turquoise glacier had bled its water down. I had my new husband there with me, we had our little pickup stuffed to the gills with everything we would need to camp and backpack our way across the state for a month, but the thought of dropping a Kastmaster into that crystalline water seemed suddenly profane. Still, the absence of the rod in my hands was like a phantom pain, as though I had lost my right arm. It was a different kind of hunger that I felt, then. It had nothing to do with food but with a desire to know that water, to feel its rush all around me, to see what secrets I might pull from its hold.

III

ANOTHER RIVER, so close to my childhood home at Pole Camp that a crow could fly there in an hour. The dry dust of summer, the cold water at my knees – all of it familiar and where I always want to be.

I've traded my tackle box of Kastmasters and Pautzkes for a dank vest whose pockets are stuffed with more terrestrials than any one angler will need in a lifetime. Somehow, I'm sure that today's hatch will be the very pattern I don't have, and the thought brings with it a tremor of panic. Caddis in every possible stage, mayflies of every material, midges so small that they defy tying, stimulators so large and flamboyant that they sail through the air like neon canaries – my eyes are bigger than my stomach, it seems, when it comes to these bits of feather and fur, my dead grandmother's sibylic words still echoing: *Lean times just around the corner, sister – you can never have too much stock in the larder.*

Bob and I have been angling these waters for years now, dry-camping for weeks with nothing to do but eat, fish, eat, read our way through the heat of the day (Bob with his slender volumes of poetry or his go-to summer fare of James Lee Burke and Evelyn Waugh, while I critique a friend's new novel manuscript or maybe revisit, as I do each year – and this is true – *The Old Man and the Sea*), fish, eat, drink wine, and fish before falling asleep beneath the stars. I can't remember exactly when we put down our poles and took up our rods, but I know that, even after nearly two decades, we are still learning – learning how to present the fly, how to mend the line, how to roll-cast, back-cast, double-haul . . . how to shoot the line rather than lob the lure. In my worn waders and boots, I stumble and slide across the free-stone bed, curse wind knots and the tangled nest of line my cast becomes when I miss a strike and jerk the rod back as though I were setting the hook in stone.

Evening is coming on, and we're at the end of a long trek – hours of walking up the trail and fishing our way back down the river – and our take-out point is just around the bend. I'm tired, my lower back is aching, but I'm happy half-in, half-out of the water, where I somehow feel most whole. We've had a good day – net-fillers but nothing that we might brag about around our nightly fire. The river has gone to shadow, and the chill in the air is real. I shiver, remind myself to look up and around, to cast my eyes to the wooded flanks of the mountains, the patches of meadow that catch the alpenglow in an otherworldly light. I cross the shallows to better access the far bank, where an aged stump tips toward the water, its roots a catacomb of places a trout might rest.

If you are an angler, you know this feeling, you know that there, right *there*, a big fish resides. You believe that if you do everything just right – if you are smart enough, careful enough, patient enough, if you are true of spirit and pure of heart – the fish will rise.

I have learned enough to take my time, to study the wind, the water, the drag, the drift. Maybe I have been fishing a Humpy, or maybe a hopper – but the shadows are deepening, the air gone cool, and I can feel that fish wanting something, feel him *hungry* for something that I might have. I rifle my pockets and patches, my magnetic tins and compartmentalized cases, but nothing seems right, not even the fairest Pale Evening Duns, the most minute of midges. I look to Bob, who fishes the river above me, his easy S-cast that I envy. In the past, I had tied my arm to the butt of my rod but to no avail – I have yet to break the habit of breaking my wrist. If this is my last cast of the day, I tell myself, I have to make it good.

I remember what a veteran angler once told me about fishing these waters. 'What are you using?' I had asked after watching him net a fat cutthroat. 'Nothing but elk-hair caddis,' he said. 'It's the only fly I carry.' I had flushed with embarrassment at my own trove of tied treasures, no less burdensome than the twenty pounds of tackle I once lugged. Still, when I open my pocket, there it is: a #12 elk-wing whose blonde hairs will make it easier to see in the graying light. I tie it on with great concentration, then position myself in the box of water below a large stone. Be patient, I tell myself and let my back-cast unfurl, the line haul out ten feet, then twenty.

And you know this story, too, or maybe this dream: the fly delicately dropping to the current just upstream of the stump, the drift dangerously close to the sun-silvered roots, and then the noise that isn't noise but the fish coming straight up out of the water like a Polaris missile (silly, I know, but these are the words that come to me). In my memory, it happens in a flash of golden light, the scarlet gill stripes and burnished sides, the thick body of him and the mouth – my god, I think, the size of that *mouth* – and then our two worlds are tethered.

Five/six rod, four-pound test, that impossible barbless hook – how can I hope to hold on? Down the river he runs, my line zinging off the spool until I fear we'll be into the backing. And then the pause, the steady dead weight like a snagged log, the reconnoitering. *Keep your rod up*, I remind myself, but its supple spine is bent to the point of breaking. And then that almost imperceptible easing up, a second's give when I can take back an inch, and then another.

By now, Bob has looked up, is curious, is watching, but I can't take my eyes off that place where my line meets the water. When I move, the fish moves with me, then darts to the side and sounds, nosing in against stone. What can

I do but hold on? When I work him around, urge him back into the swift current, he makes a streaking attempt to blow by me upstream . . . and so it goes, five minutes, then ten. Bob keeps his distance, afraid he'll spook the fish, but after another few minutes, the muscles of my arms begin to spasm. I want to call for him to help me, tell him that I can't get this fish in – not with this ludicrous rod, this fly with its insufficient hook. 'It's me and you, fish,' I say under my breath, but I am no Santiago, and this is no monstrous marlin but a Westslope Cutthroat grown bigger than most. I begin to growl as I prop my elbows on my hips and arch back, reel in, arch back. My entire body is shaking from the adrenalin, the effort as though my very life depended on landing this fish – as though I might starve to death if I don't have him. But he is the one whose hunger has brought him to this place, who is fighting for his life, and by the time I draw him close, we are both exhausted.

I plow the net, use both hands to raise it, but I'm shaking so hard that I can't slip the hook. I tell him how beautiful he is, tell him to hang on, just a minute longer as I slog to the bank where I can lay down my rod and work him free. I cradle him in the current, move him to and fro, work his gills, croon to him because that is what comes to me to do. He's as long as my arm, from my shoulder to the tip of my longest finger – he would feed my entire family, I think as I rock him in my hands, feel him pulse once, then again. He flexes the muscle of his body, and then he is gone, lost to the river's shadows, taking some part of me with him, and I am glad.

I haven't forgotten what hunger feels like – not *that* kind of hunger – but I haven't felt it for a long time. I step from the river, replete. I know that Bob and I will return to our camp, take our tepid showers beneath the limb of a white pine – nothing more than a strung-up jug of warmed water, a hose, a nozzle – that we will make a fine dinner in our open-air kitchen and tell the story of this fish and then tell it again, the story itself my Horn of Plenty. All winter, as the snow deepens and the river's seams meld to ice, I will dream my larder full.

Crossing Lines: Art, Meat, and Enlightenment in American Sport Fishing

HENRY HUGHES

O N A GRAY October morning, Bob Fultz and I motor his drift boat up the Salmon River, north of Lincoln City, Oregon. Three miles from the sea in the deep narrows, the river has a marbled turbidity, sheened here and there with oil from dozens of motorboats anchored or maneuvering into every hole. A boy in a small pram holds up a blood-streaked Chinook salmon for a photo, while a man in a new sled boat – the name *Blood Sport* stenciled on the hull – fights a big fish, his rod bending and pulsing, his friend waiting eagerly with a wide net. I can hear the whine of the man's drag as the fish makes a fierce run, tangles in another boat's anchor line, and snaps off. 'Fucking shit!' the fisherman yells across the river. When he turns, I see a pistol holstered to his hip. 'What's he gonna do?' I ask Bob. 'Shoot the fish?'

As we approach the bridge for Highway 101, the trampled, trash-strewn banks of the Salmon River are lined with more anglers slinging heavy globs of orange eggs under huge sliding bobbers or lead sinkers. Avoiding an oncoming boat, Bob steers us closer to the bank, rousing a large, flannel-coated man sitting on a cooler, smoking a cigarette. 'Better watch my line,' the man barks. Bob swings us away, and I lift my hand in a conciliatory wave. The man just stares. 'Goddamn boats,' I hear someone else grunt as an ounce of lead splashes beside us. When we clear the bridge, Bob shakes his head, saying, 'They're a rough crowd.'

Bob Fultz has been fishing the Salmon River for thirty years, and, though he's witnessed some ugly moments among the sportsmen, he can't deny the appeal of big fish concentrated in great numbers within a few well-known holes accessible to both bank and boat fishermen. It's fishing for the masses. In addition to being a natural run, the river boasts a hatchery four miles upriver that raises Chinook salmon, releasing the young smolts every August. After leaving the river and living up to five years at sea, these salmon return as what some locals call 'fall hogs.' They are magnificent creatures in silver and bronze, frequently leaping and rolling out of the water, making their way upriver to spawn.

Bob and I angle intensely for several hours, casting spinners and bait, eventually joining 'the hog line,' a ring of boats anchored around the Barn Hole, where I hook a torpedo. Bob and the anglers next to us reel up their lines to give me some fighting room. After a few minutes of deep dives and wild runs, she's in the net – a thirty-pound, chrome-bright chinook. Bob and I high-five and pop celebratory Budweisers. The older couple next to us nod admiringly. 'Real nice fish,' the woman says. 'You sure got supper for everybody.'

Bringing fish home for my family to eat is one of my earliest memories of childhood pride. I baited hooks with sandworms and caught flounder after flounder off a steel bulkhead in New York, within the roar of my father's crane, unloading gravel barges. My friends and I spent weekends in leaky boats on Long Island Sound, bottom fishing for flounder, fluke, porgies, and blackfish, or trolling through boiling schools of bluefish. We'd catch dozens of blues, giving fillets to neighbors and grilling the rest with sweet corn and clams for an August feast. In some ways, the very simplicity of those boyhood outings is pleasantly revisited on the Salmon River. 'You're getting in touch with your working-class roots,' a colleague at the university where I teach teases me.

One hundred and fifty miles east of the Salmon River, over the Santiam Pass into Central Oregon, lies the Metolius River. Emerging from springs at the basaltic base of Black Butte, the Metolius runs cold and clear through alpine forests some twenty-eight miles to Lake Billy Chinook. Walking into the pine-paneled country store at Camp Sherman in late October, I hear the woman behind the counter discussing the virtues of cane rods, while an older gentleman in a tweed jacket selects flies from the extensive display case. They speak Latin here. 'Are the *Drunella coloradensis* still hatching?' the man asks. 'Try a small paradrake or Bunse's natural dun,' responds the fluent attendant.

As for all civilized pursuits, there are considerable terms, protocols, and rules for fishing here. Only barbless hooks are permitted from Camp Sherman downstream to Bridge 99. Lead sinkers are prohibited. And no fish may be kept. Below the bridge, anglers may, in addition to flies, use artificial spinning lures, but the no-bait and catch-and-release policies cover the entire river. I couldn't help bemoaning that there would be no grilled trout to accompany the pinot gris I brought from the Willamette Valley.

There is, however, good reason to protect the fish of the Metolius. Unlike those in the Salmon River and in many other Oregon fisheries that are pumped up with hatchery offspring, the rainbow and bull trout of the Metolius are wild. For precarious and threatened populations of wild fish, catch-and-release policies are important management tools. The great sport angler Lee Wulff extended that idea, declaring, 'Game fish are too valuable to catch only once.' But many fly fishermen take the moral high ground, always release fish, and denounce eating any catch as crude, cruel, and ignorant of the higher art. Golf legend and avid fly fisherman, Jack Nicklaus, explained in a 2009 *Golf Digest* interview, 'I like to catch fish and release them. I probably haven't killed a fish that I've caught in sport fishing for twenty years. No reason to kill it.' The writer John McPhee, however, deflates the presumed nobility of catch-and-release devotions in his 2002 book, *Founding Fish*. 'I'm a meat fisherman,' McPhee says. 'I think it's immoral not to eat a fish you jerk around the river with a steel barb through the mouth. I see no other justification for doing so.'

Although the fish in the Metolius are wild, the land around the river has been tamed by educational signboards, campsites, cabins, and huge RVs. Driving the red cinder roads through the clean, thinned stands of ponderosa and lodgepole pine, one gets the sense that nature is managed but respected. I pull into a paved parking spot beside a new SUV, gather my gear, and walk down the well-worn path to the river. A man approaches a garbage can and tosses in a wrapper. 'How's the fishing?' I ask him. 'Tough,' he says. His name is Robert, and he's a physician from Bend who fishes the Metolius a few times every year. Given his Patagonia boots, waders, and wader jacket stuffed with Wheatley fly boxes, and his Simms vest and Filson hat, Robert must be wearing around two thousand dollars. His Sage rod and Abel reel might run another twelve hundred. But fly-fishing with even the best gear can humble a man, and Robert's manner is easy. 'I saw plenty of fish, but no takers.' Identifying a blue-winged olive hatch, he plied a sparkle dun until his arm got tired and his back ached. 'It's always great to be out here. If I get one or two fish, I'm happy.

But this is a very tough river.' When he asks me what's happening on the coast, I tell him about my Salmon River Chinook. 'You can have it,' Robert says. 'I don't want any part of that meat market.'

Fly fishing and catch-and-release-only restrictions have been placed on many rivers in the United States, and many proponents see correlations with angler behavior. Dorothy Schramm, founder of Flygirls of Michigan, insists 'we're much more comfortable and feel safer where there are gear restrictions.' Schramm distinguishes bait waters from fly waters – 'What we find in the fly water is manners and less swearing.' In the spinning and bait water 'it's the F-word every other word. There is trash . . . they build fires anywhere, and it's an awful experience.'

In popular culture, 'meat fishing,' catching fish to eat with spinning or conventional gear – and especially with the use of bait – is often associated with lower and middle class attitudes; catch-and-release fly-fishing is viewed as upper class. Spinning, bait casting, and trolling with heavy equipment are stereotyped as simpler, easier, and aimed at extraction; fly-fishing carries the lofty air of a more challenging, refined art, rewarded by intellectual, emotional, and spiritual satisfaction. But like most simple binaries, these orders are easily upset. Many anglers, like myself, look for beauty and art in a range of fishing styles. Many anglers cross class lines.

I tie on a pheasant-tail nymph and cast into the Metolius's blue transparency, undulating with watercress and the white-tipped fins of visible trout. The weight of the line rolls from arm and rod into satisfying, graceful loops, unfurling straight over the water. But fly casting can be more difficult than spin casting, and my fifth back-cast puts me in a bush. I untangle and continue, casting steadily for about two hours without a strike. Other fly fishermen pass and say hello, politely stepping out of the river to walk behind me.

When I least expect it – which is always the reward for expecting so long – the line tightens and there's a terrific splash of silver and pink. I take my time bringing a fourteen-inch rainbow to the net. It's a gorgeous fish with striking, red-metallic lateral bands and black spots over its fins and tail. I hold the trout in my wet hands, remove the barbless hook, look at it a moment longer, and let it go. Sound of rushing water, blue-bubbled cascades, kingfisher in a tamarack bough. How different from the outboard- and man-snarls of the Salmon River, slamming that netted chinook to the deck, and clubbing it with a bat.

Do gear, technique, and the fate of the caught fish determine the class of the person fishing? Judging from the vehicles and apparel along the Salmon

River as compared to those along the Metolius, it would be easy to speculate that the average income of the fly fishermen from Sisters and Bend is higher than the Lincoln City plunkers. But gauging class among those who fish is tricky. Many wealthy people eat the fish they catch using the freshest bait and the most expensive lures, gear, boats, and guides. And one of the best fly fishermen on our local creek sleeps in a van and collects mushrooms for a living. 'Nor is fishing a rich man's regeneration,' proclaimed Depression era president, Herbert Hoover; 'all men are equal before fish.'

Then there are the Southern bass fishing tournaments where pro anglers speed around lakes, deploy state-of-the-art tackle, and catch and release trophy bass for huge cash prizes. Though this kind of fishing appeals to the working class, it exercises the science, the technology, and the bait-free and catch-and-release principles admired by the fly-fishing elite. 'I think bass tourney fishing is soulless,' explains Richard Bunse, one of Oregon's most distinguished anglers and fishing illustrators. 'It's driven by competition with other men for the heaviest fish and money, not as a way to deepen your relationship with nature.' Bunse reminds us that fly fishermen have also organized competitive, cash-crazed televised events. 'It's not about lure fishing, bait fishing, or fly-fishing; it's about attitude.'

Perhaps, as the sociologist Pierre Bourdieu argues, economic capital is not the main force in shaping class behavior. Rather, it is the manners, tastes, activities, and attitudes we inherit and learn – our cultural capital – that determine the class we occupy. Cultural capital is, however, historically traceable to economic capital. Consider the deep associations between sport fishing and more sophisticated attitudes about nature developed in Great Britain, where river access and fishing opportunities were largely limited to the landed gentry. The culture of sport fishing maintained the values of a leisure class obsessed with fashion and manners, but also with science, literature, and art.

Although these values and styles were transplanted to the New World, fishing in America's fin-filled waters has always been less exclusive than it was back in Europe. In his *Description of New England* (1616), John Smith writes, 'Here nature and liberty afford us that freely, which in England we want, or it costs us dearly.' In the colonies, Smith exclaims, 'man, woman and child, with a small hook and line – by angling – may take diverse sorts of excellent fish, at their pleasures.' American settlers, of course, fished to feed themselves, but by the eighteenth century there were more and more accounts of pleasure fishing in America.

Recreational fishing worried our workaholic founding father, Ben Franklin, who wrote, 'I was seen at no places of idle Diversion; I never went out a-fishing or shooting.' In the early nineteenth century, Washington Irving offers a refreshing Romantic alternative in his short story 'Rip Van Winkle.' Rip has an 'aversion to all kinds of profitable labour' and 'would sit on a wet rock . . . and fish all day without a murmur, even though he should not be encouraged by a single nibble.' We think of leisure time for sports like fishing as something afforded to the middle and upper classes. But fishing has always had adherents among the poor and disenfranchised perhaps because it could put food on the table, help forget worries or, at its simplest, be done with a string and bent pin.

Recreational fishing also became immensely popular with America's growing middle class in the nineteenth and twentieth centuries, and continued to capture the imagination of writers like Ernest Hemingway, who wrote passionately about fly and bait fishing in his novels and short stories. Despite the rising number of anglers, fly-fishing was still relatively expensive until gear revolutions in the 1950s replaced silk lines and cane rods with more reasonably priced products made of nylon and fiberglass. This, combined with a proliferation of information on fly-fishing, from brochures to books, caused the sport to become very popular in the 1960s. During the 60s and 70s, fly-fishing was further celebrated by a generation of hippie or renegade fishing writers like John Gierach and Russell Chatham, and significant literary figures such as Richard Brautigan and Thomas McGuane. These fishermen rejected Franklin's capitalist overdrive, but they were not content to sit on the bank, crack a beer, and drown a worm like Rip. Instead, they drew on both the back-to-earth environmentalism of their time and the traditional aesthetics and spirituality of the enlightened angler to reshape fishing as a 'way,' in the Taoist sense, toward peace and harmony.

This tradition of contemplative fishing can be traced back to ancient China and poets like Bai Juyi – 'Though my body sits waiting for fish, / My heart wanders to the Land of Nothingness' – also to British anglers who had the time to fish and think, such as Izaak Walton, author of *The Compleat Angler, or The Contemplative Man's Recreation* (1653-1676). Walton – who used flies, lures, and bait – was one of the first writers to give sport fishing a true aesthetic and philosophical dimension, and his ideas are key to understanding the sensibility that favors fishing with 'wit, hope . . . and patience, and a love and propensity to the art itself' over a fillet quota or the most expensive gear.

In the philosophy of contemplative fishing, the angler has everything to gain; he cannot even lose a fish, 'for no man can lose what he never had.' This kind of fishing was clearly more than a means of procuring dinner or an excuse to skip work. It had become a way of being, a discipline, possibly an art – and this takes practice, knowledge, and a philosophy.

The connection between philosophy and fishing is realized in the life and work of the American writer, Henry David Thoreau, who called fishing 'the true industry of poets.' Although he had little money, the many hours Thoreau invested in angling paid off in a series of moving parables and meditations. He used worms to catch perch and pickerel for supper, but he recognized that most men 'plainly fished much more in the Walden Pond of their own natures, and baited their hooks with darkness.' Fishing was a way of sounding those darker, unconscious impulses and of connecting lofty thoughts back to nature. There's surprise and renewal, Thoreau says, 'especially in dark nights, when your thoughts had wandered to vast and cosmogonal themes in other spheres, to feel this faint jerk, which came to interrupt your dreams and link you to Nature again.'

In a comparably beautiful passage from *The Habit of Rivers* (1994), Ted Leeson writes: 'The rise of trout to a drifting insect reverberates in expanding concentric ripples, magnified iterations of a simple event that resonate outward to encompass more and more, remaining visible long after and far from the thing that made them.' Leeson goes on to say that 'the rings of the rising trout eventually comprehend the entire river,' including the person fishing. Making a distinction that might be more useful than those related to social class, Leeson believes, 'The craft of angling is catching a fish. But the art of angling is a receptiveness to these connections, the art of letting one thing lead to another until, if only locally and momentarily, you realize some small completeness.'

So perhaps it is attitude, philosophy, and art, rather than technique – fly, lure, or bait – that differentiates the people who fish. And yet fly-fishing undeniably lends itself generously to the kind of angling most revered as art. Consider the fly itself: a beautiful object, hand-tied from delicate hair and feather, lovingly described and illustrated in countless books. A good dry fly fisherman, in particular, must also know something about insects, matching a delectable natural hatch to the representative artificial in his box. The fly, along with hand-split cane rods and a smooth cast, has no artistic equals in spin or bait fishing. In *A River Runs Through It* (1976), Norman Maclean recalls his father's belief that man had fallen from grace into a state of chaos, and that 'only by picking up God's rhythms were we able to regain power and beauty.' For the Macleans, fly casting, 'an art that is performed on a four-count rhythm between ten and two o'clock,' was a sure way of regaining that divine beauty.

The best places to fly-fish are often the most beautiful wild rivers and streams. New York fly fishing guru, Nick Lyons, savored his escapes from Manhattan 'to be on the river. To be away. Alone.' But beyond the trout stream, fly-fishing is usually not the most effective way of catching fish, so the emphasis is naturally on process and experience, not merely product. For me, there's nothing déclassé about keeping and eating fish; but if, as Thoreau says, we fish the waters of our own natures, there are distinctions between people who snag salmon stacked in a pool because they want something for the smoker, and those who wade icy rivers, casting flies to wild winter steelhead in Oregon – arguably the greatest challenge in American angling, and one that is almost always crowned with a gentle release.

Exerting tremendous skill and effort over many hours to attain something nearly impossible and of indeterminate value? Sounds like art. Although art has always appealed to the upper classes, it is also true that nothing crosses the lines of social class more easily than the creation of art. Successful artists, even those with meager incomes and raggedy pedigrees, readily receive byes into high society. Consider the simple voice and music patterns in American roots and folk music, which continue to speak emotional truths to contemporary listeners. Technical mastery and sophistication are important criteria for judging art, yet the simplest work, like Lead Belly's lyrics, sometimes provides the profoundest insight.

Wouldn't it follow, then, that more simple means of sport fishing – plunking cheese baits for catfish on a sultry Louisiana night – may just as easily lead to enlightenment? Yes, indeed. And the most basic – perhaps purest – moments in fishing have been the subject of many songs, paintings, films, and works of literature. Mark Twain's poor orphan, Huckleberry Finn, tells us that he and his friend, the runaway slave, Jim, floated down the Mississippi, 'catched fish and talked.' They 'bait one of the big hooks with a skinned rabbit . . . and catch a catfish that was big as a man . . .' Fishing is symbolic of freedom and the natural ability to provide for oneself. Think also of the poor Cuban fisherman, Santiago, in Hemingway's *The Old Man and the Sea,* working his crude hand-lines baited with sardines. Santiago is, by definition, a commercial fisherman, perhaps out of the realm of this discussion. Nonetheless, his simple, faithful, thoughtful, and financially futile labors canonize him as one of the most beloved fishermen in world literature.

But if, as the media critic Marshall McLuhan claimed, 'Class in society is determined by voice,' then fly-fishing still commands the choir. American writers including Norman Maclean, Thomas McGuane, David James Duncan and Ted Leeson, and British authors Luke Jennings, David Profumo, John Andrews and Charles Rangeley-Wilson experience fly-fishing not so much as a subject written about but as a way of being. 'Wherever I go, I'm fishing the one river, the river of forgetting, where I shut out the world and lose myself,' Rangeley-Wilson writes. 'I think maybe this is all anyone is doing, no matter how they fish. All forms of fishing are good, but for me, fly fishing is best. It's my chant, my meditation, my prayer.' Is the art of fly-fishing the pinnacle to which all soulful anglers should aspire?

In the end, fly-fishing represents a way, not an arrival or a class. Perhaps there is a progression from the child swinging a worm into a pond of hungry sunfish to the seasoned angler casting streamers to wary steelhead. But the greater progression is that of the human who comes to revere and protect the environment; who catches and keeps fish with conservation, personal values, and sensible use in mind; and who learns about fish, water, and angling simply because there is much to learn. These virtues can be achieved by anyone, no matter his or her formal education, occupation, or economic state. If fishing becomes an art that deepens a person's sense of self in relation to others and nature, that's progress. I'll plunk at night with worms for muddy catfish and wake at dawn fly-casting pale duns to rising rainbows – moon and sun, master and servant, forever changing places.

I Used to Be a Fisherman

BY WESTON OCHSE

SITTING IN AFGHANISTAN, staring at the Hindu Kush rising monolithically over the protective T-Walls and HESCO barriers of my NATO military compound, I wonder what sort of rivers and streams run there. It looks like trout country, high up in those hoary mountains, snow on the ground, winds teasing the surface of the water. I can imagine long pools and miles of riffles, giving way to dramatic waterfalls where the lunkers lurk.

Do the Taliban and other insurgent fighters ever stop and fish, I wonder. Or are they so intent on the downfall of an already precariously balanced society that they never think about fishing – never aching to feel the hit of an unseen fish on a piece of bait, or a lure, or a fly so they could experience that hollow chill, followed by the unease of bringing it in, then finally either joy or frustration at the result?

You see, I used to be a fisherman, and this is how fishermen think. Sure, I'm also a military man and think about better ways to protect those I'm charged to serve, but at my core I'm a fisherman and would rather be fishing than fighting.

Or at least I used to be a fisherman.

It's been more than a decade since I was a fisherman. I can remember when I'd spend hours dreaming about fishing. I'd clean my rod and reel and practice casting in my driveway. I'd get up at five in the morning, just so I could beat the morning sun and be there when the fish awoke hungry, sleep still riddling their eyes enough so that my lure appeared to be something real and eatable. Whenever I was out for a drive, other people would look at the scenery as a whole, but I'd watch the water, carefully examining and searching for the places where I knew fish to be, then imagining me standing, casting, and retrieving.

Why I stopped fishing I can't figure out.

My mother taught me how to fish when I was just three. I had a bamboo pole with a bit of line, a bobber and a hook. This was my first non-toy. It was a tool for adventure, I was told, and I became crazed with the new adventure it gave me . . . what my mother called fishing. We lived in a lonely place called LaGrange, Wyoming, an hour north of Cheyenne. A little stream bubbled full of crappies about two miles outside of town. Every morning my mother and I would dig worms in the back yard, and every afternoon we'd go down to this stream, and I'd pull in fish as fast as my mother could bait my hook.

Even as I sit in the middle of a combat zone, hearing the crackling of automatic gunfire, I remember the joy that three-year-old version of me felt. So strong, so powerful, so enduring. How had I let it get away? Why had I stopped fishing? – because I have to tell you, I have such amazing memories of fishing.

On my grandfather's boat on Pactola Dam, South Dakota. Night fishing. Lanterns over the edge of the boat. The buzz and snap of flies and mosquitoes killing themselves in the light. Lines deep in the freezing Black Hills mountain water. Then the bang of the pole, the bend of the rod, and the sluicing of the fish so far down below it could have been in another dimension. Then the finale of each mini passion play, as I reel in a rainbow trout from the depths, so many, too many, flopping, banging, beating against the bottom of the boat their frustration at being caught, and me watching their dance, a victorious ten-year-old fisherman on top of their piscine world.

My dad and I fishing the Tellico River in the Appalachian Cherokee National Forest. Five a.m. and ready to fish. Waiting for sunrise. Raining, no one else is fishing, and we land trout after trout feeling like the day could get no better, laughing, sodden, tripping, shaking our heads at the miraculous fortune. Then driving home with a cooler full of rainbows and a head full of each snap, pull, and retrieve memory.

Or the day we discovered the new trout stream behind the row of putrescent pig farms in some backwater Tennessee county I've long since forgotten. Stench-filled paddocks. Swarms of black flies. A mysterious slow-moving Tennessee mountain creek, but cold as if fed from a series of springs. Skulking along the back of the property lines, our backs itching from imaginary buck-shot. A bend, then a toss, then a rainbow, twenty inches long, came in fighting, furious and surprised. Then another and another, 22, 24 and 25 inches. No one had fished here. The stench, the flies, the No Trespassing signs, the slow moving water, all great camouflage for a luxurious fisherman-free trout life, now turned into our secret spot.

Or when we all went camping on Tellico again and the life-and-death struggle between us and water moccasins who came up on us when we were cleaning the fish one evening, eager to eat our catch. I still remember us standing tall, hurling curses and rocks, protecting our catch, even if it meant being bitten by the ultra-poisonous viper.

Or the time when I crawled to the side of a creek on my knees, bow casting a spinner into the water, then gasping as a roll of silver the length of my arm thumped the side of my lure like a great water god showing itself, a challenge. Then the panic and the hollow fear as I bow cast once more, doing in two casts what I hadn't done in ten thousand, landing a five pound rainbow as long as my arm, the envy of a wide-eyed boy scout troop who'd fished that area the day before and had never even imagined such a giant lurking in the thin ribbon of creek.

Or the time I went fishing with my dad, when my old friend Chuck took us on his boat on the Columbia River. We fished two hard days and nary a hit. Skunked on a river one should never be skunked on. Then the next day, unplanned, we fished once more. But nothing again. Thirty minutes before we were to call it a day, a freight train took my father's line, reel screaming, hearts hammering, my father, proud man who'd taught me so much about the magic of fishing, the man who'd taught me the bow cast, brought in a twenty-five pound shining model of Piscean grandeur. Then me, ten minutes later, doing the same, gasping, fortunate, amazed, heroic, laughing.

The Hindu Kush. I first learned of it from Kipling in 'The Man Who Would Be King'. Majestic. Rising to 26,000 feet, and running 800 kilometers, it has to have trout streams. Do the children of the insurgents have fishing poles? The tribes living in the mountains, do they yearn for the stalking, the outwitting, and fighting with a twelve-inch trout, or are their attentions solely to do these things to us? What could they learn about themselves if they spent more time fishing? What would we learn if we fished rather than fought?

This august mountain range dominates my horizon, visible to my every thought, every movement, and every step. I wonder at the fishing there, knowing

I'd never be able to try my hand, blocked by a people who would see me die. I bet they were fishermen before they were fighters. If they were fishermen again, could we find a common ground, I wonder? Could we stand side-by-side, rods in hand, stalking the wildness of a Himalayan trout, eager and joyous to fish in a land of legend?

Or is that too much?

There was a moment of magic when Chuck and I were kids with dreams of lunkers, fishing for giant catfish on Chickamauga Reservoir, where legends had it they grew as large as Cadillacs. We didn't catch a catfish that day, but one did rise up, slam the bottom of our canoe, and splash dramatically on both sides of it, as if to demonstrate how immense it was and how foolish we were for trying to catch something so sovereign, so mammoth. I wrote about this in a story called *Catfish Gods*, more than fifteen years ago. I hadn't fished in years, but I still hadn't forgotten that fishing isn't just about catching. Fishing is more about being a part of something than anything else. A fisherman cares about the water and nature more than most people. How we take care of our world directly affects a person's ability to fish. A fisherman has respect for his environment and for the thing he desires most, the very fish he's trying to catch. A fisherman is introspective, honorable, patient, and covetous of time lost to those things which take away from fishing.

Then there's the solitude. Although many of us fish with friends or family, we're always fishing within ourselves. Fishing with my grandfather on the lake or my father on a river or Chuck in a canoe, we always went together, but we'd end up alone, in our minds, each of our universes balanced on the tip of our rods.

Oh, how I miss fishing.

Where had it gone? Why isn't it part of my life anymore?

So I thought a lot about fishing today. I'm not sure why. I can't tell you what brought it on. But I can say that it's something I miss terribly. I've felt incomplete without it. In fact, I'm forty-eight years old now and I don't even own a fishing pole. Where it went, I just don't know. One thing is for sure. You can't call yourself a fisherman without a fishing pole.

So here's my plan. I'm eventually going to leave Afghanistan. When I do, I'm going to get a fishing pole and some new gear and I'm going to become a fisherman again. Someone better tell my wife that we might even start camping, so she can start praying I change my mind. I want to get back in touch with the beauty of nature. When you're alone on the water, quiet as you attempt to become one with the land, there's a special beauty that you become a part of.

It's a lightness of being only fishing can afford you.

I want to feel this again. I want to do this again. I want to be a fisherman. Not because I want to catch anything. I've caught enough for a campfire circle full of stories. No. I want to be a fisherman because I want to be a part of the universe again. No more looking in. I want to be inside and looking out.

Once more I glance at the Hindu Kush. Is there a fisherman staring down at me, wondering if I'm a fisherman too?

'Not now,' I'd respond. 'Not anymore. But soon, soon I'll be a fisherman again and then you can fish in your home and I'll fish somewhere in my home, and we can be fishermen together, stalking trout instead of each other, reveling in a world where fishing is more important than fighting.'

Fishing the Ancient Headwaters

JAMES PROSEK

IT WAS NOT until we reached the hostilities in the semi-desert of south-eastern Turkey that I fully realized I was in the company of a monomaniac.

'I don't think we should go down to Catak,' I said. 'Is a trout worth all this?'

Johannes nodded his head, grinning.

'I will trade you to the Kurdish terrorists for a trout from the headwaters of the Tigris,' he said. 'They like Americans.'

We were stopped by the Turkish military not far from the Iraqi border. In the past few hours, more than a hundred armed tanks had passed us on the road.

The officer who came to the driver's door of our Land Rover was not much older than I; he wore a green uniform and carried a gun on his shoulder.

'What is your purpose for traveling to Catak?'

'Alabalik,' Johannes said. 'Trout.'

At the time it seemed like a ridiculous answer, but we had told the officers the truth: We had come to fish for trout. Our month-long journey had taken us to Greece, Turkey, Macedonia, Serbia, Bosnia, Croatia, and Slovenia in search of pristine headwaters. Now and then I paused to wonder exactly how I had come to be traveling through these places in a vehicle stuffed with fishing and camping gear, journals, vials of alcohol, glass aquariums, and cameras.

Our purpose was to discover and document subspecies of trout. Johannes Schoeffmann, age forty-seven, is a baker and an amateur ichthyologist; he has made it his goal to document various types of trout, in particular the subspecies of brown trout native to Europe and Asia. Johannes catches fish and traces them on paper with a pencil, marking down their scale counts, number of fin rays, and other characteristics. He preserves their liver tissue in alcohol, carefully labeling each vial. The tissue samples are mailed to Louis Bernatchez, a research biologist at Laval University in Quebec who is using DNA to create an evolutionary map of trout and to define the characteristics that make each lineage unique.

The theory of trout evolution holds that about 15 million years ago, the common ancestral trout separated into two branches, one of which eventually gave rise not only to the modern species of Pacific salmon, but also to the rainbow and cutthroat trout. The other branch became the ancestor of the Atlantic salmon, the brown trout, and related species. During the Pleistocene glacial epochs – the past 2 million years – climatic conditions promoted dispersal, isolation and speciation. The last glacial epoch began 60,000 to 70,000 years ago and ended 8,000 to 10,000 years ago. During the colder periods, trout dispersed throughout the Mediterranean area – the Black Sea, the Adriatic Sea – and this distribution gave rise to the diversity that Johannes and I observed on our trip.

When we started our trip I was twenty-two, fresh out of college and looking for adventure. I had been fascinated by trout for years, having grown up fishing the trout streams near my home, in Easton, Connecticut. When I was thirteen, my father cut out a small article from *Yankee* magazine about a type of trout that was once thought to be extinct but had recently been rediscovered in eight small ponds in northern Maine. The discovery of this particular fish, the blueback trout, made me wonder whether there might be other trout out there besides the rainbow, brown and brook trout that I knew of.

As a child I had painted birds, tracing the drawings of John James Audubon. Now I began documenting the various subspecies of trout, and when I was twenty, I published a book called *Trout*, an illustrated catalogue of the trout of North America. Next, I wanted to illustrate the trout of the world.

Where to begin? I had always wanted to visit the headwaters of the Tigris and the Euphrates, in eastern Turkey, since some of the earliest civilizations and probably the earliest of fishermen had established themselves between those two great rivers. I also know that the first recorded reference to fishing with an artificial fly was in a second-century text by a Roman named Claudius Aelian, who described how the Macedonians fished for trout in a river near what is now the Greek town of Thessaloniki. I wondered if the trout were still there.

I wrote to Robert Behnke, a professor of fishery biology at Colorado State University who is perhaps the world's foremost trout taxonomist. He replied that he knew of only one man who had ever fished for trout in this region, and that was Johannes Schoeffmann, who lived in St. Veit an der Glan, Austria. I wrote to Johannes, telling him I might be in Europe that summer, and he invited me to visit him.

Johannes met me at the train station in St. Veit after my seventeen-hour ride from Paris. We quickly realized that we had a communication problem: Johannes could write English but could not speak it well. I did not speak German. But we discovered that we both spoke Spanish – and the universal language of trout, of course.

Though he was twenty-five years my senior, I soon discovered Johannes to be, at least in part, my alter ego. He was left-handed as I was, drew pictures of trout, and spent spare moments dreaming of them and planning fishing trips. As a baker, he typically worked from 2 a.m. to 9 a.m., leaving plenty of daylight for fishing.

The day after I met Johannes, we traveled over the border into Slovenia, to a valley where the emerald Soca River flows – one of the most primitive and incredibly beautiful valleys I had ever seen. After a lunch of prosciutto, cheese, and red wine, we drove to the stream with the intention of catching a specimen of the native marble trout. I was not deterred by the sign next to which Johannes had parked his Land Rover – a fish with a red X over it, the universal sign for no fishing – but when I went to get my fly rod from the back of the car, Johannes shook his head.

He proceeded to put on a full-body wetsuit, hood and all, and walked, with his fins, to the edge of the stream. Within thirty seconds of jumping into the ice-cold and crystal-clear pool, he surfaced with a small marble trout cradled in his neoprene gloves, then let it slip back into the water. How could I have anticipated a man who fishes for trout with his hands?

The following day, before my train left for Paris, I told Johannes I would like to join him on his next expedition in search of trout. He said, 'I might go to Turkey next summer, maybe to Albania.'

'That would be fine,' I told him.

So in the summer of 1996 Johannes, his wife, Ida, and I embarked on a month-long trip that would take us from St. Veit to Trieste, Italy, by ferry to Igoumenitsa, Greece; through Turkey to the borders of Georgia, Iran, and Iraq; around to Greece again; to Macedonia, Serbia, Bosnia, Croatia, and Slovenia; and then back to Austria.

In our pursuit of trout we sometimes had a vague reference to follow, such as a stream mentioned in a biological paper published in Italian at the beginning of the century. Mostly, though, we followed Johannes's instincts and our own knowledge of where trout might live. We drove through mountain regions, stopped by clear streams, and used a thermometer to see if they were cold enough to support trout.

A wild-trout population requires, among other things, clean, well-oxygenated water that is typically between 52° and 72° Fahrenheit, and a stream bed with suitable spawning habitat. Such fragile, pristine ecosystems are becoming harder and harder to find. In the ten years that Johannes has been traveling to Turkey in pursuit of trout, he has seen entire populations wiped out by fishermen using explosives or nets, and stream beds silted in by road construction. He predicts that in twenty years few native trout will survive in Turkey.

In many of the countries where we traveled, there were no apparent fishing regulations. Even where regulations did exist, they were not enforced: the people there were more concerned with their immediate survival than with the future of their environment. Still, Johannes said the eight or so years of war that had devastated Bosnia, Serbia and Croatia had allowed trout populations to recover, since people had been hiding in their basements instead of fishing.

We found trout in all the countries we visited and in about half the streams we fished. The fish we caught were primarily brown trout (*Salmo trutta*), although we also caught flathead trout in southern Turkey (*Salmo platycephalus*) and marbled trout (*Salmo marmoratus*).

The more traveling we did and the more trout we saw, the more I began to realize that the naming process I was accustomed to was limited in describing variations of fish. The brown trout in every drainage differed significantly in their colors and their spots; sometimes the trout in different streams within the same drainage had different coloration and different spots.

The most beautiful trout we saw were in western Turkey, not more than eight miles from the Mediterranean coast. The paper that had been written by the Italian biologist mentioned this stream and the brown trout that inhabited it. We were staying in the town of Akcay, with a German couple who were friends of Johannes and Ida. One morning Johannes and I navigated the dirt roads through a grove of ancient, twisted olive trees and down a steep slope to the banks of the stream. The lower reaches of the stream were nearly dry, but in the headwaters, which ran through the olive orchard, the stream was remarkably pristine and cold. It was there that we caught some of the most colorful brown trout I had ever seen: bright-yellow sides, purple parr marks, and large red-and-black spots. All the fish had a peculiar oblong black spot above and behind each eye, which, from above, resembled another eye.

I fished with my fly rod and then joined Johannes, diving into the cold water. That afternoon, just miles from where we had caught the trout, we dived with our masks and snorkels in the warm Mediterranean and watched colorful little fish dart in and out of rock crevices.

Johannes's favorite river was the Krka, a crystal-clear, spring-fed stream in Croatia. This was the first time since the war began that Johannes had been to the Krka. He said there were many more trout now than on his previous trips – and larger ones – because much of the river was fenced off, owing to land mines. Along paths and roads, signs pointed to the ground, warning: MINE. We were cautious, using only well-worn paths to the stream. At one point we lowered ourselves off a bridge into the water and dived for the trout without touching the bottom. We saw brown trout that looked to be upward of seven or eight pounds, as well as a fish Johannes identified as the softmouth trout (*Salmothymus obtusirostris*). Softmouth trout live in only one other stream – the Buna River, in Bosnia, which we also visited. They are characterized by a slight overbite, presumably to facilitate feeding on insects on the river bottom. They had black spots, like brown trout, and silver and gold sides.

Our itinerary had been planned by Johannes, but at one point I asked if we could make a detour. I wanted to fish the stream in Greece that Claudius Aelian had written about eighteen centuries ago. Johannes told me before we began our trip that what appears in Aelian's text as the Astraeos River is actually the Aliakmon River. Johannes had caught trout, though very few, in tributaries of the Aliakmon. I tied the same fly that Aelian described – using ruby-colored wool and two cock's feathers – but when we reached the Aliakmon, it had been replaced by a maze of irrigation ditches diverting water from its main stem. We continued our journey and searched several tributaries of the Aliakmon near the town of Tripotamos (meaning three rivers in Greek). The water in one of the tributaries was clear, cold and trouty, and I cast my ruby-wool fly in all the likely spots, but we saw no fish. It was one of many examples during our trip of how the encroachment of human civilization has been detrimental to the survival of trout.

In its prime, I imagine, the Aliakmon must have looked something like the Vodomatis. Located near the town of Vikos-Aoos, in north-western Greece by the mountains of the Albanian border, the Vodomatis was emerald-tinged, clear and cold. Its brown trout were large, 16 to 20 inches. Their subspecies name, *dentex* – meaning 'tooth' – derives from their long teeth. Johannes told me that they were similar to the Aliakmon fish.

The Vodomatis and the other rivers we saw that still ran clear and full of trout gave us hope that preservation is possible. As I cast Aelian's fly into this stream and reeled in a beautiful brown trout with blue gill plates and cream-yellow sides, I felt as though I were participating in a centuries-long continuum that, if we are more careful with our resources, can carry on for centuries more.

Trout in Africa: A British Legacy

BILL MONROE

HERE, AT 7,200 feet and within a relative few miles of the Equator, rainbow and brown trout hover beneath cut banks and in the seams of eddies created by the rush of water over and around three-million-year-old boulders. They find quiet havens in a small stream which, but for the overhanging vines, elephant-ear type vegetation and occasional palm, looks every bit like a postcard for the middle Cascade Mountain Range.

'Don't go that way,' Victor Mutaki cautions as I assemble a fly rod and head below a bridge for a run I've spotted as we drove up. 'Not good; we have to stay upriver.'

Mutaki is packing a G3 assault rifle. While I've been known from time to time to neglect a few details the guide asks of me, I've never, ever, crossed one carrying an assault rifle.

And even if Mutaki is only the guard, not the guide, local knowledge always trumps experimentation.

I was never clear whether he was in the Kenyan army, park service or simply an employee of the Serena Mountain Lodge, an ark-like hotel built over a water hole in a setting so scenic guests forget all about the third-world challenges they've threaded to get here.

At dawn, the mountain's jagged peak is visible for an hour or two before generating its own clouds; and the night's denizens – hyenas, leopards and bush bucks – give way to Cape buffalo, water bucks and baboons.

Wild Africa is visible from every room, but the central outdoor balcony is best, with its hot coffee and soft seats, nestled like loges between signs: 'Please keep quiet' and 'Please don't feed the monkeys.'

We'd come here for the novelty of trout in Kenya, introduced by British colonials in 1908, according to our guide, Benson Maina. (Peter Kummerfeldt, the retired US Air Force survival expert who appears every year in the Pacific Northwest Sportsmen's Show at the Portland Expo Center, is a native of South Africa and said his grandfather helped plant trout in Kenya.)

We weren't prepared, however, for the silent majesty of this forest setting and its parade of *National Geographic* headliners. It's not unusual for guests to watch the kill-and-be-killed drama of wild Africa from the smaller balconies of their rooms.

At dinner each evening, they're given a list of animals they'd like to be awakened to see, if and when they appear – a unique wake-up menu for the night desk.

Trout fishing is more novelty this close to the lodge than a draw for serious anglers. There are, however, much larger trout in a lake higher on the mountain, a seven-hour drive, spike camp overnight and two-hour hike beyond the lodge. Larger trout also are found in the Aberdare Mountains, southwest of Mt. Kenya. Guards there add African lions to their protection list.

We're satisfied with our brief excursion to this small mountain stream, which also involves a visit to, of all things, a commercial trout hatchery. It's crude by American standards, but the managers proudly point out they don't have to pump water in the gravity-fed rusty pipes (no electricity). Hatchery fry aren't stocked for fishing, but rather sold to local farmers to grow for food.

The nearby Trout Tree Restaurant, for example, is an upscale eatery just off the Nairobi-Nanyuki highway offering seating built into an open tree house, three trout ponds and a nearly all-trout menu (grilled, baked, sushi, almondine, etc.).

During tea (and cake) at streamside we ask Victor about the gun, which he carries to frighten off Cape buffalo, elephants, leopards and hyenas that appear during fishing and hiking trips from the lodge.

Does he have to use it often? 'All the time,' he says.

But you can't kill the animals, right? 'Oh, no, I cannot shoot to kill any wildlife, just scare them.'

What about poachers, I ask with a bit of a smirk. 'Yes,' he says, neither smiling nor frowning. It's a simple statement of a fact of daily life for the army, park wardens and rangers. 'I can shoot to kill a poacher.'

A week or so after our fishing trip, we learn a hyena attacked a group of village women gathering firewood a short distance from the lodge, killing one of them.

I wonder whether the 2,000 Kenya shillings I tipped Victor (about $24) was enough.

Big Fish in an Enormous Pond

JEREMY WADE

SPRAY BREAKS OVER us in silvery blasts as the boat pitches in the heavy swell, splinters of cold flying through the tropical furnace. The not-quite-rhythmic pounding of hull on water is hypnotic. But the impression of time as a repeating loop is abruptly dispelled. Something has yanked one of the rods into an alarming curve and is making the reel's friction surfaces scream . . .

It would be a typical moment of big-game-fishing high drama, but for two facts. The boat's occupants are not members of that affluent club that migrates between Hawaii, the Bahamas and the Great Barrier Reef. And there is the taste of the spray: this is fresh water.

Lake Nasser is a vision of the world after the flood, with just the mountain-tops left above the water. But the aspect of this remaining land banishes any thoughts of refuge. Bare and heat-shattered, strewn with clinker-like rubble and swept with drifts of blinding sand, it all seems to be visibly in the process of crumbling beneath the surface. In places, a single line of thin greenery skirts the shore. Otherwise, water meets desert with no transition.

It is a disconcerting place: a dreamscape with a logic of its own, where the unlikely but true explanation – that it is a man-made one-off – comes as a strange relief. Created just three decades ago by the raising of the Aswan High Dam above the Nile's first cataract, it is still the subject of much inconclusive debate about its environmental consequences. For instance, is reduced fertility in the delta a fair price to pay for flood control? What is undeniable, however, is that the Nile's fish now have a huge new habitat – more than 2,000 square miles – in which all species have thrived. Doing particularly well at the top of the food chain is *Lates niloticus*, the Nile perch.

Formerly the object of one of ancient Egypt's bizarre animal-worship cults (mummified bodies were interred in a cemetery near present-day Esna), this giant relative of our village pond perch is now attracting devotees from around the world. Their offerings are gaudy caricatures of small fish, made from wood, metal, plastic or rubber, that come exaggeratedly alive when pulled through the water. Using this deceit, most first-timers on Lake Nasser catch their lifetime-biggest fish. A fifty-pounder is a realistic target for a one-week safari, but something twice or even four times that size could be just a gulp away. A fish of 213 lb (more than 15 stone) caught in December 1997 is currently awaiting ratification as the official world record. But the biggest one caught so far was too heavy for the scales available at the time. A colossal 6 ft 1½ in. long, with a girth of 59 in., it was estimated at more than 250 lb.

Two days in, our party's biggest catch stands at 77 lb, with everyone already blasé about 'twenties' and 'thirties'. In the evening, the three steel-hulled fishing boats rendezvous with the supply boat, *Bahr el-Nuba* ('The Nubian Sea'), deep inside a *khor*, an inlet, somewhere down the east bank, for supper of fried perch, miraculous fresh-baked rolls, and iced beer. As the slow kaleidoscope of night sky and flat water turns, three old hands and six first-timers swap tales of the day's events: of monitor lizards, 1,000 ft-high dust-devils, and the goat-herd with the Calvin Klein T-shirt. The exchange that follows news of a big fish lost looks set to become laughably familiar: 'Where was that?' 'I haven't a clue!' It appears I am not the only one who has lost his bearings.

I am not sure quite where it happened. The map we were each given as we set off in convoy from the High Dam at first made some sense of the vastness around us. Although more than 300 miles long, the lake is relatively narrow – steaming down the middle we could see both banks. Its alignment, most of the time, is north-south. And there is a rule of thumb that the east bank is more mountainous than the west. Orientation looked a simple enough affair.

But approach the shore and the picture changes. What appears from a distance to be a continuous steep bank breaks up into shifting fragments that slide over and behind one another like multi-layered stage scenery. These promontories, islands, and deep, branching inlets add up to 4,500 convoluted miles of shoreline. What's more, it is constantly changing, due to the annual 10 -15 ft tide that reflects rainfall half a continent away. Headlands suffering identity crises become part-time islands. Submerged pinnacles peep above the surface only to sink again two months later. For the angler this complexity means a glut of underwater features that attract and hold fish. But once inside the maze, even a momentary lapse of concentration can lose the thread. Was it that gap we came through, or that identical one over there? The sun, directly overhead, gives no clue. So navigation is entrusted to the Nubian guides, whose relatives once lived in ornamented mud houses in the villages 300 ft down, along the sunken river's course.

This anonymity of landmarks makes it hard to peg memories to any framework. After a few days they float around in no definite sequence. The family of golden jackals feeding on scraps just 30 ft from where we were dining in the moored supply boat. The snake-like vundu catfish that stuck its tentacled face out of the water right in front of me. Waking in the small hours up on the canopy of *Sobek*, one of the fishing boats – to see a red tower of light on the eastern horizon, which had me quietly perplexed until it grew into the upper horn of the tilted crescent moon. Meanwhile, wind and calm alternate, following a cycle of their own.

But for each of us, some places do etch very clear pictures in the mind. About halfway through the week, we reach a spot where the east bank suddenly falls away into the distance. We enter the *khor*, which after two hours funnels down to the mouth of Wadi Allaqi, once a caravan route from the Sudan and conduit for Nubian gold, now a flooded valley that threads far into the desert. We cross towards a prominent headland that meets the water in a vertical wall. As we approach, we see the overhangs, clefts and ledges that hint at an underwater architecture made for ambush-predators.

One possibility is to swim the lures behind the boat, a rod-length out in water 60 ft deep. But there is another option, which pits angler against fish in a way no other big-game fishing can match – I decide to stalk my quarry from the shore.

The boat noses into a cove around the side of the headland, from where a climb leads to a platform of sorts between the cliff top and the slope to the summit. Peeping over the edge, I see two fish very close in, lying along the top of a ledge: black silhouettes against the rock's carpet of pale yellowish algae. Keeping as far back as possible, I cast well beyond them. A pause of five seconds allows the lure to sink as many feet, then a few erratic cranks bring it to life, its angled diving-vane keeping it deep, out of my sight. It is hard to identify exactly what happens next – a slight flaring of fins? An inching down the ledge's slope? – but the fish are definitely aware of my offering, perhaps just from its vibrations. Intuitively, I spurt the lure forward in an escape bid...

The next moment something heavy – not one of the fish spotted – is carrying it away, impossibly far, down the submerged precipice. When it stops, there is a grating and jarring coming up the line. I picture the fish in some underwater cavern, sawing the thick monofilament leader across a ragged edge. Then it comes out, and I regain a few feet of line. But now I have to follow it along the cliff, past where the platform tilts sideways to merge with the mountainside. The slope above me looks disconcertingly like a still from a film of a rockslide, but for one reassuring detail: spiders have stitched it all together with fine-spun cat's-cradles that comb the air for lake flies.

With nearly all mental capacity taken up with footholds and rod control, the following minutes leave just snapshots in the memory: the fish jumping, mouth agape and gills flaring in a flurry of spray; Mohammed clambering down 20 sheer feet to the water; an indistinct larger form, deeper down, inscrutably shadowing the fish on the line. And then it is over: a slab of silver nearly 4 ft long lies on its side at the surface, a restraining hand gripping the lower jaw of its bucket-sized mouth. Briefly, adding a surreal touch, two other perch materialize just feet from where Mohammed is crouched, and calmly observe proceedings before melting back into the fathomless blue.

'Fifty pounds,' says Mohammed. I take a couple of photographs, then he lowers it back into the water and holds it steady. Soon it flexes from side to side, signaling that it is ready to go.

It silently launches itself from the mountainside, gliding high above the desert floor.

Garfish

JASON RIZOS

IN THE DISTANT hills of southern Missouri, four dammed and flooded tributaries form winding lakelets, ridged and folded and nestled into the Ozark Mountains. From the sky, the Lake of the Ozarks forms furious tendrils of subsidiary waterways that shock outwards from an oxbow channel, once the Osage River, and lay a fractal pattern across the land, settling into thousands of placid coves. In these waters there once lived some of the biggest freshwater fish ever found.

Stretched out straight, the Lake of the Ozarks' coastline could cover California's entire seaboard and all but fifty miles of Oregon's as well. Roadways feed through the hills, lanes narrow as they truncate and end, asphalt turns to concrete and concrete dissipates to gravel. Follow Highway 54 south through central Missouri to route W, past washboard and pot-holed gravel roads that peter out into anti-climactic conclusions of wildflower and ruined boat ramps, and you will find an exposed timber, single-room log cabin built by the grandfather of my own great-grandfather, occasionally chinked and daubed with plaster and cement over the course of ninety years.

My mother's side of the family is defined by a legacy of bitter divisions. Siblings reach adulthood, swear to never speak to one another again, and make good on that promise. So it was over subsequent generations that two factions became four, and distant relatives I heard of only in vague stories split and sold what was sixteen acres at the time of Bagnell Dam's construction in 1931. The land bifurcated not once, but twice, and fifty years later only a single four-acre slope of oak-hickory remained, and with it the family Blake, its Patriarch, my Uncle Pat, a war veteran, hermit, and testament to this time and place in history.

Down a final grassy incline to the water, a path now unsuitable for anything but off-road vehicles, a pontoon of salvaged Styrofoam and pinewood planks once floated on the still, murky waters of my family cove at the second mile marker – all marine destinations upon Lake of the Ozarks are measured by their distance in miles from Bagnell Dam. Kneeling there upon the dock, threading monofilament through the eye of a treble hook, there I was, next twisting the line with my thumb, feeding it through the first loop and pulling the knot tight. Turning over a limestone boulder yielded mud-gorged earthworms as thick as sausages. These I would impale halfway through so that the barbs would not be exposed to the many insufferable timber snags that dotted the lakebed.

This was 1986. I was nine years old.

On this particular evening I first discovered just what kind of monsters lurked in the voluminous depths of the Lake of the Ozarks. The rest of my family had rolled vulcanized rubber tractor-tire inner tubes to the cabin atop the slope, distracted with preparing the campfire and applying ointment to fresh sunburns. Thirty or so feet from the cabin, Pat had occupied a small camping trailer since returning from Vietnam. We knew we had arrived at the lake the minute we spotted the black and white POW/MIA flag hanging from the wooden porch he had built beside his trailer. Agent Orange had taken its toll on his health, as such Pat lived off a modest disability stipend from the US Army. Hair white and tightly curled, Pat wore wiry, circular John Lennon spectacles, smoked sweet-smelling tobacco from soapstone pipes he carved himself, and explained how the tonic smoke and a steady diet of channel catfish kept the dioxin contamination in his lungs at bay. Even the youngest of us kids could tell from the way he coughed that something was seriously wrong. But Pat was one tough cookie, so we figured he'd be as permanent a Lake Ozarks fixture as the family's rustic cabin with its purple painted door.

The other kids preferred swimming and plunging from a rope swing while I traversed the shoreline with my rod, aiming for still waters between patches of cat-tail and primrose. Since I had been old enough to hold a fishing rod, the mystery of what lay beneath these waters entranced me, and I reveled in that first glimpse of a fish rising up to the surface as I towed it ashore.

Pat appreciated that I enjoyed fishing as much as he, so that evening he brought with him his own fishing gear and met me there on the dock as I cast my earthworms deep into the waters of the cove. My uncle rarely engaged with the rest of the family, preferring to sip Busch beer and stoke his pipe in an orange lawn chair. His stories were imbued with a kind of magical wonder and never without an inkling of peril. Let's just say, you listened up. Pat gripped us with tales of his encounters with MoMo, the Missouri Monster, a kind of vernacular Sasquatch that seemed to exist primarily for the purpose of torturing old Pat by shaking the canvas army surplus tent in which he stored tools and landscaping gear. Sometime in the late hours of the night we would wake inside the cabin to the sound of fists furiously beating upon stretched canvas and wrenches banging on empty gas cans until my grandmother would at last yell out the window a reminder that he promised not to do that again this year.

That evening, there upon the dock Pat opened his tackle box with a priestly reverence and lit his pipe with a single match struck from the backside of his blue jeans. He sat down and let his bare feet dip into the water beside my own.

'You want to catch the big fish, do you?' he asked, not without his trademark tinge of sternness.

I hadn't really thought about it.

Pat gently lifted a single lure from among a welter of broken baubles and lead weights. 'It's called the Rattlin' Rapala. Three ninety-nine at Walmart,' he said, gazing at me over his peacenik glasses for emphasis. 'I can let you borrow it, but you can't lose it.'

I nodded, the significance of Pat's gesture beginning to dawn on me.

'Now, Jason, this is the *only way* you're going to catch the big one.'

'Big one?' I asked, skeptically, having spent the last few seasons plunking earthworms into shoals of half-pound bluegill and sunfish that struck lures without reservation.

He flashed the end of his pipe in my face and I felt the breath come out of me. 'You don't even know what you are talking about, kid,' he said gravely.

I scratched my head sheepishly. 'Well, what do you mean? How big do they get?' I looked out at the main channel in the distance, nearly a mile of water reaching from the cove where we fished to the far shore beyond, only a couple miles from the gargantuan, 2,500-foot-wide Bagnell Dam and a reservoir large enough to comfortably home a blue whale.

'There's catfish down there,' Pat insisted, his voice now a whisper. 'Never stopped growing since they put in the dam. Fifty years old now. So big you can't even haul them up.' Pat had a way of talking, whether he was serious did not matter, in fact, he was probably never serious, always messing with us kids, but we always listened and whatever it was he was talking about, we took it as gospel. 'Some the size of a Volkswagen. One hundred thirty feet deep they swim . . .'

I was stricken by the mere thought of it. I had seen a Volkswagen Beetle before. Short, squat, with buggy fish-eyes and in my mind turning blackish-green, growing thick, whip-like whiskers and spiny dorsal fins.

'. . . lurking about,' Pat continued, 'water black as night, hungry . . . searching for fish. Or, well . . . you know.'

'People?' I asked, choking on my words.

'I sure as heck wouldn't try swimming out there in the channel,' he said.

'But we are safe here? By the dock?'

He thought about this, took a contemplative draw from his pipe, and then nodded. 'I think so.'

'You can't catch them?' I asked, my mind reeling, heart racing.

'Ain't nobody strong enough to reel in a fish that size.'

'Then how do you know how big they are?'

Pat stoked his pipe, thick ribbons of smoke wafting orbits around his head. 'You're a smart kid, you know that?'

I shook my head.

'Tell you what,' he said, 'you promise you don't lose it, you can borrow this here lure. You promise me now.'

'Yes sir,' I said. 'I promise.' I flashed the Cub Scout three-finger salute. Pat handed over the lure. The entire lake bottom was awash in countless, invisible snags. I had lost a dozen rubber crawfish in just the first day of this trip. Making matters worse, largemouth bass are known to swim laterally, as soon as they are hooked, and find the nearest underwater log or tree stump around which they will wind and cleat your fishing line. This creates no uncertain difficulty for the would-be angler, who has to take this into consideration and strike a balance between reeling too hard and too fast – breaking the line with the savage fight this fish puts up – and letting out some line only to have the beast tangle it around the first log it finds.

'You know how to cast out far?' Pat asked after a long silence.

'Yes sir,' I said. Earlier that summer, at the Beaumont Jamboree, I took first place in the Cub Scout casting competition in both distance and accuracy, striking a paper plate in field at seventy-five yards.

At dusk, as shadows from the trees reach out into the lake, catfish and bass venture in from the cold depths and peruse minnows in the shallow waters. Upon the edge of the dock, I casted parallel to the shore, beyond the line of shadow drawn by the setting sun and into the predatory waters where Pat promised bass as big as fourteen pounds.

My Snoopy brand spin caster and four-foot rod were no match for behemoths like these, but Pat never pointed this out, so there I was fishing for them anyway. The Snoopy rod would later see its demise at the hands of such a fish. The one time I finally hooked into one it was like I had caught hold of Earth's rotational axis itself. The fish yanked my line and ratcheted the drag so fast it sounded like a bullfrog croaking in a kettle drum, and I could only watch helplessly as all fifty yards of 14 lb test flew out to completion and the little toothy dial on the drag snapped and sent tiny brass nuts and springs into the air around me. The fish threatened to pull me into the water, were it not for the two-by-four handrail Pat had nailed into the terminus of the dock, around which I had wrapped my free arm. Before I even had a chance to turn the crank, the reel let out a helpless, tinkling death rattle, the knot fastening the line yielded and the trembling monofilament popped and vanished into the water. I was certain I had hooked into one of those Volkswagen-sized catfish.

But another summer would pass before that event. That night, after Pat crept back up the hill, I snagged the Rapala on the first cast. My best bet was to pull the line in the opposite direction and unhook the snag. Dock fishing meant this was an impossibility, but I was desperate to rescue the lure that had cost $3.99 at the local Walmart. Recovering the lure meant rowing Pat's ruined metal johnboat out into the cove in order to gain the proper angle for dislodging the snag.

Grasshoppers and June bugs assaulted the boat's aluminum hull as I crunched through the tall fescue surrounding it. A constellation of arachnids held firm to the boat's interior after I flipped it over in the grass. Grim, hairless, the stuff of nightmares, smooth, pallid legs spoke more of the seriousness of the brown recluse's bite than the tiny brown violin on its thorax. I counted three. The only hope this vessel had for salvation was a Molotov cocktail to the hull. I wasn't about to climb aboard.

I returned to the dock. I winced and pulled hard against the snag and tried desperately to coax it free. But at last the line snapped and there I was, watching the fatal fishing line trickle and sink into the soup when a faint sloshing sound issued from behind me. I turned to look at what might have been one of Pat's empty Busch beer cans nuzzling the shore, but what I saw instead would rip my nine-year-old subconscious asunder.

A fish, six feet in length, but narrow as a python, rested motionlessly atop the water. Bony, striated diamonds of greenish brown led to a grisly beak overwhelmed with long, needle-like teeth, splayed in every vicious and impractical direction. The fish floated idle three feet from where I stood.

There is a type of fear that seizes the conscious mind, recommends that solid memories not form and instead some psychological housekeeping takes place in sudden anticipation of one's carnal departure from this world. All of these things happened in rapid succession as this fish made its incursion into my mind. But even the most horrific and onerous beasts of the natural and imaginative realms have the decency to devour their hapless victim in this sudden moment of discovery. This fish, which at the time I had no knowledge of, *the alligator gar*, gave me no such luxury. It preferred to remain semi-motionless, supping small beakfuls of air as I watched in agonizing horror.

Such is the way real world terror outstrips those devised by the conjurations of fiction. I was made to bear witness to this creature and to entertain thoughts of how and why such a thing could be made to exist whatsoever. Agonizing time expired until at last a grim, truncated caudal fin waved ominously into motion and the entire thing rolled down and forward beneath the dock like the vile tentacle of the *Diagna* that haunts the trash compactor aboard the Death Star.

During what was no doubt some sort of fugue state, I had evidently carried my intact body up the hill leading to the cabin, night having fallen by now, at least as far as the forest was concerned. My recounting of the tale to those around the campfire was not one of excitement or intrigue, nor was it of terror or fear, rather, one of total imminent doom. There is an alligator in the lake, I confessed, and it is going to kill me.

I vaguely recall the bursts of laughter that followed, and in all fairness I had already identified as a child capable of specious recollections of the imaginary sort. But my family, however bucolic and poor, were strictly terrestrial, largely suburban, and had zero knowledge of the alligator gar. They would not believe me. They blamed Pat for putting such notions into my head in the first place. Pat, warming his hands before the campfire, wore a stricken countenance but remained silent on the matter. Eyes wide through glistening round lenses, he pegged me with a look of total and unabashed credulity.

The vehemence with which I refused to enter the water the next day did nothing to help corroborate my story and the alligator gar would never show up again. There, upon the shore, as my cousins splashed gleefully in the fatal waters around the dock, I clasped my knees in my arms and rocked mournfully until Pat, witness to my state, offered wisdom I recall axiomatically to this day: 'You can't be a pussy all your life, Jason.' Determined not to in fact live as a pussy the remainder of my life, I retrieved one of the sticky, black inner tubes and embarked upon the stygian abyss, the only one of the adolescent cousins and siblings to enjoy the lake in possession of nihilistic agony of being devoured by this creature that had in no way been the product of my overactive imagination. Something had come unglued in my head that weekend as I *swam anyway*.

I spent the following school year regaling fellow fifth-graders of the fearsome brute I had encountered and began researching other mythic and speculative creatures in earnest. A world of fictional and semi-fictional occultism opened up before me. I embarked on a spiritual journey, read tales of horror and mayhem, and immersed myself in mythology and folklore, certain at least some had to be true. Truth, for that matter, became irrelevant. The world I held as true became mere speculation in light of what Pat had promised to exist and what I had seen with my own eyes. My trauma from that day was soothed by the sheer exhilaration provided by chronicles of fantastic realms. It was this year that I discovered I must write these things down, I must tell stories fantastic and true, some more fantastic than true, some more true than fantastic. But I did not know where along this spectrum the story of the Lake of the Ozarks Leviathan would fall.

The next summer, *Jaws: The Revenge* found its way into theaters and proved that predatory fish could track their victims across hemispheres, thus confirming the monster I had encountered could be lurking just about anywhere I traveled. Vivid nightmares of fish were routine. A recurring dream of mine, though less frequent today, I find myself high above a small, transparent body of water, such as a small lake or a river, my perspective allowing me to see fish impossibly large for the water they inhabit, beginning with prize catfish. I spot dizzyingly massive fish creeping about, bony pike the size of orca whales, until it becomes clear I am much closer to the water than when the dream began and beholding these fish causes me to collapse helplessly in a state of shock and fear, until I at last fall into the water, and desperately kick my legs against the current in a vain attempt to struggle ashore before the fish, whether accidentally or on purpose, begin gently masticating my torso. Thankfully, I always wake soon after this occurs.

A strange obsession with fish and the invisible potential for what lies deep within large bodies of water followed me well into college. Though squarely a student of writing and literature, I committed myself to double-majoring in Biological Sciences. And I was no doubt the only student within the Ichthyology lecture hall who wore a strained rictus of terror and fear as the professor droned on about the bizarre and uncanny physiology of fishes on this planet.

It was during the winter semester of 1997 that a taxonomical guide simply titled *Missouri Fish* yielded the answer I had spent a decade in search of. There it was, the alligator gar, *Atractosteus spatula*, drawn in colored pencil and accompanied by vital statistics:

> a ray-finned euryhaline fish related to the bowfin, considered one of few living fossils, retaining morphological features of early ancestors, such as a broad snout and dual rows of sharp teeth, used for capturing and impaling prey. Capable of growing up to ten feet in length and weighing over 300 lbs, these fish –

The words were blurred by tears before I could finish reading the entry.

Library patrons turned their heads in my direction as I sniffed loudly and wiped my eyes with the back of my hand.

'It's just a goddamn fish,' I remember sputtering through maniacal laughter.

> They do not have scales, rather, they are armored with hard, diamond-shaped ganoid enamel plates that are nearly impenetrable, their bodies torpedo shaped, they are stalking, ambush predators, primarily piscivores, but will ambush and eat small water fowl and even mammals.

I continued reading this real-life *Necronomicon*, hair clasped in white-knuckled fists, my gaping mouth frozen and crooked like a tetanus patient.

> Diet studies have revealed fishing tackle and boat engine parts in their digestive systems. Their method of ambush is to float a few feet below the surface, and wait for unsuspecting prey to swim within reach. They lunge forward, and with a sweeping motion grab their prey, impaling it on their double rows of sharp teeth.

A campus security guard gently tapped my shoulder and asked if I needed any help.

With all the distractions and frugality that accompanies university life, I had not visited my family's cabin at the Lake of the Ozarks for several years. But after reading this, and feeling a strange combination of vindication and luck that I had not become scrawny prey for that gigantic fish ten years ago, I left that day for the lake. Much had changed in that time: the lake had endured a long trajectory of reckless misuse so that today the Lake of the Ozarks is no longer thought of as a sport fisher's paradise, but a swirling tempest of sewage, ringed by concrete seawalls, forever mauled by retching power yachts piloted by drunken neophytes.

Pockets of ice crunched beneath the tires of my car as I scratched down the gravel road leading to the cabin. The road thus far had been ominously bereft of bait and tackle shops. I thought about how Pat had passed away the previous autumn, metastatic carcinomas in both lungs. An argument between my mother and that part of the family meant that I had not attended the funeral. It was strange not to see his trailer and POW/MIA flag. The cabin itself looked worse for wear, the once buckled roof had partially caved in and the iconic purple screen door had chipped and faded to the point that only vague indications of its original color remained.

On a nail within the well's pump house, the rubber daisy-flower keychain still hung, along with the cabin's deadbolt key. The cabin had been burgled, apparently repeatedly, and anything of value had been either hauled off or burned in a campfire outside. An old wooden baby crib still lay in the rafters beneath an abandoned wasp nest on the ceiling. Flabby, deflated, black inner tubes drooped down from the rafters like Dali clocks, accented with orange Styrofoam life vests. A single brown bamboo cane fishing pole remained, butchers' twine leader tied to one end. I stood on the old picnic table, slid the rod carefully from the rafters and made my way down the hill.

There had been a drought the previous summer and the lake level that January had reached its lowest point in decades. The cove had been transformed into a rock-filled gully. The once floating dock lay prostrate like a sorrowful penitent on the barren lakebed, its steel tether festooned with ribbons of lacey, dry algae. I stepped down from the bank and out into a sea of softball-sized chunks of limestone. I could walk clear across the cove, if I wanted to, the lake reduced to just a meager channel in the distance, where no boats roamed.

A withered and ancient oak stump lay there among the rocks. Hung within its bleached roots was a shrine of desiccated fishing lures and line, measuring decades of artificial bait technology. I reached out and took one of them in my fingers. The casing rattled as I turned it over in my hand. Pat's Rapala. $3.99 at Walmart. All the mysteries of the deep laid barren and sober before me. Beyond this shrine of lures, nothing, there was nothing at all.

I squatted, sat down on the ground and let the old bamboo cane rod fall and click on the rocks. The stark January sun beat down shamelessly from above, chasing every shadow, exposing every contour of the parched lakebed. In six months' time, the main channel would be over-run with jet skis and Scarab power boats. Sleek, certain lines of blue and red painted fiberglass, tall rooster tails of petrol-infused lake water spraying the air behind them, leaving colorful, oily rainbows upon the surface. The alligator gar now only fable, spectacle of memory, a tale told as fiction.

On Dry-Cow Fishing As a Fine Art

RUDYARD KIPLING

IT MUST BE clearly understood that I am not at all proud of this performance. In Florida, men sometimes hook and land, on rod and tackle a little finer than a steam-crane and chain, a mackerel-like fish called 'tarpon,' which sometime run to 120 pounds. Those men stuff their captures and exhibit them in glass cases and become puffed up. On the Columbia River sturgeon of 150 pounds are taken with the line. When the sturgeon is hooked the line is fixed to the nearest pine tree or steamboat-wharf, and after some hours or days the sturgeon surrenders himself, if the pine or the line do not give way. The owner of the line then states on oath that he has caught a sturgeon, and he, too, becomes proud.

These things are mentioned to show how light a creel will fill the soul of a man with vanity. I am not proud. It is nothing to me that I have hooked and played 700 pounds weight of quarry. All my desire is to place the little affair on record before the mists of memory breed the miasma of exaggeration.

The minnow cost 18 pence. It was a beautiful quill minnow, and the tackle-maker said that it could be thrown as a fly. He guaranteed further in respect to the triangles – it glittered with triangles – that, if necessary, the minnow would hold a horse. A man who speaks too much truth is just as offensive as a man who speaks too little. None-the-less, owing to the defective condition of the present law of libel, the tackle-maker's name must be withheld.

The minnow and I and a rod went down to a brook to attend to a small jack who lived between the clumps of flags in the most cramped swim that he could select. As a proof that my intentions were strictly honorable, I may mention that I was using a little split-cane rod – very dangerous if the line runs through weeds, but very satisfactory in clean water, inasmuch as it keeps a steady strain on the fish and prevents him from taking liberties. I had an old score against the jack. He owed me two live-bait already, and I had reason to suspect him of coming up-stream and interfering with a little bleak-pool under a horse-bridge, which lay entirely beyond his sphere of legitimate influence. Observe, therefore, that my tackle pointed clearly to jack, and jack alone; though I knew that there were monstrous perch in the brook. The minnow was thrown as a fly several times and, owing to my peculiar and hitherto unpublished methods of fly throwing, nearly six pennyworth of the triangles came off, either in my coat-collar, or my thumb, or the back of my hand. Fly fishing is a very gory amusement.

The jack was not interested in the minnow, but towards the twilight a boy opened a gate of the field and let in some twenty or thirty cows and half a dozen cart-horses, and they were all very much interested. The horses galloped up and down the field and shook the banks, but the cows walked solidly and breathed heavily, as people breathe who appreciate the Fine Arts.

By this time I had given up all hope of catching my jack fairly, but I wanted the live-bait and bleak-account settled before I went away, even if I tore up the bottom of the brook. Just before I had quite made up my mind to borrow a tin of chloride of lime from the farmhouse – another triangle had fixed itself in my fingers – I made a cast, which for pure skill, exact judgment of distance and perfect coincidence of hand and eye and brain, would have taken every prize at a bait-casting tournament. That was the first half of the cast. The second was postponed because the quill minnow would not return to its proper place, which was under the lobe of my left ear. It had done thus before, and I supposed it was in collision with a grass tuft, till I turned round and saw a large red and white bald-faced cow trying to rub what would be withers in a horse with her nose.

She looked at me reproachfully, and her look said as plainly as words: 'The season is too far advanced for gadflies. What is this strange disease?'

I replied, 'Madam, I must apologize for an unwarrantable liberty on the part of my minnow, but if you will have the goodness to keep still until I can reel in, we will adjust this little difficulty.'

I reeled in very swiftly and cautiously, but she would not wait. She put her tail in the air and ran away. It was a purely involuntary motion on my part: I struck. Other anglers may contradict me, but I firmly believe that if a man had foul-hooked his best friend through the nose, and that friend ran, the man would strike by instinct. I struck, therefore, and the reel began to sing just as merrily as though I had caught my jack. But had it been a jack, the minnow would have come away. I told the tackle-maker this much afterwards and he laughed and made allusions to the guarantee about holding a horse.

Because it was a fat innocent she-cow that had done me no harm the minnow held – held like an anchor-fluke in coral moorings – and I was forced to dance up and down an interminable field very largely used by cattle. It was like salmon fishing in a nightmare. I took gigantic strides, and every stride found me up to my knees in marsh. But the cow seemed to skate along the squashy green by the brook, to skim over the miry backwaters and to float like a mist through the patches of rush that squirted black filth over my face.

Sometimes we whirled through a mob of her friends – there were no friends to help me – and they looked scandalized; and sometimes a young and frivolous cart-horse would join in the chase for a few miles, and kick solid pieces of mud into my eyes; and through all the mud, the milky smell of kine, the rush and the smother, I was aware of my own voice crying: 'Pussy, pussy, pussy! Pretty pussy! Come along then, puss-cat!'

You see it is so hard to speak to a cow properly, and she would not listen – no, she would not listen.

Then she dropped, and the moon got up behind the pollards to tell the cows to lie down; but they were all on their feet, and they came trooping to see. And she said, 'I haven't had my supper, and I want to go to bed, and please don't worry me.'

And I said, 'The matter has passed beyond any apology. There are three courses open to you, my dear lady. If you'll have the common sense to walk up to my creel, I'll get my knife and you shall have all the minnow. Or, again, if you'll let me move across to your near side, instead of keeping me so coldly on your off side, the thing will come away in one tweak. I can't pull it out over your withers. Better still, go to a post and rub it out, dear. It won't hurt much, but if you think I'm going to lose my rod to please you, you are mistaken.'

And she said, 'I don't understand what you are saying. I am very, very unhappy.'

And I said, 'It's all your fault for trying to fish. Do go to the nearest gate-post, you nice fat thing, and rub it out.'

For a moment I fancied she was taking my advice. She ran away and I followed. But all the other cows came with us in a bunch, and I thought of

Phaeton trying to drive the Chariot of the Sun, and Texan cowboys killed by stampeding cattle, and 'Green Grow the Rushes, O!' and Solomon and Job, and 'loosing the bands of Orion,' and hooking Behemoth, and Wordsworth who talks about whirling round with stones and rocks and trees, and 'Here we go round the Mulberry Bush,' and 'Pippin Hill,' and 'Hey Diddle Diddle,' and most especially the top joint of my rod.

Again she stopped – but nowhere in the neighborhood of my knife – and her sisters stood moonfaced round her. It seemed that she might, now, run towards me, and I looked for a tree, because cows are very different from salmon who only jump against the line, and never molest the fisherman. What followed was worse than any direct attack. She began to buck-jump, to stand on her head and her tail alternately, to leap into the sky, all four feet together, and to dance on her hind legs. It was so violent and improper, so desperately unladylike, that I was inclined to blush, as one would blush at the sight of a prominent statesman sliding down a fire escape, or a duchess chasing her cook with a skillet. That flopsome abandon might go on all night in the lonely meadow among the mists, and if it went on all night – this was pure inspiration – I might be able to worry through the fishing line with my teeth.

Those who desire an entirely new sensation should chew with all their teeth, and against time, through a best waterproofed silk line, one end of which belongs to a mad cow dancing fairy rings in the moonlight; at the same time keeping one eye on the cow and the other on the top joint of a split-cane rod. She buck-jumped and I bit on the slack just in front of the reel; and I am in a position to state that that line was cored with steel wire throughout the particular section which I attacked. This has been formally denied by the tackle-maker, who is not to be believed.

The wheep of the broken line running through the rings told me that henceforth the cow and I might be strangers. I had already bidden goodbye to some tooth or teeth; but no price is too great for freedom of the soul.

'Madam,' I said, 'the minnow and twenty feet of very superior line are your alimony without reservation. For the wrong I have unwittingly done to you I express my sincere regret. At the same time, may I hope that Nature, the kindest of nurses, will in due season –'

She or one of her companies must have stepped on her spare end of the line in the dark, for she bellowed wildly and ran away, followed by all the cows. I hoped the minnow was disengaged at last, and before I went away looked at my watch; fearing to find it nearly midnight. My last cast for the jack was made at 6.23 p.m. There lacked still three and a half minutes of the half-hour; and I would have sworn that the moon was paling before the dawn.

'Simminly someone were chasing they cows down to bottom o'Ten Acre,' said the farmer that evening. "Twasn't you, sir?'

'Now under what earthly circumstances do you suppose I should chase your cows? I wasn't fishing for them, was I?'

Then all the farmer's family gave themselves up to jam-smeared laughter for the rest of the evening, because that was a rare and precious jest, and it was repeated for months, and the fame of it spread from that farm to another, and yet another at least three miles away, and it will be used again for the benefits of visitors when the freshets come down to spring. But to the greater establishment of my honor and glory, I submit in print this bald statement of fact, that I may not, through forgetfulness, be tempted later to tell how I hooked a bull on a Marlow Buzz, how he ran up a tree and took to water, and how I played him along the London road for thirty miles, and gaffed him at Smithfield. Errors of this kind may creep in with the lapse of years, and it is my ambition ever to be a worthy member of that fraternity who pride themselves on never deviating by one hair's breadth from the absolute and literal truth.

Bats, Bushes, and Barbless Hooks

ERIC WITCHEY

IT FRUSTRATES ME that insight often comes from frustration, but it's not quite as bad when it comes from frustration while flipping fly line in a lake or river. After all, I've had a habit of dealing with frustration while angling ever since my earliest fishing memory, in which I was out with my father, whom we often called PapaRon, on the Clear Fork River in Ohio.

PapaRon was spin-casting bait and light lures for smallmouth bass, and I was his bait hunter. The bit where I flipped rocks and hunted hellgrammites for him was wonderful. I was low, quick, and filled with the joy of the hunt and the helping. The bit where I hid from an icy thunderstorm while standing in the wind shadow of my father and a big maple tree was the frustrating part.

Under that tree, my father provided a stoic model of the pleasures of the outdoors. Meanwhile, my fifty-pound body fought to stop shivering and to keep my father from seeing me cry.

I failed on both counts.

PapaRon, however, was kind and encouraging. He said things like, 'Thank you for helping me stay warm under this tree. You've been a big help today.'

My child fisherman-self grinned ear-to-ear, and my little body got so pumped full of endorphins that my brain became permanently imprinted with angling, no matter how frustrating, as a positive experience. Add a lifetime of many other joyful experiences with my father, my family, others, and just myself, and my adult fisherman ended up feeling pretty good after any angling day – no matter what the mix of frustrations and joys.

And isn't that really the whole of the Zen of angling? The pleasures come from anticipations, from exertions, from preparations, from surprises, and from both the successes and failures. All these things lead to that moment of simple clarity and silence of mind we seek from our experiences in nature. The joy of angling is, in at least a part, the experience of opening to the natural world and emptying the mind of the useless chatter and worry of our normal days. As one good friend of mine says, 'I don't go to the river to catch fish as much as I go to the river to fill my head with its sound. It's a good day if I can go home, close my eyes, and hear only the river.'

Angling is, as most anglers know, a meditation in the truest traditions of mindfulness. Tying a cinch knot can be a pure moment of being here now. Untangling a rat's nest can be an exercise in patience that includes recognizing our frustration and letting it go.

This is the nature of our experiences when we sally forth on the adventure that comes from trying to trick a fish into sticking itself in the lip with a curved, pointy bit of wire.

Frustration is just part of the package.

Personally, my mind is most completely washed clean by fly fishing in high mountain streams and tarn lakes. I like to take a four-weight rod into tiny streams where precise casts under low bushes yield small, nervous trout, which I try with all my heart to release unharmed. I like to take my six-weight backpacking rod to the high country lakes and find quiet places in late summer where I can stretch out my casts to the limits of my skill and let dry flies settle onto glassy lakes.

I'm pretty much always a barbless catch-and-release guy. I have been since the day I saw PapaRon absently reach out his spin-caster rod tip (and double-, treble-hooked Rapala) toward a passing woodpecker on the wing. Much to his surprise, and mine, he actually hooked the poor bird. The ensuing chaos, blood, and pain taught me that barbs are not anybody's friend. When the bird was freed and PapaRon had cleaned off his hands, rod, and Rapala, he turned to me and said, 'Eric, if you go out often enough, you will experience some very surprising things.'

In addition to what I learned about unintentional cruelty from that moment of surprising gore and casual, accidentally inflicted pain, I have come to a place in life where I rarely feel the need to kill a fish. Occasionally, while in the high country, I eat a few fish. And, like the First Nations People who were here long before me, I thank the fish for participating in sustaining my life.

I love fish – living fish even more than the fish on my plate.

The iridescence of a rainbow's sides, the aggression of a cutthroat attack, the general arrogance of a German brown's carnivorous view of the world – these things make me happy. Perhaps I personify the fish more than I should, but I don't care. I am, after all, a writer by trade. Imagination and empathy don't stay home when I go out with rod and fly.

In fact, I'll just say it up front. This is a fish tale.

I'm often accused of exaggerating, as are all anglers. However, I will point out that I am meticulous and precise in my recounting of my angling experiences. I became this way because of Dick Martin, who was a freelance writer who used to, and may still, write for magazines like *Field & Stream* and *Outdoor Life*. Not only was he PapaRon's good friend and companion on many fishing trips, he was a biology teacher in my high school.

Science-type people might read this. I really don't want people to think my fiction spills over into my biology, and I especially don't ever want to meet Dick Martin (in this life or the next) and have to explain how I lied in print about fishing.

OK, a fish may grow by an inch or so in the telling and retelling.

After all, I can't hold my hands up exactly the same distance from one another every time. And, as I said, I have no photographic proof of what I'm about to recount.

All I have to keep me honest is the memory of PapaRon and Dick Martin. I think they would both approve of the story of how I discovered two new types of angling.

One sunny, late July day in the years after PapaRon passed and before selfies and GoPro cameras, my pursuit of the peace provided by high mountain trout brought me new levels of frustration, and my frustrations brought me to the discovery of the aforementioned types of angling. Both have since taken their place in my grand pantheon of angling pleasures.

In spite of the lack of photographic evidence, I must point out that I have many times proven, and will continue to take great pleasure in proving, the results of the moments of insight that came from my frustration.

How? I simply show people the new angling methods. Seeing is, as they say, believing.

After two days of packing, in that long ago July, I finally planted my feet on the shallow slope of a stone shelf that descended gently from a low patch of kinnikinnick scrub in alpine tundra into the clear, glass surface of a tarn lake.

For those who are sticklers for such things, the actual lake's name is Lower Ice Lake. It is in the Entiat Mountains in the Glacier Peak Wilderness near the City of Wenatchee in Washington State in the USA. I don't recommend the hike for the untrained. The last mile is almost 1,500 feet of treacherous, nearly vertical ascent through wet, loosely attached tundra plants. That's a story for another day and another page.

Perfection, at least for me, is pretty much defined by a lake backed by sheer scarps and edged on at least one side by accessible bank with clear casting room.

The evening was beginning to cool. An ant swarm had just ended. Large cutthroat cruised the submerged edge of my stone shelf. Through the crystal water, I watched them picking up sinking ants, and my angler's pride, totally not Zen thing that it is, made me grin in anticipation.

I had brought sinking tippet. I had brought sinking ant patterns. I had at least an hour before true sunset.

Life was good. I was as near heaven as I could get.

It is a perverse truth of the universe that when anglers believe themselves near to heaven, the gods of line and fly are about to laugh.

I rigged up.

I flipped flies.

In my mind's eye, I saw myself landing sixteen inch high-lake cuts – bringing them gently to my carefully wetted hand, keeping them in the water, and quietly, respectfully, gripping the barbless hook with forceps and slipping the hook from their mouths. In my imagination, they nodded to me, thanked me for the game, and swam back to their world of ant, tiny snail, and caddis dinners.

My casting was perfect. I swear, I felt the loading and unloading of the rod more completely than ever in my life before or since. My hand felt the light tug of the loaded rod on the back cast. I know to the microsecond when to push, when to pull, when to let my wrist break to create adjustments in laying the line down on that perfect lake.

An osprey called to me. A mountain goat watched from the wall of rock across the lake. The low sun off my right shoulder even caught spray from my line and made little rainbows.

Since GoPro cameras didn't exist yet, and because my father had occasionally fished with a camera crew present, I wished for my own camera crew.

Oh, the gods of angling were having fun. I just didn't know it yet.

So, I put my ant pattern on the water, let it sink, and watched a giant cut rise like a missile from a rock shadow and, as cuts often do, hit hard.

Some anglers lament that cuts will often hit hard but give a weak fight. Personally, I like that streaking attack and the fact that the fight does little damage to the fish.

So, I set the hook.

Perhaps I was more excited than I realized.

Instead of hooking that first, glorious attacker, the ant streaked up out of the water and actually hit me in the face. Line piled in the water and on the rock at my feet.

Suddenly, my fantasy camera crew was no longer welcome on my sunset rock.

I missed the hook set. I had no fish. I had a rat's nest of tangles. And I had my first frustration of the evening.

Many years of practice had taught me the ritual patience needed in that moment, so I cursed lightly and settled onto my butt to untangle before trying again.

Unfortunately, when I got to the final flip and twist of tangled leader before my ant pattern would be free, I discovered that the hook was broken where the shank meets the bend. The ant pattern was fine, but all that was left of my barbless, kind-hearted hook was a tiny bit of curve that suggested that once there had been more steel.

Figuring the hook had been flawed, I shrugged off the setback and replaced the fly.

Finally, once more settled into the magic of my perfect moment on the lake, and only a little bit miffed that I had lost ten minutes of daylight, I pulled out line, roll casted for some length, then false casted to get the distance I wanted. Finally, I shot a little line and let my new fly settle ten feet in front of a visible, cruising cut.

The fish wasn't as big as the first, which I estimated to be at least, oh, as long as my arm and as fat as my water bottle.

Hm ... OK, PapaRon and Dick Martin. I'm sorry. It was between twelve and fourteen inches. Water obscured my view. It was big enough to have that odd sort of square-backed head cuts get when they are big enough. That's as precise as I can get.

However, the new fish was certainly just as aggressive.

Congratulating myself on two hits on my first two casts, I set the hook.

Again, the fly came free. The mess wasn't as bad, but my frustration went way up. The goat was a bit surprised by my vocabulary. I think it blushed.

Embarrassed again, I quickly regrouped and put my fly back in the water.

Again, I set the hook and missed.

And again.

The goat learned more new words. The osprey went home.

The experience made no sense to me. I knew how to set a hook. I knew the timing. The hits made it very clear that I had the right fly. My casting was spot on.

After twenty minutes of continuous, inexplicable failure, frustration moved inexorably toward the kind of anger known only by an angler who repeatedly misses visible, aggressive strikes.

These are the kinds of moments that destroy fishing rods. It's like a golfer who misses ten consecutive gimme putts, explodes in rage, and breaks his four-hundred dollar putter in half.

Luckily, I had stood in storms under trees as a child, so I just sat down on the rock and stared at the lake for a few, precious pre-sunset minutes.

The sun ignored me and dropped lower and lower. The surface of the lake became opaque. Rational thought returned, as it occasionally does.

I decided to put a dry fly on because I could no longer see the trout under the surface. My reasoning was that if I couldn't see the trout, I couldn't see an underwater strike. If I were going to break my streak of missed fish, I would need to see the hit. If the fish wouldn't hit a surface fly, that was OK. Better to have no hits than miss another fish.

Claiming that my frustration resulted in an insight that caused me to choose a big, especially fat red humpy pattern would be a lie. In truth, I chose the pattern because it was big and had high-contrast white hackle that would make it easy to see in the waning light.

While returning my ant pattern to my fly box, I discovered that the hook was missing. The break was in exactly the same place as the first ant. Silently, I swore to find the name of the hook brand and never buy that brand again.

Floating tippet tied in, humpy on, casting still smooth and spot-on, I laid out thirty feet of line and let the humpy settle.

To my great joy, the water erupted around my new fly.

I set the hook.

The fly came at me like an angry hornet. The fish swam away.

This time, I immediately checked the fly.

Broken.

The sun, like the osprey, decided to leave. The goat continued to watch.

My perfect evening fishing had become a nightmare of mysterious equipment failure, lost fish, and damaged pride.

I had maybe a half hour before I would have to stop trying. By law, I had only an hour to fish after sunset anyway. Sometimes, the law provides a good way to save face.

As fast as I could, I tied on a new humpy. As fast as I could, I pulled line, rolled, and false casted to get my distance.

During a back cast, the fly snagged.

Of course it did. Evenings of perfection while angling do not tolerate urgency. The angling gods laughed. I suspect that even the goat watching from the cliff across the lake laughed, but I could no longer make out its face and don't know what goat noises really mean.

I set down my rod and followed the line back up the gentle slope of my shelf of rock.

The fly was hooked on a little lip of stone, a two-inch tall cliff that cut across the otherwise featureless shelf. There, near my snagged fly, I found half a hook.

They say that laughter is the release of tension, and I had certainly gotten very tense. I laughed. The goat made a noise. I decided that it could be in my tribe. We were bonding.

That earlier feeling I had that I could feel the line loading and that I knew the exact moment to push my rod forward turned out to be my hooks breaking on a rock. Every first cast had resulted in a hookless fly. Only my current humpy, probably because my cast was weak and hurried, had survived the test of stone.

I unhooked my humpy, reorganized my line, and set out to get a cast that didn't destroy my fly.

Confidence renewed, joy intact, imagination functioning again, my vision of giant cuts coming to hand returned. All that was needed was a shift in the angle of my back cast. Keep the fly high behind. Almost touch the water in front. I'd get a little less distance on my cast. I'd get maybe two false casts – no more.

Good plan.

The gods laughed.

My first full back-cast did not return. I turned, expecting to see my hook caught on the rock again.

Instead, the line ended in the thick of the low kinnikinnick.

That wasn't so bad. Somehow, hooking the foliage on the back cast seemed almost normal.

I followed the line to the scrub.

Something in the scrub moved.

My new angling calm and optimism left like the sun and osprey.

Low light and thrashing are not a good combination when the imagination has spent the evening building and rebuilding angling dreams. Adrenaline became my new companion.

The thrashing in the kinnikinnick reminded me of PapaRon's woodpecker. It thrashed for a few seconds, then it went quiet. If we reached for it, it thrashed again, making things much worse.

While I considered the unlikely possibility that I had snagged a bird, my thrashing thicket stilled.

Hoping my fly would come free, I tugged on the line.

The thrashing started again.

I gently tugged again, and I found that the line lifted and the thrashing stopped.

From the brush, I lifted a couple feet of line that ended in a terrified little brown bat. For Dick Martin, that's *Myotis Lucifugus.*

Not many people think of bats as cute, but this one looked at me with big, sad, black eyes. The hook's eye and hook shank stuck out of its mouth just like it would had I actually caught a fish that evening. Hanging helplessly by my humpy, the bat seemed to know I was trying to help it. At least, that's what my imagination told me.

I murmured calming words and prayed to the gods of angling and rabies before pulling my forceps from my vest. Just as I would have for a fish I hoped to release unharmed, I slid the forceps jaws along the line until I could grasp the hook shank.

Barbless hooks are a blessing to all bats.

A quick flick freed the hapless creature. Like a healthy, rested fish set to water, the bat flipped in the air, opened its wings, skimmed the surface of the kinnikinnick, and disappeared into the night.

Now, I can't say if it was frustration or anger or embarrassment, or just laziness, but when I went back to my rod and reset for my next cast, I decided that it wouldn't be right to hook either a bat or a fish at this point in my evening. In truth, what I decided was that it would be quite a bother. So, I deliberately cut the hook off my humpy.

For about ten minutes – until it was just too dark to see – I put the fly on the water and counted myself a successful angler if a fish rose to the fly.

That, and I might embarrass myself in front of a goat again. I'm not sure I could bear that.

The bat fishing tale, which is what most of my friends call it, is one of those tales that everyone thinks the angler made up. Luckily, my frustration that night in the mountains led me to two insights and two new kinds of angling.

The first insight was that my personal angling experience didn't actually require me to hook a fish. In fact, all I really needed was to trick the fish into hitting my fly. On many trips since, I have spent time practicing the relaxing art of hookless, no-catch angling. Sometimes, hookless fishing is exactly the kind of relaxing I need. The river or lake still cleanses my mind. The fish still come out to play. My flies never snag rocks, scrub, or bats. Since I usually don't plan to eat the fish, I just trick them without sticking a pin through their lips. If they rise to my fly, I have succeeded in reading the water, the weather, the fish, and the food. The hit is my success, and setting the hook, fighting the fish, bringing it to hand, and releasing it would just interfere with my moment of bliss. I'm sure it interferes with the fish's plans for the day as well.

The second insight, the one that led to the second type of fishing that was born that night, is that a true angler need not necessarily be a fisherperson. Hookless angling can take the eyes and mind off the water and focus them for a while, for about a half hour just after sunset, on the sky.

An open field, a broad sky, a decent fly rod, and a big, hookless humpy is all an angler needs to prove to friends and family that bat angling is not only possible, it is another lens through which to view this amazing, fragile world. In fact, I suspect that the next stage of evolution for my bat angling will be standing in the field holding a forgotten rod and staring at the sky in silent awe. In the context of the Zen of the universe, is that any different than standing at the edge of a tarn lake or stream staring in silent reverie at the water until the mind and soul are cleansed?

The Ethics of Skipping School

ERIC J. CHAMBERS

I WAS CONFUSED THE evening during my freshman year of high school as my mom spoke on the phone for a bit, cryptically couching language so as to disguise the topic and her feelings towards it. That wasn't entirely unusual, as during the days of the family land-line telephone, private conversation required a code language of sorts. What did surprise me was that after a few minutes of her exchange, she hollered at me and said that the call was for me.

Skeptically, I greeted whoever was on the line, and heard Grandpa's friendly voice on the other end.

'You want to go fishing tomorrow?' he asked, mischievously.

'Tomorrow is Wednesday, Grandpa, I have school.'

'Well, no shit, Sherlock, but the salmon are in, and thick. Teeny said they were knocking them dead yesterday,' he implored. 'Teeny' was a longtime friend of Grandpa's who still fishes prodigiously today, and catches more than anybody.

'Mom will never let me skip school to fish, you know that.'

'Already taken care of, Sonny Boy. Your mom is my daughter, after all. You just need to be at my house by 6:30 in the morning.'

Still confused, but liking where circumstances were heading, I told him I'd be there bright and early. I hung up the phone and glanced, carefully, at my conservative mother.

'That's really OK with you?' I asked, knowing that in addition to being the woman who disciplined our most significant childhood mishaps with a ping-pong paddle, she also happened to be the attendance clerk at the middle school, and was well-versed in the district's truancy policies.

'You are old enough to make your own decisions now,' she said. 'Plus, two unexcused absences must occur before the student is required to miss a sporting event, so you should be OK for cross-country.'

My mind raced as it occurred to me that not only was my mother enabling this excursion, but she was citing the loophole through which I would avoid all formal consequences.

As children, we are often taught in school or otherwise to view the world through the lens of ethical legalism. It's a convenient shortcut to lay out a code of arbitrary rules and convince the world that it is somehow inherently moral to follow them, as opposed to having to take the time to describe the validity of each. But in this case, rules were being broken, and for something as fun and trivial as salmon fishing.

Were I not in adolescence, and thus gifted with the ability to sleep deeply for prolonged periods, I probably wouldn't have gotten a wink that night. But I slept hard and morning came quickly, landing me at Grandpa's house right on time. He was in the midst of filling his coffee thermos when I arrived, and he packed a bag of smoked fish to snack on, along with lunch and a couple of Halloween-sized candy bars, rarely eaten but always handy in case his pancreas had a flash of functionality, rendering his insulin shot too powerful and plummeting his blood sugar.

We loaded up the boat and headed to the dock, which was busy despite being a weekday, and the early hour. Grandpa cursed at the sight of Teeny's rig, already parked with an empty boat trailer, indicating he was in the water and fishing before we arrived, a circumstance that makes one feel simultaneously lazy and amateurish, no matter how early it is.

Clouds of blue smoke filled the air as Grandpa fired up his 75-horsepower Johnson motor and prepared to jet up to the Power Line Hole, where people were reporting great success. The flavor of anticipation welled up on the back of my tongue, as Chinook boiled on top of the water across from the dock. They were in, no doubt, and we'd be tangling with them soon.

Not even an hour later we were trolling spinners under the Power Lines when my rod shook quickly and erratically, the unmistakable sign of a good Chinook hook-up. 'Fish on!' I announced, glancing away from the action quickly enough to see Grandpa's age-carved perma-frown lift from longitude to latitude.

Back in those days nearly everybody on the river knew each other, so etiquette hovered around its all-time high. As the troll of nearby boats would approach a boat with a fish on, all of the fishermen in the approaching vessel would reel up and pass the action slowly, so as to avoid being an unnecessary hazard for the lucky fisherman.

As I fought the fish, my eye caught the unmistakable outline of one particular approaching boat. Grandpa must have seen it at the time, because he juiced the trolling motor ever so slightly, turning the boat so as to expose the broadside of the action to the forthcoming vessel. He was experiencing the joy of watching his grandson fight a fish right in front of Teeny.

I had the good fortune of a few successful fishing seasons under my belt by that point, so I had built enough confidence to revel in our audience nearly as much as Grandpa. Teeny reeled up, but instead of motoring on by to continue fishing, or turning around and leaving in disgust as he often did even though he was good friends with Grandpa, he drifted in the water fifty yards or so from our boat, watching the conclusion of the fight.

Truth be told, I horsed in the last fifteen feet of line quicker than I should have, because I didn't want to miss the chance to have Teeny watch Grandpa hoist the netted fish out of the water. While Grandpa would have normally chastised me for such an action, he didn't seem to mind this time, and we got the fish to the boat and netted quickly and successfully. We slapped high five, and he clubbed the decent Chinook.

Only then did he look up, 'discovering' that Teeny was nearby, and feigning surprise as he asked him if he had seen the fish.

'Nice fish, Bud, I see the old grandkid is outdoing you again today,' Teeny responded.

'Good thing I brought him along,' Grandpa responded. 'We need somebody who can catch fish.'

Teeny turned his boat to return upriver when Grandpa caught him with one final question. 'Any luck yet?'

Teeny didn't look back as he continued in the opposite direction, but shook his head in disappointment, answering Grandpa's inquiry, much to our satisfaction.

The fishing that day was, in fact, quite hot. It seemed at least one boat was fighting a fish in succession all day long, regardless of the tide. Our next opportunity came a little over an hour later when Grandpa's rod had two small bumps and then a hard bend, usually a sign of being snagged on the bottom.

He put the boat in neutral and retrieved his rod from the holder, pulling back on the line to diagnose the issue.

Thump, thump, thump, his rod tip shook, and he retrieved line for thirty seconds or so before he made the mandatory announcement that he had, in fact, hooked a fish. To this day I am so excited when I hook up that announcing the condition is a reflex, and I shout it with joy – sometimes embarrassingly premature, misdiagnosing the tug of the bottom of the river. Grandpa had reached a point of salty maturity where he could restrain enthusiasm long enough to be sure beyond a doubt that he had hooked a fish, and sometimes slow-play it to such an extent that I'm certain he was making sure he had it sufficiently hooked, in case he lost the fish in the first few moments and wanted to play it off like it was the bottom.

I sprang to action and grabbed the net, still wet from retrieving my own fish out of the water. I gave it an exaggerated wave in the air, unnecessarily notifying nearby boats that we were fighting a fish. In my tour-de-pride with the net I noticed that, downriver just a ways, floated our familiar friend.

'Teeny is here again, Grandpa.'

'I know that; I saw him before I hooked the fish,' he responded.

I tried to imagine how Grandpa, facing upriver as he steered the boat, noticed Teeny a few hundred yards downriver of our position. I suppose after a few decades of chasing each other around the river, the two of them never really lost track of the other's position.

Grandpa fought the fish just as he fought most of them late in his life, taking nothing for granted and playing it longer than necessary. I netted his exhausted fish and hoisted it over the side of the boat, retrieving his lure from the Chinook's jaw and preparing my own rod to resume fishing. With conditions this terrific, we couldn't afford to have our rigging out of the water. As we let out our lines and began fishing, we passed by Teeny. Grandpa held up two fingers, as if Teeny hadn't been present for both. Teeny mustered the energy to feign surprise, and returned a thumbs up, himself still fishless.

Late in the afternoon, half the boats already off the river, I hooked another fish in the same spot I had landed my fish that morning. It ended up being almost identical to the morning fish, both bucks and both of decent size. I feathered this one in a bit more, since Teeny wasn't around and I had the benefit of watching Grandpa delicately retrieve his fish earlier in the day. It was hooked deeply, and we had no problem getting it into the boat.

For the first time in my life I tagged a second fish in a single day, meaning that I had reached the bag-limit on the Yaquina. Cultures and religions across the world celebrate coming-of-age with sacraments and traditions. For Catholics, it is the right of Confirmation. Jewish teens celebrate a Bar Mitzvah. In Islam it's a Sehra, and in Protestant Christianity it is Baptism, a ceremony I would enjoy a few years later, upriver on the Yaquina. In salmon fishing, the ritual is called limiting out, and that afternoon I transformed from boy to fisherman.

We could have stayed on the river and worked for Grandpa's second fish, but he had limited out plenty of times, and with over 75 pounds of Chinook already in the boat, we really didn't need a fourth fish. As we tied up at the dock to wait our turn at the ramp, Grandpa saw Teeny a couple boats in front of us in line, and chatted him up a bit. Teeny, it turns out, had gone fishless on one of the hottest fishing days of the year. We reveled in the fact, even as we sympathized with him, though truth be told it never bothers us when Teeny catches fish. Valley fishermen, on the other hand, well, that's a different matter. We'll play around, but we never root against a friend.

Childhood ethics are too often based on legalism, out of necessity, I suppose. Real-world ethics are based on a much wider framework, and I learned that afternoon what my mom knew all along: if education was the goal, school was the second-best place for me to be that day. The river was the finest classroom available, with a grizzled old substitute teacher holding class.

Though I didn't necessarily appreciate it enough at the time, the fact that I have multiple memories of 'discussing' rules with my mother until 2 a.m. after she had already repeated her rationale a dozen times, gives me hope that I might also have it in me to treat my own kids with the same respect and give them an ethical foundation based on tangible explanations and patience.

There comes a time in life, for most people anyway, when one pulls up to a red light at 1 a.m., looks around in every direction for a few prolonged moments, sees nobody in sight, and decides that green is just a color. Kant described high ethics through his Categorical Imperative. John Stuart Mills suggested that Utilitarianism best organized behavior in society. Grandpa Bud just knew the fish were in the river, and that mattered, and school could wait for a day. Mom's complicity took me in an instant from Old Testament to New. It transformed me from Saul to Paul, he on the road to Damascus, and me floating beneath the Power Lines on the Yaquina.

As a parent now, too often I catch myself exclaiming the familiar explanation, 'Because I told you to.' I cringe each time, trying hard to banish the phrase from my lexicon. I owe my children more than simple legalism, and an explanation rooted in something of substance only takes a moment, whether they accept it or not. There will come a time when our kids will need to weigh right and wrong with something more complex than rules, and I want them to have some experience sorting out such matters.

Without a Backward Cast:
Notes of an Angler

KATHARINE WEBER

*T*ROUT ARE MYSTERIOUS. *They're quiet and graceful, the oak trees of the fish forest. Mackerel, on the other hand, are noisy fish, tough and clever. They fight like hell. I've had a one-pound mackerel bend a fishing rod practically under the boat in waters off the coast of Maine. Between the two lie bass, who are middle-of-the-road fish, non-controversial. Sunfish one catches intentionally only if one is under the age of twelve; they're stupid and weak, a very lower-class fish. I have never met a sturgeon, but I have a hunch that they are downright intellectual (perhaps a bit dark and Russian, too). Salmon are, without a doubt, the most intelligent of fish; they also have an excellent sense of humor.*

Why this excursion into fish personalities? Knowing what and who is on the other end of the line is as important as knowing the rules of the game. This is the heart of it, the essential lure: the one-to-one challenge between angler and fish.

The first time I ever held a fishing rod was at a stocked lake in Minnesota when I was seven years old. I don't think I cast the line or landed the fish, but the rod was put into my hands for a few minutes after a trout had been hooked, and I remember the thrill of the tension and pulse of the struggling fish. My family was not athletically inclined, and I think this was not so much a sporting occasion as it was a diversionary way of finding something to eat. I hung around the table where the fish was being cleaned and was given a lump of quartz that I had spotted on a low shelf next to some discarded fishing nets. I treasured the snowy cluster of crystals, which seemed to me much purer and more desirable than the fish flesh it resembled.

The next time I fished was even less authentic. My grandmother paid three dollars at the World's Fair in New York for me to have the privilege of dangling a baited hook in front of some pathetic-looking trout that were milling around in a two-foot-deep plastic pond. I think I was entitled to fifteen minutes. (Three dollars for fifteen minutes' worth of opportunity to hook an anemic trout was absurdly steep, and this was 1964).

I hooked a fish and had absolutely no idea what to do next, but the fish, which had probably been through this several times that day, gave only a few feeble attempts at shaking the hook, and I finally hauled it out of the water, where it flopped in the air on the end of my line. The man who ran the concession offered to wrap it up so I could take it home, which I was very interested in doing, but my grandmother, conscious of 90° August heat and an entire day still ahead of us at the fair, briskly declined and told me that I would rather put the dear, dear cunning little fish back, wouldn't I? I looked back over my shoulder as I was led away for some nice Belgian waffles and saw my fish swimming again in the tepid water with the other fish, some of whom were swimming backwards and upside down.

At this point in my life, fishing held no real fascination for me. I was not to become a fisher for another ten years.

When I was twenty, I met Nick. After a few months it was clear that we would be married and spend the rest of our lives together. We went to Ireland for our honeymoon. We took along a spinning rod, just in case, and ended up spending almost every day of our two weeks wading in freezing rivers, casting for salmon. The underbrush grows very close to the water along the Ilen River, and most zealous back-casts ended up in a tangled line and a lost lure. The rivers were all flooded and swollen that autumn, and we never caught a thing. But I acquired a respect for the salmon of Ireland. One chilly afternoon we saw a couple of salmon just larking in a pool – our casts were probably a source of amusement for them – and one fish jumped clear out of the water, danced on his tail and nipped away. We were enchanted. We spent more time sliding in cow dung across farmers' fields, finding a clear spot where one could cast with impunity, and we warmed up after cold mornings on the rivers at the West Cork Hotel in downtown Skibbereen, where the dinners (lunches to you) consisted of wondrous heaps of roast pork or mutton or beef and four or five kinds of potatoes, piled in mounds on your plate by red-faced young women too shy to look you in the eye. Eating was an exercise in excavation.

I think I had not been happier than during some of those moments standing in my new wellingtons in some marsh waiting for my turn to fish – to cast and cast and cast. That's mostly what fishing is. We cast our arms off, developed strategies, talked to the fish, lied about what we'd seen to other fishermen and planned out routes with the primitive map issued along with the fishing license by the wizened little man who perched behind an official litter of rubber stamps at the license office in Skib. We had one rod and one license between us.

You don't see many women fishing in Ireland, and the ones you do see are usually English or German. We saw one other couple fishing, and they had fixed up a strange rig with sand eels and several hooks, which seemed rather joyless to us. They caught many trout. We preferred our system. We caught nothing. But I developed a certain amount of skill in casting, although I still to this day, because of the undergrowth of the Ilen, tend to throw more of a side-arm than an overhead cast.

A year later, we moved into the eighteenth-century Connecticut farm-house where we live today. One of the features that attracted us to this bit of countryside is the small lake on the adjoining property, which while not exactly teeming with fish does allow one frequent glimpses of ducks, geese and resident herons, depending on luck and time of day.

What one sees is, of course, one of the main attractions of fishing. Fishing takes you to some incredibly beautiful locations and then gives you the excuse to stand there all day and enjoy yourself. You would never fall asleep while fly casting; in fact, wading and casting are vigorous forms of exercise. It's also a game of skill, not a game of waiting, as polefishing must be. The rules of the game are that you are a person who can't see beneath the surface of the water terribly well and you can't use any equipment that isn't sporting (no submachine guns, X-ray devices, drag nets, dynamite and – with a finer calibre of sportsmanship in mind – no multiple hooks and no unfair techniques such as jig-hooking, which is a nasty way of getting a hook into any part of a salmon, without the salmon's co-operation). The fish have their fish sensibilities and the advantage of home territory. The object of the game is for you to make the fish think that your lure or fly or bait is a delicious little morsel swimming free and clear, and if he goes for it you have to have the skill to outmaneuver and land him. The object of the game for the fish is not to be fooled. For him, it's a matter of life and death.

Three summers after Ireland, Nick and I felt ready to move on to more serious fishing. We learned of a fishing camp in northern New Brunswick, Canada, and decided to spend five days there in mid-July. To get to Jim Black's fishing camp, you fly to Presque Isle, Maine, where someone from the camp meets you, and you are then driven a couple hours north. The Tobique River, a tributary of the Serpentine, flows past the camp, and most of the outlying wilderness is owned by big paper conglomerates; the only traffic is huge logging trucks that go by empty in the morning and come out of the woods in early evening piled high with tree-length logs.

We were in for a bit of culture shock. The Blacks' television set was on every hour of the day. Their daughter possibly never went outside the entire time we were there. (And we ended up spending ten days there.) At the edge of civilization, these people were closer to suburbia than we were, living just outside New Haven.

Our lodging consisted of a log cabin with a sagging double bed and a wood stove. It had the luxury of its own spring-fed sink and toilet. This meant that occasionally a tiny fish would find its way into the toilet bowl, which can be very disconcerting, for both you and the fish, first thing in the morning.

The first afternoon conditions were all wrong for catching a fish, but we were impatient and it was a good time for me to learn how to fly cast. Nick quickly recalled most of what his father had taught him about casting on a memorable father-son fishing trip to Lake Parmacheene in New Hampshire. And I was eager to move on from the known, safe waters of spinning into the more subtle, cerebral currents of fly fishing. I was given some hip waders about four sizes too big, and with a slow leak in one knee. But with four layers of socks, there was so little room for water the leak never became more than a nuisance.

Careful not to wade any deeper than within a couple of inches of the tops of my waders, I slowly learned how to lay the fly down on the water. In fly casting, you pull out line from the reel with your left hand and hold it bunched in a loose loop, while with your right arm you whip the rod back and forth overhead, from eleven o'clock to two o'clock. As you whip the rod, you let it take more and more line, which you unreel and feed with your left hand, until you have thirty or forty feet of line in the air, in constant motion. With all this line whipping back and forth over your head, you are now ready to make a cast. You throw the line forward in a smooth, continuous sweep so that the line travels forward in a perfect horizontal unrolling, and with a little flick, the fly is laid down on the surface of the water without a splash. When an expert fly fisher casts, it's a beautiful thing to watch. It seems effortless and perfect, and it can be hard to believe that this process is human invention and not a natural occurrence.

Even on that bright afternoon, I felt the tension and alertness one feels in the presence of the possibility of a strike. We fished both dry and wet flies, the dry flies sitting on the surface of the water, the wet sinking an inch or so. One casts slightly upstream, floats the fly and then lifts it off the water with a quick, splashless flick before it reaches the end of the floating line and begins to drag. A dragging fly or needless flailing in the water discourages the salmon.

Salmon, we learned, don't strike at flies because of hunger, but out of irritation or sport. They don't eat at all in the fresh water, and any salmon killed on a river will have a clean gullet. Apparently, Atlantic salmon gather under the ice in the Davis Straits and gorge themselves on shrimp and not much else, which would certainly account for the unique flesh of a salmon. When salmon return to their rivers, it is only to spawn. Salmon invariably find their way back to the river in which they themselves were spawned, and some guides swear that they even come back to the same rock pools in the river, year after year. Stocked salmon have a piece of back fin clipped off for identification. Their spawn, obviously, have complete fins. When Jim's wife Nita landed a naturally spawned fish on our fourth day there, she looked at its back fin and declared, 'This here is God's own fish,' with evident satisfaction.

Our routine was to get up at 5.30 every morning, before sunrise, have a preliminary breakfast, and then fish from six until about 9.30, when the mist would have burned off completely and it would be too bright to fish. We would then go back to camp, have a more serious breakfast, usually with eggs from Nita's chickens, and then go back to bed. At one we would have lunch. In the afternoon we played cribbage, read, bicycled down the road to look at the same three pairs of hand-knit socks made by the church ladies and offered for sale in the only store in town, or visited with members of Nita's voluminous family, who were perpetually dropping in. My favorite was her toothless brother Murray, about whom it was darkly hinted that he tied salmon flies made from his own pubic hair.

One afternoon, after yet another fishless morning, Jim and Nita took us on a hike into an area with mountain streams. We hooked dozens of very small rainbow trout, on worms, feeling no guilt because Jim felt they were trapped in a pool created by a new beaver dam and that there were too many fish to survive. The trout were delicious pan-fried in bacon fat, eaten with fried eggs and bacon and toast.

One late morning, Jim poled our canoe over the rock pool we'd been fishing, and we could count seven fat salmon. We knew they were there. We fished with greater determination.

One afternoon we saw two baby bobcats tumbling together across the path in the woods.

Jim demonstrated excellent moose calls.

Our five days stretched into ten, and we never hooked any salmon.

We were back the following summer, in August this time. My mother, a bird-watcher, joined us. Jim had aged visibly, and Jim Jr. was our guide. On the third of our eight days there, we went trout fishing on the Serpentine, on a stretch accessible only after an hour of driving on dirt followed by a strenuous hour of climbing. Trout flies are smaller and lighter, and it was a windy day. I had cast a few times, standing in deep midstream. (Nick's Christmas present to me had been chest waders with felt soles, and a fishing vest.) A gust of wind took my fly in mid-cast and carried it back into my left eye. I yelled for Nick with what must have been a terrible voice; he was at my side in seconds. He gently took my hand away from my eye and saw that the fly was just barely caught in the skin of my eyelid. He freed it, and then the two of us clung together shaking. We both knew that because I am blind in my right eye, that little trout fly had come very close to changing my life. My one piece of advice to all who would fish: wear sunglasses. We retrieved Nick's rod, which he had flung in the bushes on the bank, and waded upstream around a bend where Jim Jr. and my mother were waiting. They didn't hear my scream over the roaring current. We never told anyone about what happened.

Two days later I killed my salmon. (I don't know why, but one says 'killed' with salmon, just as one rides with the 'hounds,' never the 'dogs.')

Choosing a fly at any given moment, is, I suppose, a science, but as with picking horses at the track, whimsy can be as successful as any more consistent method. I would generally change flies after a few casts; my selections were based on intuition and what I thought I might be in the mood for if I were a salmon. On that morning, the fog lifted early, and we were discouraged and ready to quit.

I felt as though the salmon had defeated us, as though it was Us and Them. When they refuse to engage, the relationship between we who fish and those who are fish remains entirely theoretical. What we want – and I include in that 'we' anyone who has ever dangled a worm on a bent pin off the side of a bridge as well as aristocratic sportsmen flying elite waters for thousands of dollars a day – is the one-to-one engagement. The I and Thou of it all.

That morning on the Tobique, I was restless and bored. It wasn't happening. I changed to a brown fairy, a handsome wet fly, for my last few casts of the morning. I knew the salmon were there. Coaxing one to strike had become an urgent, almost archaic wish to attract, to compel. I was sending signals to a distant planet.

Three casts later I felt that unmistakable surge of something alive on the line. Salmon, when hooked, have been known to try anything to get off the line: for every two fish hooked, only one is landed. The reel was singing as the fish took off downstream. As soon as I felt a slack, I reeled in like crazy, keeping a tension without pulling in too sharply, which would break the line. Then the fish would run the line out again, and I could see that I was getting near the backing on the reel. There would be occasional pauses while he changed direction or rested, and I would reel it all back in. I felt the fish tiring. Way upstream, I thought I saw another salmon jumping clear of the water, but it was my fish trying to jump the hook. I tried to keep the line taut. Suddenly I felt a strange new tension on the line. The fish was rolling over and over on the line. 'That dirty fish!' declared Nita, 'You bring him in and tell him to stop those games.'

I reeled the fish in closer, and Nita warned me that if he went near the rocks he might try to saw the line between two ledges. We could see the fish clearly for the first time; it was much bigger than I had realized. The fish went out for one more weak run, and then I reeled in as tightly as I dared; Jim Jr. made a deft pass with the net, and we had our fish. It weighed a little over ten pounds. I saw that I had hooked the fish, a female as it turned out, solidly in the lip. But there was only one turn left in the knot I had made to tie the brown fairy, and I had used five. Another few minutes and the fish would have been off the line with the fly. The fish could then have worked the fly out of its lip by scraping along the river bottom. Jim Jr. killed the fish with one blow with a rock. It was awful. Inert, solid, the salmon was transformed forever. But, still, I had earned it. We would eat it, smoked, and I would salt her sacs full of eggs, too, for delicious caviar. When a salmon dies, it's a death far more profound than the last fierce flappings of a mackerel in a bucket. I was both appalled and elated. Nina broke the spell when she pointed out the cuts in the tail and back fins, caused by the line when the fish had stood on its tail and rolled. Nita said, 'You did real marvelous.'

Fishing *is* marvelous: there is the challenge, the tuning of a skill, the aesthetic. But mainly there is the irresistible urge to tangle with the mysterious and unknown, to rely on intuition and hunches. You do it for those moments of casting your thoughts beneath the surface of the water to see if you can conjure up a fish.

When I was little, I thought there were actual fish in the sky after rain, and I would always strain my eyes to see them between a rainbow's bars of color. The swimming spots in my eyes that resulted were, I convinced myself, what people meant by 'rainbow trout.'

My mind still makes that leap when I fish for rainbows – a particularly brilliant fish can make me believe again that water is not its only element.

Trout-Fishing in the Traun

HENRY VAN DYKE

'Those who wish to forget painful thoughts do well to absent themselves for a time from the ties and objects that recall them; but we can be said only to fulfil our destiny in the place that gave us birth. I should on this account like well enough to spend the whole of my life in travelling abroad if I could anywhere borrow another life to spend afterwards at home.'
— William Hazlitt, *On Going a Journey*.

THE PECULIARITY OF trout-fishing in the Traun is that one catches principally grayling. But in this it resembles some other pursuits which are not without their charm for minds open to the pleasures of the unexpected – for example, reading George Borrow's *The Bible in Spain* with a view to theological information, or going to the opening night at the Academy of Design with the intention of looking at pictures.

Moreover, there are really trout in the Traun, *rari nantes in gurgite*; and in some places more than in others; and all of high spirit, though few of great size. Thus the angler has his favourite problem: given an unknown stream and two kinds of fish, the one better than the other; to find the better kind, and determine the hour at which they will rise. This is sport.

As for the little river itself, it has so many beauties that one does not think of asking whether it has any faults. Constant fullness, and crystal clearness, and refreshing coolness of living water, pale green like the jewel that is called aqua marina, flowing over beds of clean sand and bars of polished gravel, and dropping in momentary foam from rocky ledges, between banks that are shaded by groves of fir and ash and poplar, or through dense thickets of alder and willow, or across meadows of smooth verdure sloping up to quaint old-world villages – all these are features of the ideal little river.

I have spoken of these personal qualities first, because a truly moral writer ought to make more of character than of position. A good river in a bad country would be more worthy of affection than a bad river in a good country. But the Traun has also the advantages of an excellent worldly position. For it rises all over the Salzkammergut, the summer hunting-ground of the Austrian Emperor, and flows through that most picturesque corner of his domain from end to end. Under the desolate cliffs of the Todtengebirge on the east, and below the shining ice-fields of the Dachstein on the south, and from the green alps around St. Wolfgang on the west, the translucent waters are gathered in little tarns, and shot through roaring brooks, and spread into lakes of wondrous beauty, and poured through growing streams, until at last they are all united just below the summer villa of his Kaiserly and Kingly Majesty, Francis Joseph, and flow away northward, through the rest of his game-preserve, into the Traunsee. It is an imperial playground, and such as I would consent to hunt the chamois in, if an inscrutable Providence had made me a kingly kaiser, or even a plain king or an unvarnished kaiser. But, failing this, I was perfectly content to spend a few idle days in fishing for trout and catching grayling, at such times and places as the law of the Austrian Empire allowed.

For it must be remembered that every stream in these over-civilised European countries belongs to somebody, by purchase or rent. And all the fish in the stream are supposed to belong to the person who owns or rents it. They do not know their master's voice, neither will they follow when he calls. But they are theoretically his. To this legal fiction the untutored American must conform. He must learn to clothe his natural desires in the raiment of lawful sanction, and take out some kind of a license before he follows his impulse to fish.

It was in the town of Aussee, at the junction of the two highest branches of the Traun, that this impulse came upon me, mildly irresistible. The full bloom of mid-July gaiety in that ancient watering-place was dampened, but not extinguished, by two days of persistent and surprising showers. I had exhausted the possibilities of interest in the old Gothic church, and felt all that a man should feel in deciphering the mural tombstones of the families who were exiled for their faith in the days of the Reformation. The throngs of merry Hebrews from Vienna and Budapest, amazingly arrayed as mountaineers and milk-maids, walking up and down the narrow streets under umbrellas, had Cleopatra's charm of an infinite variety; but custom staled it. The woodland paths, winding everywhere through the plantations of fir-trees and provided with appropriate names on wooden labels, and benches for rest and conversation at discreet intervals, were too moist for even the nymphs to take delight in them. The only creatures that suffered nothing by the rain were the two swift, limpid Trauns, racing through the woods, like eager and unabashed lovers, to meet in the middle of the village. They were as clear, as joyous, as musical as if the sun were shining. The very sight of their opalescent rapids and eddying pools was an invitation to that gentle sport which is said to have the merit of growing better as the weather grows worse.

I laid this fact before the landlord of the hotel of the Erzherzog Johann, as poetically as I could, but he assured me that it was of no consequence without an invitation from the gentleman to whom the streams belonged; and he had gone away for a week. The landlord was such a good-natured person, and such an excellent sleeper, that it was impossible to believe that he could have even the smallest inaccuracy upon his conscience. So I bade him farewell, and took my way, four miles through the woods, to the lake from which one of the streams flowed.

It was called the Grundlsee. As I do not know the origin of the name, I cannot consistently make any moral or historical reflections upon it. But if it has never become famous, it ought to be, for the sake of a cozy and busy little Inn, perched on a green hill beside the lake and overlooking the whole length of it, from the groups of toy villas at the foot to the heaps of real mountains at the head. This Inn kept a thin but happy landlord, who provided me with a blue license to angle, for the inconsiderable sum of fifteen cents a day. This conferred the right of fishing not only in the Grundlsee, but also in the smaller tarn of Toplitz, a mile above it, and in the swift stream which unites them. It all coincided with my desire as if by magic. A row of a couple of miles to the head of the lake, and a walk through the forest, brought me to the smaller pond; and as the afternoon sun was ploughing pale furrows through the showers, I waded out on a point of reeds and cast the artful fly in the shadow of the great cliffs of the Dead Mountains.

It was a fit scene for a lone fisherman. But four sociable tourists promptly appeared to act as spectators and critics. Fly-fishing usually strikes the German mind as an eccentricity which calls for remonstrance. After one of the tourists had suggestively narrated the tale of seven trout which he had caught in another lake, WITH WORMS, on the previous Sunday, they went away for a row, (with salutations in which politeness but thinly veiled their pity,) and left me still whipping the water in vain. Nor was the fortune of the day much better in the stream below. It was a long and wet wade for three fish too small to keep. I came out on the shore of the lake, where I had left the row-boat, with empty bag and a feeling of damp discouragement.

There was still an hour or so of daylight, and a beautiful place to fish where the stream poured swirling out into the lake. A rise, and a large one, though rather slow, awakened my hopes. Another rise, evidently made by a heavy fish, made me certain that virtue was about to be rewarded. The third time the hook went home. I felt the solid weight of the fish against the spring of the rod, and that curious thrill which runs up the line and down the arm, changing, somehow or other, into a pleasurable sensation of excitement as it reaches the brain. But it was only for a moment; and then came that foolish, feeble shaking of the line from side to side which tells the angler that he has hooked a great, big, leather-mouthed chub – a fish which Izaak Walton says 'the French esteem so mean as to call him Un Vilain.' Was it for this that I had come to the country of Francis Joseph?

I took off the flies and put on one of those phantom minnows which have immortalised the name of a certain Mr. Brown. The minnow swung on a long line as the boat passed back and forth across the current, once, twice, three times – and on the fourth circle there was a sharp strike. The rod bent almost double, and the reel sang shrilly to the first rush of the fish. He ran; he doubled; he went to the bottom and sulked; he tried to go under the boat; he did all that a game fish can do, except leaping. After twenty minutes he was tired enough to be lifted gently into the boat by a hand slipped around his gills, and there he was, a lachsforelle of three pounds' weight: small pointed head; silver sides mottled with dark spots; square, powerful tail and large fins – a fish not unlike the land-locked salmon of the Saguenay, but more delicate.

Half an hour later he was lying on the grass in front of the Inn. The waiters paused, with their hands full of dishes, to look at him; and the landlord called his guests, including my didactic tourists, to observe the superiority of the trout of the Grundlsee. The maids also came to look; and the buxom cook, with her spotless apron and bare arms akimbo, was drawn from her kitchen, and pledged her culinary honour that such a *prachtkerl* should be served up in her very best style. The angler who is insensible to this sort of indirect flattery through his fish does not exist. Even the most indifferent of men thinks more favourably of people who know a good trout when they see it, and sits down to his supper with kindly feelings. Possibly he reflects, also, upon the incident as a hint of the usual size of the fish in that neighbourhood. He remembers that he may have been favoured in this case beyond his deserts by good-fortune, and resolving not to put too heavy a strain upon it, considers the next place where it would be well for him to angle.

Hallstatt is about ten miles below Aussee. The Traun here expands into a lake, very dark and deep, shut in by steep and lofty mountains. The railway runs along the eastern shore. On the other side, a mile away, you see the old town, its white houses clinging to the cliff like lichens to the face of a rock. The guide-book calls it 'a highly original situation.' But this is one of the cases where a little less originality and a little more reasonableness might be desired, at least by the permanent inhabitants. A ledge under the shadow of a precipice makes a trying winter residence. The people of Hallstatt are not a blooming race: one sees many dwarfs and cripples among them. But to the summer traveller the place seems wonderfully picturesque. Most of the streets are flights of steps. The high-road has barely room to edge itself through among the old houses, between the window-gardens of bright flowers. On the hottest July day the afternoon is cool and shady. The gay little skiffs and long, open gondolas are flitting continually along the lake, which is the main street of Hallstatt.

The incongruous, but comfortable, modern hotel has a huge glass veranda, where you can eat your dinner and observe human nature in its transparent holiday disguises. I was much pleased and entertained by a family, or confederacy, of people attired as peasants – the men with feathered hats, green stockings, and bare knees – the women with bright skirts, bodices, and silk neckerchiefs – who were always in evidence, rowing gondolas with clumsy oars, meeting the steamboat at the wharf several times a day, and filling the miniature garden of the hotel with rustic greetings and early Salzkammergut attitudes. After much conjecture, I learned that they were the family and friends of a newspaper editor from Vienna. They had the literary instinct for local colour.

The fishing at Hallstatt is at Obertraun. There is a level stretch of land above the lake, where the river flows peaceably, and the fish have leisure to feed and grow. It is leased to a peasant, who makes a business of supplying the hotels with fish. He was quite willing to give permission to an angler; and I engaged one of his sons, a capital young fellow, whose natural capacities for good fellowship were only hampered by a most extraordinary German dialect, to row me across the lake, and carry the net and a small green barrel full of water to keep the fish alive, according to the custom of the country. The first day we had only four trout large enough to put into the barrel; the next day I think there were six; the third day, I remember very well, there were ten. They were pretty creatures, weighing from half a pound to a pound each, and coloured as daintily as bits of French silk, in silver gray with faint pink spots.

There was plenty to do at Hallstatt in the mornings. An hour's walk from the town there was a fine waterfall, 300 feet high. On the side of the mountain above the lake was one of the salt-mines for which the region is celebrated. It has been worked for ages by many successive races, from the Celt downward. Perhaps even the men of the Stone Age knew of it, and came hither for seasoning to make the flesh of the cave-bear and the mammoth more palatable. Modern pilgrims are permitted to explore the long, wet, glittering galleries with a guide, and slide down the smooth wooden rollers which join the different levels of the mines. This pastime has the same fascination as sliding down the balusters; and it is said that even queens and princesses have been delighted with it. This is a touching proof of the fundamental simplicity and unity of our human nature.

But by far the best excursion from Hallstatt was an all-day trip to the Zwieselalp – a mountain which seems to have been especially created as a point of view. From the bare summit you look right into the face of the huge, snowy Dachstein, with the wild lake of Gosau gleaming at its foot; and far away on the other side your vision ranges over a confusion of mountains, with all the white peaks of the Tyrol stretched along the horizon. Such a wide outlook as this helps the fisherman to enjoy the narrow beauties of his little rivers. No sport is at its best without interruption and contrast. To appreciate wading, one ought to climb a little on odd days.

Ischl is about ten or twelve miles below Hallstatt, in the valley of the Traun. It is the fashionable summer-resort of Austria. I found it in the high tide of amusement. The shady esplanade along the river was crowded with brave women and fair men, in gorgeous raiment; the hotels were overflowing; and there were various kinds of music and entertainments at all hours of day and night. But all this did not seem to affect the fishing.

The landlord of the Königin Elizabeth, who is also the Burgomaster and a gentleman of varied accomplishments and no leisure, kindly furnished me with a fishing license in the shape of a large pink card. There were many rules printed upon it: 'All fishes under nine inches must be gently restored to the water. No instrument of capture must be used except the angle in the hand. The card of legitimation must be produced and exhibited at the polite request of any of the keepers of the river.' Thus duly authorised and instructed, I sallied forth to seek my pastime according to the law.

The easiest way, in theory, was to take the afternoon train up the river to one of the villages, and fish down a mile or two in the evening, returning by the eight o'clock train. But in practice the habits of the fish interfered seriously with the latter part of this plan.

On my first day I had spent several hours in the vain effort to catch something better than small grayling. The best time for the trout was just approaching, as the broad light faded from the stream; already they were beginning to feed, when I looked up from the edge of a pool and saw the train rattling down the valley below me. Under the circumstances the only thing to do was to go on fishing. It was an even pool with steep banks, and the water ran through it very straight and swift, some four feet deep and thirty yards across. As the tail-fly reached the middle of the water, a fine trout literally turned a somersault over it, but without touching it. At the next cast he was ready, taking it with a rush that carried him into the air with the fly in his mouth. He weighed three-quarters of a pound. The next one was equally eager in rising and sharp in playing, and the third might have been his twin sister or brother. So, after casting for hours and taking nothing in the most beautiful pools, I landed three trout from one unlikely place in fifteen minutes. That was because the trout's supper-time had arrived. So had mine. I walked over to the rambling old inn at Goisern, sought the cook in the kitchen and persuaded her, in spite of the lateness of the hour, to boil the largest of the fish for my supper, after which I rode peacefully back to Ischl by the eleven o'clock train.

For the future I resolved to give up the illusory idea of coming home by rail, and ordered a little one-horse carriage to meet me at some point on the high-road every evening at nine o'clock. In this way I managed to cover the whole stream, taking a lower part each day, from the lake of Hallstatt down to Ischl.

There was one part of the river, near Laufen, where the current was very strong and waterfally, broken by ledges of rock. Below these it rested in long, smooth reaches, much beloved by the grayling. There was no difficulty in getting two or three of them out of each run.

The grayling has a quaint beauty. His appearance is aesthetic, like a fish in a Pre-Raphaelite picture. His colour, in midsummer, is a golden gray, darker on the back, and with a few black spots just behind his gills, like patches put on to bring out the pallor of his complexion. He smells of wild thyme when he first comes out of the water, wherefore St. Ambrose of Milan complimented him in courtly fashion: 'Quid specie tua gratius? Quid odore fragrantius? Quod mella fragrant, hoc tuo corpore spiras.' But the chief glory of the grayling is the large iridescent fin on his back. You see it cutting the water as he swims near the surface; and when you have him on the bank it arches over him like a rainbow. His mouth is under his chin, and he takes the fly gently, by suction. He is, in fact, and to speak plainly, something of a sucker; but then he is a sucker idealised and refined, the flower of the family. Charles Cotton, the ingenious young friend of Walton, was all wrong in calling the grayling 'one of the deadest-hearted fishes in the world.' He fights and leaps and whirls, and brings his big fin to bear across the force of the current with a variety of tactics that would put his more aristocratic fellow-citizen, the trout, to the blush. Twelve of these pretty fellows, with a brace of good trout for the top, filled my big creel to the brim. And yet, such is the inborn hypocrisy of the human heart that I always pretended to myself to be disappointed because there were not more trout, and made light of the grayling as a thing of naught.

The pink fishing license did not seem to be of much use. Its exhibition was demanded only twice. Once a river guardian, who was walking down the stream with a Belgian Baron and encouraging him to continue fishing, climbed out to me on the end of a long embankment, and with proper apologies begged to be favoured with a view of my document. It turned out that his request was a favour to me, for it discovered the fact that I had left my fly-book, with the pink card in it, beside an old mill, a quarter of a mile up the stream.

Another time I was sitting beside the road, trying to get out of a very long, wet, awkward pair of wading-stockings, an occupation which is unfavourable to tranquillity of mind, when a man came up to me in the dusk and accosted me with an absence of politeness which in German amounted to an insult.

'Have you been fishing?'

'Why do you want to know?'

'Have you any right to fish?'

'What right have you to ask?'

'I am a keeper of the river. Where is your card?'

'It is in my pocket. But pardon my curiosity, where is YOUR card?'

This question appeared to paralyse him. He had probably never been asked for his card before. He went lumbering off in the darkness, muttering 'My card? Unheard of! MY card!'

The routine of angling at Ischl was varied by an excursion to the Lake of St. Wolfgang and the Schafberg, an isolated mountain on whose rocky horn an inn has been built. It stands up almost like a bird-house on a pole, and commands a superb prospect; northward, across the rolling plain and the Bavarian forest; southward, over a tumultuous land of peaks and precipices. There are many lovely lakes in sight; but the loveliest of all is that which takes its name from the old saint who wandered hither from the country of the 'furious Franks' and built his peaceful hermitage on the Falkenstein. What good taste some of those old saints had!

There is a venerable church in the village, with pictures attributed to Michael Wohlgemuth, and a chapel which is said to mark the spot where St. Wolfgang, who had lost his axe far up the mountain, found it, like Longfellow's arrow, in an oak, and 'still unbroke.' The tree is gone, so it was impossible to verify the story. But the saint's well is there, in a pavilion, with a bronze image over it, and a profitable inscription to the effect that the poorer pilgrims, 'who have come unprovided with either money or wine, should be jolly well contented to find the water so fine.' There is also a famous echo farther up the lake, which repeats six syllables with accuracy. It is a strange coincidence that there are just six syllables in the name of 'der heilige Wolfgang.' But when you translate it into English, the inspiration of the echo seems to be less exact. The sweetest thing about St. Wolfgang was the abundance of purple cyclamens, clothing the mountain meadows, and filling the air with delicate fragrance like the smell of lilacs around a New England farmhouse in early June.

There was still one stretch of the river above Ischl left for the last evening's sport. I remember it so well: the long, deep place where the water ran beside an embankment of stone, and the big grayling poised on the edge of the shadow, rising and falling on the current as a kite rises and falls on the wind and balances back to the same position; the murmur of the stream and the hissing of the pebbles underfoot in the rapids as the swift water rolled them over and over; the odour of the fir-trees, and the streaks of warm air in quiet places, and the faint whiffs of wood-smoke wafted from the houses, and the brown flies dancing heavily up and down in the twilight; the last good pool, where the river was divided, the main part making a deep, narrow curve to the right, and the lesser part bubbling into it over a bed of stones with half a dozen tiny waterfalls, with a fine trout lying at the foot of each of them and rising merrily as the white fly passed over him – surely it was all very good, and a memory to be grateful for. And when the basket was full, it was pleasant to put off the heavy wading-shoes and the long rubber-stockings, and ride homeward in an open carriage through the fresh night air. That is as near to sybaritic luxury as a man should care to come.

The lights in the cottages are twinkling like fireflies, and there are small groups of people singing and laughing down the road. The honest fisherman reflects that this world is only a place of pilgrimage, but after all there is a good deal of cheer on the journey, if it is made with a contented heart. He wonders who the dwellers in the scattered houses may be, and weaves romances out of the shadows on the curtained windows. The lamps burning in the wayside shrines tell him stories of human love and patience and hope, and of divine forgiveness. Dream-pictures of life float before him, tender and luminous, filled with a vague, soft atmosphere in which the simplest outlines gain a strange significance. They are like some of Millet's paintings – 'The Sower,' or 'The Sheepfold' – there is very little detail in them but sometimes a little means so much.

Then the moon slips up into the sky from behind the hills, and the fisher-man begins to think of home, and of the foolish, fond old rhymes about those whom the moon sees far away, and the stars that have the power to fulfill wishes – as if the celestial bodies knew or cared anything about our small nerve-thrills which we call affection and desires! But if there were Some One above the moon and stars who did know and care, Some One who could see the places and the people that you and I would give so much to see, Some One who could do for them all of kindness that you and I fain would do, Some One able to keep our beloved in perfect peace and watch over the little children sleeping in their beds beyond the sea – what then? Why, then, in the evening hour, one might have thoughts of home that would go across the ocean by way of heaven, and be better than dreams, almost as good as prayers.

The Holy Anglers

CHARLES BRADFORD

'The greater number of them [Christ's disciples] were found together, fishing, by Jesus, after His Resurrection.'

– Izaak Walton

'. . . certain poor fishermen coming in very weary after a night of toil (and one of them very wet after swimming ashore) found their Master standing on the bank of the lake waiting for them. But it seems that He must have been busy in their behalf while he was waiting; for there was a bright fire of coals on the shore, and a goodly fish broiling thereon, and bread to eat with it. And when the Master had asked them about their fishing he said: 'Come, now, and get your breakfast.' So they sat down around the fire, and with His own hands he served them with the bread and the fish.'

– Henry Van Dyke

'The first men that our Saviour dear
Did choose to wait upon Him here
Blest fishers were . . .'

– W. Basse

'I would . . . fish in the sky whose bottom is pebbly with stars.'

– Henry David Thoreau

THE PRINCIPAL FISHES of the Sea of Galilee today are the same as they were two thousand years ago – bream and chub. These were taken in olden times by both net and hook and line.

The fishermen whom Christ chose as His disciples – Peter, Andrew, James, and John – were professional net fishermen, but hook and line fishing was a favorite pastime of the well-to-do Egyptians as well as the poor people who could not afford a net.

Weirs not unlike the modern article were used in the Holy Land in Bible time, excepting on Lake Gennesaret, where the law of the land forbade them.

The bream and the chub were eaten alike by rich and poor people. Wayfarers roasted them over chip fires in the groves and on the lake shores, housewives boiled and broiled them, and the wealthy man served them at his banquets. 'Moses, the friend of God,' writes Izaak Walton, in his immortal *Compleat Angler*, quoting from Lev. xi., 9, Deut., xiv., 9, 'appointed fish to be the chief diet for the best commonwealth that ever yet was. The mightiest feasts have been of fish.'

Our Saviour 'fed the people on fish when they were hungry.' The species is not alluded to in the Biblical paragraph, but no doubt the fish feasts of the Lord were mostly of chub and bream. Jesus loved fishermen and was in their society most of His time. No other class of men were so well favored by Him. He inspired St. Peter, St. John, St. Andrew, and St. James, poor fishermen, who drew their nets for the people, and these four fishermen, declares Father Izaak, 'He never reproved for their employment or calling, as he did scribes and money changers.'

The Lord's favorite places of labor and repose – the places He most frequented – were near the fishes and fishermen. 'He began to teach by the seaside. His pulpit was a fishing boat or the shore of a lake. He was in the stern of the boat, asleep. He was always near the water to cheer and comfort those who followed it.' And Walton tells us that 'when God intended to reveal high notions to His prophets He carried them to the shore, that He might settle their mind in a quiet repose.'

Bream and chub are not monster fishes – they do not average the great weights of the tarpon and the tuna; they are of the small and medium-size species; so, if the apostles were pleased with 'ye gods and little fishes,' we mortals of today should be satisfied with our catch, be it ever so small.

Observations of the Bream

FROM *THE COMPLEAT ANGLER* BY IZAAK WALTON

Pisc. THE BREAM being at a full growth is a large and stately fish; he will breed both in rivers and ponds: but loves best to live in ponds, and where, if he likes the water and air, he will grow not only to be very large, but as fat as a hog: he is by Gesner taken to be more pleasant or sweet then wholesome; this fish is long in growing, but breeds exceedingly in a water that pleases him; yea, in many ponds so fast, as to overstore them, and starve the other fish.

He is very broad with a forked tail, and his scales set in excellent order; he hath large eyes and a narrow sucking mouth; he hath two sets of teeth, and a lozenge-like bone, a bone to help his grinding. The Melter is observed to have two large melts, and the female two large bags of eggs or spawn.

Gesner reports, that in Poland a certain and a great number of large Breams were put into a pond, which in the next following Winter was frozen up into one entire ice, and not one drop of water remaining, nor one of these fish to be found, though they were diligently searched for; and yet the next Spring when the ice was thawed, and the weather warm, they all appeared again. This Gesner affirms, and I quote my author, because it seems almost as incredible as the Resurrection to an Atheist. But it may win something in point of believing it, to him that considers the breeding or renovation of the silk-worm, and of many insects. And that is considerable which Sir Francis Bacon observes in his *History of Life and Death*, fol. 20, that there be some herbs that die and spring every year, and some endure longer.

But though some do not, yet the French esteem this fish highly, and to that end have this proverb: 'He that hath Breams in his pond is able to bid his friend welcome.' And it is noted, that the best part of a Bream is his belly and head.

Some say, that Breams and Roaches will mix their eggs, and melt together, and so there is in many places a bastard breed of Breams, that never come to be either large or good, but very numerous.

The baits good to catch this Bream are many. First, paste made of brown bread and honey, Gentles, or the brood of wasps that be young, and then not unlike Gentles; and should be hardened in an oven, or dried on a tile before the fire; or there is at the root of docks, or flags, or rushes in watery places, a worm not unlike a maggot, at which Tench will bite freely. Or he will bite at a grasshopper with his legs nipped off in June and July, or at several flies under water, which may be found on flags that grow near to the water side. I doubt not but that there be many other baits that are good, but I will turn them all into this most excellent one, either for a Carp or Bream, in any river or mere: it was given to me by a most honest and excellent angler, and hoping you will prove both, I will impart it to you.

1. Let your bait be as big a red worm as you can find, without a knot. Get a pint or quart of them in an evening in garden walks, or chalky commons after a shower of rain; and put them with clean moss well washed and picked, and the water squeezed out of the moss as dry as you can, into an earthen pot or pipkin set dry, and change the moss fresh every three or four days for three weeks or a month together, then your bait will be at the best.

2. Having thus prepared your baits, get your tackling ready and fitted after this sort. Take three long angling rods, and as many and more silk, or silk and hair lines, and as many large swan or goose-quill floats. Then take a piece of lead made after this manner, and fasten them to the lower ends of your lines. Then fasten your link-hook also to the lead, and to the end of your line, let there be about a foot or ten inches between the lead and the hook, but be sure the lead be heavy enough to sink the float or quill under water, and not the quill to bear up the lead. Note, that your link next the hook may be smaller than the rest of your line, if you dare adventure for fear of taking the Pike or Perch, who will assuredly visit your hooks, till they be taken out (as I will shew you afterwards) before either Carp or Bream will come near to bite. Note also, that when the worm is well baited, it will crawl up and down, as far as the lead will give leave, which much entices the fish to bite without suspicion.

3. Having thus prepared your baits, and fitted your tackling, repair to the river, where you have seen them to swim in schools or shoals in the Summer time in a hot afternoon, about three or four of the clock, and watch their going forth of their deep holes and returning (which you may well discern) for they return about four of the clock most of them seeking food at the bottom, yet one or two will lie on the top of the water, rolling and tumbling themselves, whilst the rest are under him at the bottom, and so you shall perceive him to keep sentinel: then mark where he plays most, and stays longest (which commonly is in the broadest and deepest place of the river), and there, or near thereabouts, at a clear bottom, and a convenient landing place, take one of your angles ready fitted as aforesaid, and sound the bottom, about eight or ten foot deep, two yards from the bank is the best. Then consider with your self, whether that water will rise or fall by the next morning by reason of any water-mills near, and according to your discretion take the depth of the place, where you mean after to cast your ground-bait, and to fish, to half an inch; that the lead lying on or near the ground-bait, the top of the float may only appear upright half an inch above the water.

Thus you having found and fitted for the place and depth thereof, then go home and prepare your ground-bait, which is next to the fruit of your labours to be regarded.

The Ground-Bait

You shall take a peck, or a peck and a half (according to the greatness of the stream, and deepness of the water, where you mean to angle) of sweet gross-ground barely-malt, and boil it in a kettle (one or two warms is enough) then strain it through a bag into a tub (the liquor whereof hath often done my horse much good) and when the bag and malt is near cold, take it down to the water-side about eight or nine of the clock in the evening, and not before; cast in two parts of your ground-bait, squeezed hard between both your hands, it will sink presently to the bottom, and be sure it may rest in the very place where you mean to angle; if the stream run hard or move a little, cast your malt in handfuls the higher upwards the stream. You may between your hands close the malt so fast in handfuls, that the water will hardly part it with the fall.

Your ground thus baited, and tackling fitted, leave your bag with the rest of your tackling, and ground-bait near the sporting-place all night, and in the morning about three or four of the clock visit the water-side (but not too near) for they have a watch-man, and are watchful themselves.

Then gently take one of your three rods, and bait your hook, casting it over your ground-bait, and gently and secretly draw it to you till the lead rests about the middle of the ground-bait.

Then take a second rod and cast in about a yard above, and your third a yard below the first rod, and stay the rods in the ground, but go your self so far from the water-side, that you perceive nothing but the top of the floats, which you must watch most diligently, then when you have a bite, you shall perceive the top of your float to sink suddenly into the water; yet nevertheless be not too hasty to run to your rods, until you see that line goes clear away; then creep to the waterside, and give as much line as possibly you can: if it be a Carp or Bream, they will go to the farther side of the river, then strike gently, and hold your rod at a bent a little while; for if you both pull, you are sure to lose your game, for either your line or hook, or hold will break; and after you have overcome them, they will make noble sport, and are very shy to be landed. The Carp is far stronger and mettlesome than the Bream.

Much more is to be observed in this kind of fish and fishing, but it is far fitter for experience and discourse than paper. Only thus much is necessary for you to know, and to be mindful and careful of, that if the Pike or Perch do breed in that river, they will be sure to bite first, and must first be taken. And for the most part they are very large, and will repair to your ground-bait, not that they will eat of it, but will feed and sport themselves amongst the young fry, that gather about and hover over the bait.

The way to discern the Pike and to take him, if you mistrust your Bream hook, (for I have taken a Pike a yard long several times at my Bream-hooks, and sometimes he hath had the luck to share my line.)

Take a small Bleak, or Roach, or Gudgeon, and bait it, and set it alive among your rods two foot deep from the cork, with a little red worm on the point of the hook, then take a few crumbs of white-bread, or some of the ground-bait, and sprinkle it gently amongst your rods. If Mr. Pike be there, then the little fish will skip out of the water, but the live-set bait is sure to be taken.

Thus continue your sport from four in the morning till eight, and if it be a gloomy windy day, they will bite all day long. But this is too long to stand to your rods at one place, and it will spoil your evening sport that day, which is this: About four of the clock in the afternoon repair to your baited place, and as soon as you come to the water side, cast in one half of the rest of your ground-bait, and stand off: then whilst the fish are gathering together (for there they will most certainly come for their supper), you may take a pipe of tobacco; and then in with your three rods as in the morning: You will find excellent sport that evening till eight of the clock; then cast in the residue of your ground-bait, and next morning by four of the clock visit them again for four hours, which is the best sport of all; and after that let them rest till you and your friends have a mind to more sport.

From St. James Tide until Bartholomew Tide is the best, when they have had all the Summers food, they are the fattest.

Observe lastly, that after three or four days fishing together, your game will be very shy and wary; and you shall hardly get above a bite or two at a baiting: then your only way is to desist from your sport about two or three days; and in the mean time (on the place you late baited, and again intend to bait) you shall take a turf of green, but short grass, as big or bigger than a round trencher; to the top of this turf, on the green side, you shall with a needle and green thread fasten one by one as many little red worms as will near cover all the turf: Then take a round board or trencher, make a hole in the middle thereof, and through the turf placed on the board or trencher, with a string or cord as long as is fitting, tied to a pole, let it down to the bottom of the water for the fish to feed upon without disturbance about two or three days; and after that you have drawn it away, you may fall to, and enjoy your former recreation.

The Angler

WASHINGTON IRVING

'This day Dame Nature seem'd in love,
The lusty sap began to move,
Fresh juice did stir th' embracing vines,
And birds had drawn their valentines.
The jealous trout that low did lie,
Rose at a well-dissembled flie.
There stood my friend, with patient skill,
Attending of his trembling quill.'
                    – Sir Henry Wotton

IT IS SAID that many an unlucky urchin is induced to run away from his family and betake himself to a seafaring life from reading the history of Robinson Crusoe; and I suspect that, in like manner, many of those worthy gentlemen who are given to haunt the sides of pastoral streams with angle-rods in hand may trace the origin of their passion to the seductive pages of honest Izaak Walton. I recollect studying his *The Complete Angler* several years since in company with a knot of friends in America, and moreover that we were all completely bitten with the angling mania. It was early in the year, but as soon as the weather was auspicious, and that the spring began to melt into the verge of summer, we took rod in hand and sallied into the country, as stark mad as was ever Don Quixote from reading books of chivalry.

One of our party had equalled the Don in the fullness of his equipments, being attired cap-a-pie for the enterprise. He wore a broad-skirted fustian coat, perplexed with half a hundred pockets; a pair of stout shoes and leathern gaiters; a basket slung on one side for fish; a patent rod, a landing net, and a score of other inconveniences only to be found in the true angler's armory. Thus harnessed for the field, he was as great a matter of stare and wonderment among the country folk, who had never seen a regular angler, as was the steel-clad hero of La Mancha among the goatherds of the Sierra Morena.

Our first essay was along a mountain brook among the Highlands of the Hudson – a most unfortunate place for the execution of those piscatory tactics which had been invented along the velvet margins of quiet English rivulets. It was one of those wild streams that lavish, among our romantic solitudes, unheeded beauties enough to fill the sketch-book of a hunter of the picturesque. Sometimes it would leap down rocky shelves, making small cascades, over which the trees threw their broad balancing sprays and long nameless weeds hung in fringes from the impending banks, dripping with diamond drops. Sometimes it would brawl and fret along a ravine in the matted shade of a forest, filling it with murmurs, and after this termagant career would steal forth into open day with the most placid, demure face imaginable, as I have seen some pestilent shrew of a housewife, after filling her home with uproar and ill-humor, come dimpling out of doors, swimming and curtseying and smiling upon all the world.

How smoothly would this vagrant brook glide at such times through some bosom of green meadowland among the mountains, where the quiet was only interrupted by the occasional tinkling of a bell from the lazy cattle among the clover or the sound of a woodcutter's axe from the neighboring forest!

For my part, I was always a bungler at all kinds of sport that required either patience or adroitness, and had not angled above half an hour before I had completely 'satisfied the sentiment,' and convinced myself of the truth of Izaak Walton's opinion, that angling is something like poetry – a man must be born to it. I hooked myself instead of the fish, tangled my line in every tree, lost my bait, broke my rod, until I gave up the attempt in despair, and passed the day under the trees reading old Izaak, satisfied that it was his fascinating vein of honest simplicity and rural feeling that had bewitched me, and not the passion for angling. My companions, however, were more persevering in their delusion. I have them at this moment before eyes, stealing along the border of the brook where it lay open to the day or was merely fringed by shrubs and bushes. I see the bittern rising with hollow scream as they break in upon his rarely-invaded haunt; the kingfisher watching them suspiciously from his dry tree that overhangs the deep black millpond in the gorge of the hills; the tortoise letting himself slip sideways from off the stone or log on which he is sunning himself; and the panic-struck frog plumping in headlong as they approach, and spreading an alarm throughout the watery world around.

I recollect also that, after toiling and watching and creeping about for the greater part of a day, with scarcely any success in spite of all our admirable apparatus, a lubberly country urchin came down from the hills with a rod made from a branch of a tree, a few yards of twine, and, as Heaven shall help me! I believe a crooked pin for a hook, baited with a vile earthworm, and in half an hour caught more fish than we had nibbles throughout the day!

But, above all, I recollect the 'good, honest, wholesome, hungry' repast which we made under a beech tree just by a spring of pure sweet water that stole out of the side of a hill, and how, when it was over, one of the party read old Izaak Walton's scene with the milkmaid, while I lay on the grass and built castles in a bright pile of clouds until I fell asleep. All this may appear like mere egotism, yet I cannot refrain from uttering these recollections, which are passing like a strain of music over my mind and have been called up by an agreeable scene which I witnessed not long since.

In the morning's stroll along the banks of the Alun, a beautiful little stream which flows down from the Welsh hills and throws itself into the Dee, my attention was attracted to a group seated on the margin. On approaching I found it to consist of a veteran angler and two rustic disciples. The former was an old fellow with a wooden leg, with clothes very much but very carefully patched, betokening poverty honestly come by and decently maintained. His face bore the marks of former storms, but present fair weather, its furrows had been worn into an habitual smile, his iron-gray locks hung about his ears, and he had altogether the good-humored air of a constitutional philosopher who was disposed to take the world as it went. One of his companions was a ragged wight with the skulking look of an arrant poacher, and I'll warrant could find his way to any gentleman's fish-pond in the neighborhood in the darkest night. The other was a tall, awkward country lad, with a lounging gait, and apparently somewhat of a rustic beau. The old man was busy in examining the maw of a trout which he had just killed, to discover by its contents what insects were seasonable for bait, and was lecturing on the subject to his companions, who appeared to listen with infinite deference. I have a kind feeling towards all 'brothers of the angle' ever since I read Izaak Walton. They are men, he affirms, of a 'mild, sweet, and peaceable spirit;' and my esteem for them has been increased since I met with an old *Tretyse of fishing with the Angle*, in which are set forth many of the maxims of their inoffensive fraternity. 'Take good hede,' sayeth this honest little tretyse, 'that in going about your disportes ye open no man's gates but that ye shet them again. Also ye shall not use this forsayd crafti disport for no covetousness to the encreasing and sparing of your money only, but principally for your solace, and to cause the helth of your body and specyally of your soule."

I thought that I could perceive in the veteran angler before me an exemplification of what I had read; and there was a cheerful contentedness in his looks that quite drew me towards him. I could not but remark the gallant manner in which he stumped from one part of the brook to another, waving his rod in the air to keep the line from dragging on the ground or catching among the bushes, and the adroitness with which he would throw his fly to any particular place, sometimes skimming it lightly along a little rapid, sometimes casting it into one of those dark holes made by a twisted root or overhanging bank in which the large trout are apt to lurk. In the meanwhile he was giving instructions to his two disciples, showing them the manner in which they should handle their rods, fix their flies, and play them along the surface of the stream. The scene brought to my mind the instructions of the sage Piscator to his scholar. The country around was of that pastoral kind which Walton is fond of describing. It was a part of the great plain of Cheshire, close by the beautiful vale of Gessford, and just where the inferior Welsh hills begin to swell up from among fresh-smelling meadows. The day too, like that recorded in his work, was mild and sunshiny, with now and then a soft-dropping shower that sowed the whole earth with diamonds.

I soon fell into conversation with the old angler, and was so much entertained that, under pretext of receiving instructions in his art, I kept company with him almost the whole day, wandering along the banks of the stream and listening to his talk. He was very communicative, having all the easy garrulity of cheerful old age, and I fancy was a little flattered by having an opportunity of displaying his piscatory lore, for who does not like now and then to play the sage?

---

* From this same treatise it would appear that angling is a more industrious and devout employment than it is generally considered: 'For when ye purpose to go on your disportes in fishynge ye will not desyre greatlye many persons with you, which might let you of your game. And that ye may serve God devoutly in saying effectually your customable prayers. And thus doying, ye shall eschew and also avoyde many vices, as ydelness, which is principall cause to induce man to many other vices, as it is right well known.'

He had been much of a rambler in his day, and had passed some years of his youth in America, particularly in Savannah, where he had entered into trade and had been ruined by the indiscretion of a partner. He had afterwards experienced many ups and downs in life until he got into the navy, where his leg was carried away by a cannon-ball at the battle of Camperdown. This was the only stroke of real good-fortune he had ever experienced, for it got him a pension, which, together with some small paternal property, brought him in a revenue of nearly forty pounds. On this he retired to his native village, where he lived quietly and independently, and devoted the remainder of his life to the 'noble art of angling.'

I found that he had read Izaak Walton attentively, and he seemed to have imbibed all his simple frankness and prevalent good-humor. Though he had been sorely buffeted about the world, he was satisfied that the world, in itself, was good and beautiful. Though he had been as roughly used in different countries as a poor sheep that is fleeced by every hedge and thicket, yet he spoke of every nation with candor and kindness, appearing to look only on the good side of things; and, above all, he was almost the only man I had ever met with who had been an unfortunate adventurer in America and had honesty and magnanimity enough to take the fault to his own door, and not to curse the country. The lad that was receiving his instructions, I learnt, was the son and heir-apparent of a fat old widow who kept the village inn, and of course a youth of some expectation, and much courted by the idle gentleman-like personages of the place. In taking him under his care, therefore, the old man had probably an eye to a privileged corner in the tap-room and an occasional cup of cheerful ale free of expense.

There is certainly something in angling – if we could forget, which anglers are apt to do, the cruelties and tortures inflicted on worms and insects – that tends to produce a gentleness of spirit and a pure serenity of mind. As the English are methodical even in their recreations, and are the most scientific of sportsmen, it has been reduced among them to perfect rule and system. Indeed, it is an amusement peculiarly adapted to the mild and highly-culti-vated scenery of England, where every roughness has been softened away from the landscape. It is delightful to saunter along those limpid streams which wander, like veins of silver, through the bosom of this beautiful country, leading one through a diversity of small home scenery – sometimes winding through ornamented grounds; sometimes brimming along through rich pasturage, where the fresh green is mingled with sweet-smelling flowers; sometimes venturing in sight of villages and hamlets, and then running capriciously away into shady retirements. The sweetness and serenity of Nature and the quiet watchfulness of the sport gradually bring on pleasant fits of musing, which are now and then agreeably interrupted by the song of a bird, the distant whistle of the peasant, or perhaps the vagary of some fish leaping out of the still water and skimming transiently about its glassy surface. 'When I would beget content,' says Izaak Walton, 'and increase confidence in the power and wisdom and providence of Almighty God, I will walk the meadows by some gliding stream, and there contemplate the lilies that take no care, and those very many other little living creatures that are not only created, but fed (man knows not how) by the goodness of the God of Nature, and therefore trust in Him.'

I cannot forbear to give another quotation from one of those ancient champions of angling which breathes the same innocent and happy spirit:

> Let me live harmlessly, and near the brink
> Of Trent or Avon have a dwelling-place;
> Where I may see my quill, or cork, down sink,
> With eager bite of pike, or bleak, or dace;
> And on the world and my creator think:
> Whilst some men strive ill-gotten goods t' embrace;
> And others spend their time in base excess
> Of wine, or worse, in war or wantonness.
>
> Let them that will, these pastimes still pursue,
> And on such pleasing fancies feed their fill;
> So I the fields and meadows green may view,
> And daily by fresh rivers walk at will,
> Among the daisies and the violets blue,
> Red hyacinth and yellow daffodil.†

On parting with the old angler I inquired after his place of abode, and, happening to be in the neighborhood of the village a few evenings afterwards, I had the curiosity to seek him out. I found him living in a small cottage containing only one room, but a perfect curiosity in its method and arrangement. It was on the skirts of the village, on a green bank a little back from the road, with a small

---

† J. Davors.

garden in front stocked with kitchen herbs and adorned with a few flowers. The whole front of the cottage was overrun with a honeysuckle. On the top was a ship for a weathercock. The interior was fitted up in a truly nautical style, his ideas of comfort and convenience having been acquired on the berth-deck of a man-of-war. A hammock was slung from the ceiling which in the daytime was lashed up so as to take but little room. From the centre of the chamber hung a model of a ship, of his own workmanship. Two or three chairs, a table, and a large sea-chest formed the principal movables. About the wall were stuck up naval ballads, such as 'Admiral Hosier's Ghost,' 'All in the Downs,' and 'Tom Bowling,' intermingled with pictures of sea-fights, among which the battle of Camperdown held a distinguished place. The mantelpiece was decorated with sea-shells, over which hung a quadrant, flanked by two wood-cuts of most bitter-looking naval commanders. His implements for angling were carefully disposed on nails and hooks about the room. On a shelf was arranged his library, containing a work on angling, much worn, a Bible covered with canvas, an odd volume or two of voyages, a nautical almanac, and a book of songs.

His family consisted of a large black cat with one eye, and a parrot which he had caught and tamed and educated himself in the course of one of his voyages, and which uttered a variety of sea-phrases with the hoarse brattling tone of a veteran boatswain. The establishment reminded me of that of the renowned Robinson Crusoe; it was kept in neat order, everything being 'stowed away' with the regularity of a ship of war; and he informed me that he 'scoured the deck every morning and swept it between meals.'

I found him seated on a bench before the door, smoking his pipe in the soft evening sunshine. His cat was purring soberly on the threshold, and his parrot describing some strange evolutions in an iron ring that swung in the centre of his cage. He had been angling all day, and gave me a history of his sport with as much minuteness as a general would talk over a campaign, being particularly animated in relating the manner in which he had taken a large trout, which had completely tasked all his skill and wariness, and which he had sent as a trophy to mine hostess of the inn.

How comforting it is to see a cheerful and contented old age, and to behold a poor fellow like this, after being tempest-tost through life, safely moored in a snug and quiet harbor in the evening of his days! His happiness, however, sprung from within himself and was independent of external circumstances, for he had that inexhaustible good-nature which is the most precious gift of

Heaven, spreading itself like oil over the troubled sea of thought, and keeping the mind smooth and equable in the roughest weather.

On inquiring further about him, I learnt that he was a universal favorite in the village and the oracle of the tap-room, where he delighted the rustics with his songs, and, like Sindbad, astonished them with his stories of strange lands and shipwrecks and sea-fights. He was much noticed too by gentlemen sportsmen of the neighborhood, had taught several of them the art of angling, and was a privileged visitor to their kitchens. The whole tenor of his life was quiet and inoffensive, being principally passed about the neighboring streams when the weather and season were favorable; and at other times he employed himself at home, preparing his fishing-tackle for the next campaign or manufacturing rods, nets, and flies for his patrons and pupils among the gentry.

He was a regular attendant at church on Sundays, though he generally fell asleep during the sermon. He had made it his particular request that when he died he should be buried in a green spot which he could see from his seat in church, and which he had marked out ever since he was a boy, and had thought of when far from home on the raging sea in danger of being food for the fishes: it was the spot where his father and mother had been buried.

I have done, for I fear that my reader is growing weary, but I could not refrain from drawing the picture of this worthy 'brother of the angle,' who has made me more than ever in love with the theory, though I fear I shall never be adroit in the practice, of his art; and I will conclude this rambling sketch in the words of honest Izaak Walton, by craving the blessing of St. Peter's Master upon my reader, 'and upon all that are true lovers of virtue, and dare trust in His providence, and be quiet, and go a-angling.'

Soldiers by the Side of the Road

KEVIN MALONEY

THE BEST CHEESEBURGER I ever had was from a diner called Deschutes Crossing on the Warm Springs Indian Reservation. In 2009, the restaurant was shut down by a health inspector, but in the late 1980s my dad and I stopped there after a long day of trout fishing on the Deschutes River. The burger was your basic lettuce-tomato-and-pickle number, but it tasted like the body and blood of Christ. I don't remember if I caught a trout that day, but I remember that burger. Maybe the cows were different back then. Maybe they ate grass and roamed wild over Montana hillsides, crapping under the stars. I don't know. But I'm still looking for that feeling – driving home in the dark with a full belly and meaty burps, my dad's hairy knuckles on the wheel, our hip waders and fly rods in the backseat, Mt. Hood looming in the west like a purple tipi floating above the desert.

It's one of the few memories I have of just the two of us. Most of my memories involve the whole family piled in a minivan on the way to Yellowstone or Glacier National Park, my brother and I fighting in the backseat, my dad's murderous glare in the rearview mirror warning us that if he had to pull over there'd be hell to pay. But on the handful of occasions we went fly-fishing, it was just my dad and I. My brother didn't see the point of driving a hundred miles, then hiking a mile and a half through rattlesnake country to stand in an ice-cold river practicing an inefficient form of catch-and-release when you could buy a Filet-O-Fish from McDonald's for 99 cents. But my dad, for all his business savvy and Republican values, was a romantic. I'd call him an artist if he hadn't spent the better part of his life trying to convince me that art is a hobby, not a career, and that happiness consists of a steady paycheck and a 401K.

This morning he's conducting a symphony. He holds his hands in front of him, maneuvering them in gentle 4/4 movements, directing an orchestra that no one else can hear. Occasionally one of his hands leaves its rhythmic dance and goes up to his forehead, where he picks at a bloody scab. Brittany, my sister-in-law, grabs the guilty hand and lowers it to his side.

'No, John,' she says. 'You're hurting yourself.'

My dad mumbles something incoherent. With his puckered mouth and closed eyes, he looks oddly like a baby.

My mom asks if he wants water.

He shakes his head no.

She asks if he'd like to see a priest.

He doesn't respond.

She says, 'Squeeze my hand if you want to see a priest.'

She waits for him to squeeze, but he doesn't.

His catheter bag hangs placenta-like on the side of the bed, full of blood. I can only look at him for so long before my eyes drift to the TV hanging from the ceiling. It's tuned to the US Open. Tiger Woods is trying to rally after shooting a career worst 10-over-par on opening day. He lines up for his second shot on the 10th and knocks it deep into a field of hay. The anguish on his face is unmistakable. It says, 'I was great once. What the hell happened?'

My dad was a hobbyist. Bikes, guns, woodworking, HAM radio. He wanted 'the best' of everything, but as soon as he'd identified his ideal purchase and charged it to his credit card, he moved on to the next hobby. The evidence was in our garage: custom Trek touring bike, diamond-bladed table saw, Kenwood TS-990S HAM radio with thirty-foot antennae in the backyard. And in the gun safe – God knows how many shotguns, handguns, and assault rifles.

In 1988, the hobby that occupied my dad more than any other was fly tying. Every night after dinner he grabbed a can of Diet Coke from the front hall closet and disappeared into the garage, where, among half-deflated basketballs and canisters of gasoline, he spun bird feathers around fishing hooks, tying artificial flies with names like 'Parachute Adams,' 'Woolly Bugger,' and 'Elk Hair Caddis.' I loved watching him work. There was something disorienting and beautiful about his 300-pound frame hovering over such a tiny object, glancing at his fly-tying manual, back at his fly, back at the manual, his meaty fingers barely fitting into the handles of his scissors as he snipped the loose thread and held the fly up for inspection. 'Not bad, eh?'

He was never one to say an unprompted 'I love you,' but if I expressed even the slightest interest in his hobby of the moment, he considered it his moral imperative to buy me whatever I needed to become just as obsessed as he was. Which is how I found myself sitting at my very own fly-tying station one day, attempting to tie a Royal Coachman, that uniquely beautiful fly with its peacock herl, red silk corset, and tail of elk hair. When my dad saw the result, he said, 'Well, I guess you'll need your own pair of hip waders. We have to test that beauty on the river.'

I don't remember who the Blazers were playing that night. Maybe it wasn't even the Blazers; it could have been Monday Night Football. Whatever it was, I was sitting in my parents' living room eating pizza and watching a game on TV. During the commercials my mom complained about their recent vacation to the American south-west. The day they'd arrived at Zion National Park, the US government had shut down due to an argumentative, incompetent Congress. She described how the frustrated tourists had taken matters into their own hands, sneaking past blockades to photograph the beautiful orange cliffs. 'But they wouldn't even let us in at the Grand Canyon. The entire park was under lock and key. I can't believe it. I say we get rid of the lot of them, Republican and Democrat, and vote in a whole new Congress!'

My dad, usually more than willing to engage in a political argument, seemed distracted. 'Yeah,' he said, fidgeting uncomfortably in his chair. 'Ridiculous.' After my mom ran out of things to say about the art galleries of Sedona and her visit with an old friend in Palm Springs, she gave my dad a meaningful look that seemed to say, 'OK, your turn.' My dad nodded and turned down the volume on the TV. 'Kevin,' he said. 'There's something I have to tell you.'

One of the duties of my job at the time involved writing copy for healthcare websites. I'd written an article on prostate cancer, and from the small amount of research I'd done, I knew it was one of the more operable cancers. The worst-case scenario usually involves the removal of the prostate and the installation of a pump so that a man can continue getting erections. As long as it's caught early, it's one of the 'good' cancers. But as my mom went into the details of my dad's medical plan, there was no mention of surgery. Instead she talked about an experimental form of radium and a trip to Seattle to see a specialist. 'I wish we'd caught it earlier,' said my dad. 'But I'm just glad we caught it.'

I left their house more confused than angry. What they hadn't told me, what they'd implied but failed to say out loud, was that my dad's cancer had metastasized and was no longer operable. There were tumors in his spine, cancerous cells in his blood and bones. What he'd described as a minor annoyance like a flat tire or broken filling, was 'metastatic prostate cancer,' an aggressive, late-stage disease with a 100% mortality rate.

The stretch of river we fished was a short hike north of the US-26 Bridge where the Shitike Creek joins the Deschutes. On the east side of the river, a narrow trail runs along the water, pockmarked with signs warning: TRESPASSERS WILL BE SHOT / SURVIVORS WILL BE SHOT AGAIN. On the west side of the river is reservation land, a thousand-square-mile parcel of high desert where three tribes – the Wasco, Tenino, and Paiute – settled after an 1855 treaty relinquished their rights to the much larger tract of land they'd inhabited for over 10,000 years. In our half-dozen trips to the Deschutes, we only saw them once: two men with long black hair walking along the opposite bank carrying fishing rods. I asked my dad why we never fished that side of the river. He said it belonged to the Indians. It was sovereign land, in effect its own country. They didn't have to follow the same regulations we did; they still fished with dip-nets up near Sherar's Bridge. I looked up at the sloping hill of sagebrush and orange rock. Their side was more or less identical to our side, but knowing it was tribal land charged it with beauty and mystique.

I thought of the terrible stories I'd heard in school: smallpox blankets, broken treaties, plains of buffalo exterminated to deprive the Indians of food. How Crazy Horse defeated General Custer at the Battle of Little Big Horn, only to watch his people starve to death in the cold winter of 1876-77. I didn't know the particular tragedy of the Warm Springs tribe, but as we drove home that night I noticed the ramshackle houses and rusted-out cars parked along the highway. I tried to imagine being caught between worlds. One glorious but gone. The other here but broken.

He's not moving his hands today. Since he stopped eating last week, his body is consuming its own fat for fuel. The flesh has pulled away from his face, giving his nose a beaklike appearance. My mom sits in the chair next to him saying, 'Squeeze my hand if you want to see a priest.' She says it over and over until she feels something that might be a squeeze.

The problem is we don't know any priests. We haven't been to church in decades, and we're not sure how to go about finding one who will perform last rites on a non-parishioner. Is there Yelp for this kind of thing? My sister-in-law googles 'Catholic church Lake Oswego' and explains our situation over the phone. Namely, that my dad is a non-church-going Catholic who'd like to receive last rites. We think. That is, he sort of squeezed my mom's hand a few minutes ago when she asked him for the twentieth time if he'd like to see a priest. Luckily, Father Kern isn't allowed to judge us. That's God's job. He says he'll be right over.

The closest thing I have to religion is a deep affection for the short stories of Flannery O'Connor and the occasional visit to the Tibetan Buddhist meditation center, but when Father Kern walks into my dad's darkened hospital room and begins reading the 'Anointing of the Sick,' I get a chill. *The grace of our Lord Jesus Christ and the love of God and the fellowship of the Holy Spirit be with you all.* He sprinkles my dad with holy water, and the truth of what is happening suddenly sinks in. My dad is dying. Not someday but imminently.

Father Kern asks us to join him in prayer. I fold my hands together and, despite years of rejecting Christianity, find that I'm praying and that tears are running down my face. The scene is straight out of a Renaissance painting, all shadow and light. The priest hovers over my dad like a dark bird. I'm witnessing both my father's death and all death, and as I make the sign of the cross over my heart, I hope that, despite Richard Dawkins and two thousand years of science, Jesus is up there, listening.

There was the momentary sound of a spinning disc, the arm of a laser positioning itself over the first track, a burst of zydeco accordion from the car's speakers, followed by a tender, boyish voice, singing. In the late 1980s my dad was swept up in the baby boomer mania for Paul Simon's *Graceland*. We listened to it driving back and forth between the suburbs and the city, and on long drives to Seattle or eastern Oregon. With its images of the Mississippi Delta and salvation at Elvis Presley's mansion, it was the soundtrack of the American highway, of fathers and sons pilgrimaging to find meaning in a meaningless world.

On the drive to the river I felt pressure to talk to my dad, to describe the bipolar life of an insecure, hormonal seventh-grader, but on the drive home we were exhausted and traveled across the high desert listening to *Graceland*. I pressed my head against the passenger window and felt the vibrations of the road. I pretended to sleep, while looking through my squinting eyelashes at the distant lights in the *terra incognita* of the desert, drifting slowly to the right like boats on a river. I thought about the vastness of the universe and the smallness of our lives, and trembled at the idea that I was going to die one day and that death lasts forever.

'Where are we?' I asked.

'Still a long way to go,' said my dad. 'Go back to sleep.'

I returned my face to the window, to the hemisphere of stars and sagebrush and black canyons. The ponderosas gave way to firs and hemlocks and the snowy peak of Mt. Hood hovered before us like the head of a decapitated ghost.

Hospice says it could happen any day now. Our extended family arrives to say goodbye. Nephews and nieces and their kids, one in her first year of high school, another about to leave for his first year of college. They take turns going into my dad's room, speaking their final words to him. My ninety-four-year-old Scottish grandmother arrives, pushing herself on a walker. She's already lost a husband and daughter, both to cancer. As I leave the room, she leans over my dad and cries, 'My baby. My poor sweet baby.' The following morning my thirteen-year-old daughter arrives from Vermont to spend the summer with me. I ask if she wants to see her Papa one last time. She says yes. I lead her into the dark room and my dad opens his eyes. 'What are you doing here?' he asks. I tell him that Sabine just flew in from Vermont, that she'll be spending the summer with us. 'Oh good,' he says and immediately falls back into his morphine stupor.

The next night my mom calls at one o'clock in the morning and says that my dad is dead. I get dressed and drive from Portland to Lake Oswego. I-5 is eerily empty. The radio is playing bad pop music. I scan from station to station, trying to find something that matches what I'm feeling, but I don't even know what I'm feeling. I'm in shock. I just need something to keep me focused so I don't drive into a concrete barrier. The care facility is bustling with activity. The nurses have put out coffee and cookies. They ask if there's anything they can do for me. I'm not even sure what they're saying. 'No, no, nothing. I'm fine.' When I walk into my dad's room, he's propped up with pillows, in the exact same position where I left him. No one has touched him yet. His skin is strangely yellow and his mouth hangs open as if his final act was to be awestruck by the beautiful world he was leaving. I sit down on the sofa next to him. My only thought is that whatever this is, it isn't my dad. It hasn't been him for a while now. But I'm amazed by whatever this is. The shell of a molted insect. The flesh that both was and wasn't him.

Hospice arrives to prepare my dad for the coroner. Behind closed doors, they clean and dress him in sweatpants and a t-shirt, the outfit he will be cremated in. When they finish, they tell us this is our last chance to see him. While my brother and I linger in the doorway, my mom walks up to my dad, squeezes his hand, and tells him she loves him. She turns to leave and we follow her out to her car.

The fish haven't been biting all day. We try one fly after another, but nothing's working. There are periodic ripples in the water but not many. The sun dips lower in the horizon, painting the canyon walls red. There's a cold wind coming off the river, spreading the chill from our legs to our hands. Finally my dad takes a deep breath through his nostrils. 'Well, bud. What do you think?' I nod. We reel in our lines, pack our gear, and begin the mile-and-a-half trek back to the car. About a quarter-mile from the parking lot, I notice a hand-made sign nailed to a tree that I didn't notice on the way in. It says:

IN MEMORY OF BOB TATE,
ONE HELL OF A FISHERMAN
1921-1986

We stand there a minute, doing math, then continue down the trail.

Chasing the Chrome

BILL HEAVEY

THE FIRST TIME I met Mikey Dvorak, he asked if he could borrow fifty bucks.

At the time I thought he was a bum. I still think he's a bum, but in the same way that an itinerant Buddhist monk is a bum. Except Mikey's spiritual path was chasing steelhead.

I met Mikey through Kirk Lombard, a hardcore angler in San Francisco, who told me that if I really wanted to meet a 'true fishing nomad' I should meet Mikey, a steelhead addict who had no fixed address and never seemed to have more than a few bucks on him. But it didn't seem to bother him. 'All he cares about is being where the fish are,' Kirk said. That's why Mikey often slept in his truck – not on a pad in the back so he could stretch out, but upright in the driver's seat because the rest of the truck was too full of gear. 'And he's such a maniac that he sleeps on the ramp.'

'I'm afraid I don't follow.'

'When Mikey's steelhead fishing, he wants to be the first guy on the river. So, the night before, he backs his drift boat down the ramp, puts the truck in park, and conks out. The next morning, the first guy at the ramp finds Mikey there. The guy is pissed and bangs on Mikey's window to wake him up. At which point Mikey wakes, apologizes, and launches. So he's on the river ahead of anybody else.'

I had to meet this guy.

A few days later the three of us headed down the California coast to chase white seabass, a highly mobile fish that migrates up from Baja California as the ocean warms in spring. We hoped to intercept some around Monterey. I dug myself a hole in the backseat of Mikey's truck, which was crammed to the roof with fishing and camping gear, as well as a great deal of stuff that should have been in a landfill. Mikey said that the police had recently stopped him on this very stretch of road because his truck fit the profile of a meth user's vehicle. The cops had searched it thoroughly. Actually, Mikey said, the stop had been a good thing. The cops turned up tackle that he'd given up for lost.

I was already captivated by the guy. He named every bird we saw at surprising distances, and when I asked how, he explained that he was doing it by the birds' flight characteristics, which were generally more distinctive than markings. He talked about all kinds of fish, their life cycles, what biologists knew and what they still hadn't figured out.

It was just outside Monterey that he asked for the fifty bucks. I gave him the money, but I also pointed out that I was leaving in three days and asked how he proposed to pay me back. 'No problem,' he said. 'I just need a battery for the boat.'

'You're losing me, Mikey.'

'Oh, right,' he said, as if the connection was so obvious that he hadn't bothered to explain. 'We need the battery. So we buy one, fish for two days, and then return it for the refund.' In my world, owning a motorboat implied that you also owned the battery needed to start the motor. In Mikey's world, I soon realized, only the present mattered. The past was done, the future abstract. If you live in the moment and care about fishing, there are only two important questions. Where are the fish? What do I need to go fishing for them right now?

In a way, I admired that Mikey had freed himself from the unproductive worries that so often kept me, like most people, from being fully present in the moment. Mikey, Kirk had said, was a barely legal walking disaster in the real world. He had a cellphone only because his sister, frustrated at never knowing where he was, bought him one. He forgot things, lost things, routinely showed up late or not at all, and failed to follow through on promises. But put him around a fish and he became focused, intent, and tireless.

For the next two days, the three of us and our new battery bobbed around on six-foot swells in the Pacific in a fourteen-foot skiff, jigging our brains out. The only other boats we saw were tankers and container ships on the horizon. Just half a mile away, waves that had traveled thousands of miles across the ocean hurtled against the coastal cliffs with thunderous claps. At some point

I realized that we had nothing but life jackets if anything were to happen. And no safe beach to swim to. I didn't want to think about this too hard, so I asked Mikey what it was about steelhead for him. He shrugged, as if to say that the answer was ineffable, but he gave it a try. 'They're the most mysterious, smartest, toughest fish I've ever seen.

'Think about it. A steelhead gets born in a particular patch of gravel in the river, spends a couple of years growing, and then decides to head down to the ocean. Which is not a safe place for a smolt. Everything out there wants to eat it. It spends a couple of years fattening up at sea, maybe swims halfway around the world. Then – if it's the one or two fish in a hundred that makes it – it'll beat its brains out to return to the same patch of gravel, you know? Amazing. And you don't know when or if they're gonna show up. They're just really tough, smart fish.'

Over the years he'd had steelhead strike so viciously that they yanked rods out of the holders on his drift boat. 'Three times that's happened. Right outta something designed to hold your rod no matter what. And they were good outfits – $500 ones, Loomis and Lamiglas rods with Shimano Calcutta reels. How can you not love a fish that wild, with that much heart?'

We fished hard for two whole days and never got a bite. By the time I left, however, I'd vowed that if I ever got the chance to go steelheading with Mikey Dvorak, I'd jump on it. The season along the California coast usually ran from late December or January through March, he said. It all hinged on getting enough rain to raise the rivers so the fish could get over the bar and swim up.

The call came two years later.

It had been an unusually dry year, Mikey told me, but the rains had finally come in mid-February. The fishing was fantastic.

By the time I booked a flight, however, there had been too much of a good thing. The rivers were unfishable – high, fast, and muddy. I delayed my departure a week. A week later, as I was checking in at the airport, Mikey called again to ask if I could delay for two more days. I couldn't.

'What the hell,' he said. 'We'll just have to do the best we can.'

I was standing outside baggage claim at the San José airport when he drove up. There's something about guys like Mikey that threaten certain types of people. I could see every cop within sight eyeballing the truck, driver, and trailered drift boat as if all three might blow up. 'Mikey,' I asked, sliding into the passenger seat, 'what is it about you that freaks everybody out?'

'Beats me, man.' I got the feeling that Mikey was so accustomed to this phenomenon that it hardly registered anymore.

It was late. We'd sleep that night on the forty-four-foot boat he kept in a marina near Half Moon Bay, then drive north tomorrow, looking for whichever steelhead river would clear up first. Mikey said the boat was a 1949 naval rescue vessel that he'd bought at auction, along with the commercial ocean salmon fishing license attached to it. It had seemed like a way to make some money. In fact, he'd had a remarkably good first year, bringing in 23,000 pounds of salmon, worth more than $100,000.

Mikey's boat was a floating version of his truck, the hands-down winner of any Most Derelict Vessel contest in the large marina. I suspected that Mikey was less than an authority on seamanship, and I damn sure knew the boat would have failed any inspection. And yet Mikey had somehow succeeded in a very competitive industry. As long as fish were involved, Mikey found a way.

I bunked that night on a narrow bench in the wheelhouse. Mikey bid me good night and disappeared into the hold. Presumably he had a bed down there somewhere. In a way, it was a shame the harbor police didn't have a profile of a meth user's boat. A good search was exactly what the boat needed.

The next morning we rolled north. 'We're chasing the chrome,' Mikey said, referring to the silvery appearance of a steelhead fresh from the ocean. The longer the fish stayed in the river, the more they reverted to rainbow trout colors. Fifty miles north of San Francisco was like being in another state. Everything changed. The towns were small, and each was smaller than the one before. It was redwood country: trees with tops you couldn't see growing on steep, rugged mountains. Mikey started making phone calls to half a dozen guiding buddies. All the steelhead rivers – the Napa, Russian, Noyo, Eel, Van Duzen, Trinity, Mad, Klamath, and Smith – were blown out. 'We're probably screwed for the next two days wherever we go,' he said.

Which river would clear first depended on a multitude of factors: today's level; how much rain had fallen and how much more might come; the extent to which degradation from lumbering, mining, and the cultivation of grapes and marijuana increased the river's run-off; and the river's record of recovery after rains in recent years. There were so many factors in play that it was impossible to take them all into account. Mikey sifted the data and decided to bet on the Smith, one of the most intact river systems in the state. It had received the least rain and had the most favorable forecast, at that moment anyway. It was also 350 miles north. Off we went.

As we drove, I asked Mikey if this was the same Pathfinder we'd driven in two years ago to chase white seabass. 'No, this is the second I've had since then.' Mikey, I was to learn, bought Pathfinders exclusively, never paid more than a grand, and drove them until the wheels came off. 'But only the first generation, '85 to '95. Those were tanks, man. After '96, they got all round and fruity-looking. Stopped being a truck, you know?' This was his sixth. He'd bought it a year ago, with 200,000 miles on it. He'd put on 66,000 since then. I asked what he'd paid. 'Seven hundred and twenty-two bucks,' he said. And smiled.

'Sounds like you've got the truck thing down,' I said.

'Yeah, but I got a problem with boats.'

'How so?'

'I can't get rid of 'em. I've got six right now.'

These included the 17-foot drift boat we were towing, a 9-foot Avon inflatable, a 14-foot Wahoo, a 16-foot Wellcraft ('in a marina in Alameda'), a 20-foot Mako, and the 44-foot salmon boat. This inconsistency – the way he could be brutally practical about trucks and completely sentimental about boats – was typical Mikey. 'It's hard to explain,' he said. 'But a boat, it becomes, I don't know, *who I am*. And they're not all great boats. But there are things about my own personality that I don't like, OK? But I'm stuck with them. I can't disown them. Does that make sense?' Of course it didn't. But I understood it.

We found a motel in Crescent City, close to the river, and woke the next morning to light rain. By now, having discovered that my phone could get on the Internet, Mikey was borrowing it every hour. The reports he was looking at said the rain might stop. It didn't. Soon it was raining hard. Mikey decided we should head up into Oregon and check the Chetco. 'It's on the other side of a ridge that sometimes splits the weather systems,' he explained. This seemed like a fool's errand. An unrelenting downpour like this one was anything but localized. But we went anyway. It was raining just as hard in Oregon.

Mikey didn't despair. The thing, it seemed, was to maintain momentum, keep chasing. He took me to the house of a guiding buddy in the area, Jim Burn. Jim knew the Smith as well as anybody. The two of them sat in front of Jim's computer for the next several hours, poring over water levels and weather reports while I played with Jim's dog.

The guides were as different as two guys could be and share the same passion for steelhead. Mikey's boat, for example, while neater than his truck, was still pretty funky. Jim's boat was spotless. He even had a 'bra' to protect it from debris when towed.

Eventually they concluded that there was no use even trying to fish the river until the next day. They adjourned to Jim's garage and spent the next two hours in what seemed to be a longstanding ritual, in which each showed off his newest lures while energetically insulting the other's. Each had hundreds of steelhead plugs, the most prized of which were 'pre-Rapala' Storm Wiggle Warts, Magnum Warts, Wee Warts, and PeeWee Warts. After Rapala acquired Storm in the late 1990s, I was told, they destroyed the original Storm molds and moved production to China. The new ones had lost the distinctive 'hunting' action of the best Storms. They had steel rattles rather than lead, which resulted in a harsher sound. The plastic was different. They were disasters. Now, they told me, old Storm lures in rare or desirable patterns went for as much as $100 on eBay. Mikey showed Jim one of his favorites, a pearl-colored PeeWee Wart that he'd recently bought for $50 from a seller called Plugwhore. It was a tiny thing, but Mikey maintained that its action was fantastic. 'Oh, yeah, I've bought from Plugwhore,' Jim said, then explained in detail why Mikey's lures, both in general and individually, sucked. Mikey returned the favor.

While the finer points escaped me, I did learn a bit of plug terminology. A light-colored lure with a red back was said to have a 'rash.' Black glitter was a 'Michael Jackson.' Black-and-white was a 'cop.' Silver-and-black was an 'Oakland Raider.' And chrome pink with a black bill was a 'Dr. Death.'

It wasn't until the next day, the fourth of the trip, that we finally threw a line in the water. And that was bank fishing, throwing weighted clusters of salmon roe rolled in borax, the better to make the eggs adhere to one another, into the Smith. I think Mikey and Jim knew the river was too high, that the fish were hunkered down until the water cleared. But maybe fishing when you knew damn well it was pointless was an act of faith, a demonstration of your humility to the river gods.

The Smith dropped a foot over the course of that day (we marked the changing levels with branches stuck into the bank), but in eight hours of fishing, not one of our three rods got so much as a bump. A few people stopped by to chat with Jim and ask about the river. By this time, Mikey had tired of telling people I was an outdoor writer. His new story was that – despite looking like a middle-aged bald guy – I was actually a Make-A-Wish kid with one of those premature aging diseases who wanted to catch a steelhead before what would be his eleventh and, tragically, final birthday. Mikey said that it was his mission to make that happen.

We tried again for a few hours the next morning in a deep gorge of the river, the descent into which required holding my rod in my mouth so I could use all four limbs. The Smith is a gorgeous river, but parts of it were just plain scary. Fall off your rock where we were, for example, and you wouldn't be coming up anytime soon. Back at the truck, Mikey decided our last, best shot was a small river 150 miles south, which he forbade me to name. I didn't question his choice. Neither did Jim, who followed us.

When we left the coastal highway, it was like finding another world inside another world, one even more remote and beautiful. We crossed a range of mountains, corkscrewing our way up over dirt roads through country where you'd go for miles without seeing a house. We rounded a bend and were looking at miles of undeveloped coastline, rocks the size of houses in the surf, which broke hundreds of yards offshore. 'Wow, Mikey, this is incredible,' I said.

'My happy place,' he said. 'It's known but not really known. I mean people know it's here, but most of them think it's just another steelhead river.' I didn't. I thought we'd landed in paradise.

We got to the river itself an hour before sunset. Mikey wanted to back the boat in and throw plugs from it for a while, get reacquainted with the water, maybe catch a fish. Jim countered that Mikey, as usual, had everything ass-backward.

'Look, we don't know where we're staying. We don't know where we're going to eat tonight. The way to do this is get squared away tonight and do it right first thing in the morning.'

'C'mon, Jim,' Mikey coaxed. 'For once in your life just relax and go with it. Fish for half an hour and then we'll go figure all that out. There's still time.'

For the next half hour, they argued. Jim was by the book, linear, logical. Mikey was seat-of-the-pants, intuitive, eccentric. It was like listening to two halves of my brain fight each other. By the time they finished, my head hurt and it was too late to fish.

Since it was all coming down to the next day, Mikey wanted to see if he could get some local intel. About 9 p.m., he swung the truck into a mostly deserted campground. When he saw a drift boat by one of the occupied sites, he made a beeline for it. 'We come in peace!' Mikey bellowed. The boat belonged to an elderly couple, who had evidently just finished dinner and were talking quietly by the light of a kerosene lantern, their dishes stacked before them. It was hard to tell what they made of the little dude with a full beard and a bush of hair tucked up into a wool hat. But they smiled as if nothing was out of place.

They listened as Mikey told them the Make-A-Wish story. They knew he was full of it but didn't seem to mind. At a certain moment, however, the woman looked at Mikey curiously, cocked her head, and said, 'Why, don't you know that you can't *plan* to catch a steelhead? Goodness! Everybody knows that. All you can do is go someplace where the fish might be, wait until the water looks right, fish it hard, and hope you get lucky.'

'Absolutely!' Mikey agreed.

No one had bothered to tell me this, the first principle of steelhead fishing. Maybe, to guys like Mikey and Jim, it's so obvious that it doesn't bear mentioning. I'd slowly been making my way toward this fact on my own, but it was striking to hear it confirmed by a third party.

The man said that he hadn't even put the boat in today. Tomorrow would be a little better, but the river needed at least two rainless days to fish well. Back at the truck, Mikey announced that he'd figured it out. If we were to have any chance on the river, it was essential that I ride in the trailered boat, drink deeply of whiskey, and savor the soft night air rushing by. 'You need to do this, dude,' Mikey declared. 'Trust me. The river needs to know you're here. Plus, it's just awesome.'

Mikey went on for a bit, making it sound like a carnival ride one moment, a solemn duty the next. It was, of course, an idiotic thing to do. But something had changed. We were chasing the chrome and I was in the grips of the chase. Mikey had sucked me into his world. What we were doing had become a pilgrimage, a quest. And although I still wanted terribly to catch a steelhead, I wanted even more to be true to the spirit of the trip, which meant giving it everything I had.

Thirty seconds later, I was sitting in the boat's front chair, a rope in one hand, a bottle of bourbon in the other, both feet braced against the front rail, the liquor burning my throat as I howled at the moon. I rode the trailered boat over bumps and potholes, around curves and plunging down straightaways. It was, on the one hand, a moron's steeplechase, requiring nothing more than a total lack of common sense. But it was also glorious, flying through the night air with only stars above and the river somewhere close. I realized that whatever happened tomorrow, everything would turn out fine. I had, unbeknownst to myself, entered Mikey's world, the eternal present. The future would bring whatever it brought. The important thing was *now*. And no matter how it turned out, I was now taking one hell of a ride.

A few minutes of this turned out to be about all I really needed. I jarred my back pretty hard a few times. Through the back window, I could see Mikey and Jim, gesturing to each other. They had resumed their argument. It had become quite animated. They weren't looking back and couldn't hear no matter how loudly I shouted. There wasn't anything in the boat I could throw onto the roof of the truck except my shoe, which I couldn't really get to because I needed both feet to brace myself. It was another five miles before Mikey finally decided to check on me, at which point I told him to stop the damn truck.

Back at the little cottage we'd rented for the night, Mikey and Jim continued arguing. It was like listening to an old married couple rehash the same feud endlessly. Then, just before lights-out, I heard Jim's voice from the other room. It sounded different, almost plaintive. 'Mikey, you think the river might drop eighteen inches overnight?'

'Yeah, maybe.'

'And maybe it'll even get another six inches of visibility?'

'Yeah, could be,' Mikey said. He sounded like a parent reassuring a child that there was indeed a Santa Claus.

'OK. Good night.'

The next day, we set out early. Mikey was at the oars, while Jim and I were plugging, in which you let out line fifteen, maybe twenty yards, engage your reel, and let the current impart action to your lure. Meanwhile, the guide rows to counteract the current and put your plug in the spots that might hold fish. In essence, it's the guide rowing the boat who does the fishing. 'It's not the most romantic way to fish,' Mikey said. 'But in this kind of water, it's your best bet.'

Just then, Jim's rod arced. 'Fish on!' he cried, letting the fish fully take the plug before setting the hook. He passed the rod to me. I suddenly felt like the Make-A-Wish kid Mikey had made me out to be. I'd done nothing to catch this fish. But I dutifully reeled it in anyway. It fought hard, but not remarkably so, and within a minute or two I'd landed what both guides deemed an 11-pound hen, her sides bright. Both guides were adamant about releasing the fish quickly, and did so.

We were pumped at having hooked a fish so soon after launching. As time went by without another hook-up, we began to despair of the quick-fish curse, that peculiar deal in which the omen of all-day success turns out to be false. We changed lures. Since we weren't finding fish in the fishy spots, Mikey began fishing unconventional ones. That didn't work, either.

Jim hooked another fish late in the float and again handed me the rod. I'm still not sure what I did wrong. Maybe I pressed it too hard. Maybe Jim should have cut more of his line off after the first fish. I saw the fish leap once in fast water, then the lure was gone.

It was over. It was late afternoon, and Mikey and I had 250 miles to cover to get back to the marina. My plane was leaving at seven the next morning.

As we drove south, I tried to sort through what I was feeling. There was some disappointment, but I was surprised at how insignificant it seemed. I would have liked to have caught more fish, but we had succeeded. We'd chased the chrome and landed one freshie. I was tired, but it was the pleasant fatigue of having done everything you could. I had no regrets.

About 150 miles north of San Francisco, Mikey left the highway. Within minutes we were bombing down dirt roads on which we saw almost no other vehicles. 'Mikey, what's up?' I asked.

'This is one of the forks of the Eel,' he said. 'Got one last spot we gotta try. We'll get back later, but you can sleep on the plane.'

I smiled. *How*, I wondered, *could you not love a guy like Mikey?*

We arrived at a small house, a little ranch, at the bottom of a dead-end road. 'I know these folks,' he said. 'Good people.'

It felt to me as if we'd just bailed out of the highway arbitrarily and driven down an anonymous dirt road. 'What do you mean, you know these people?' I asked. 'There must be hundreds of roads just like this one up and down the coast. What'd you do, drive down every one and ask if you could fish?'

Mikey looked at me. 'Pretty much,' he said, 'if it bordered a steelhead river. Most of these people have let me park on their land and sleep in the truck at one time or another.' He parked, left me in the truck while he went to have a word with the owners, and returned to tell me everything was cool.

There was maybe an hour of light left. We rigged up quickly, tying on sacks of red roe and slinky sinkers beneath slip bobbers on spinning rods, and headed for the water. The bushes were so thick that there were only a couple of places you could cast from. It had been a long shot from the start, but I cast to a pool on the far side and drifted my bait through it half a dozen times. Then I moved to another spot, which involved climbing a boulder, and threw again. And then it was dark. We'd fished the sun all the way down. We'd given it everything we had. I felt a tremendous exhilaration.

As we drove back toward the highway, Mikey was already talking about how I'd have to come back next year, how we'd nail it. We stopped for gas. Mikey asked if he could borrow a few bucks. I said yes.

117

Magic Hooks

BRIAN ALLEN CARR

WHEN I WAS young, I would spend my summers and long weekends at my grandmother's beach house in Galveston, Texas. That town suffered, suffers still, in the wake of hurricanes which have battered it senseless. On record, it's been hit a dozen times. The biggest, baddest has come to be called the Galveston Hurricane of 1900. At the time, it would have been nameless. Up to 12,000 people died. The most recent was Ike in 2008. It claimed eighty-four. Alicia, a storm I slept through on the kitchen floor of First Presbyterian Church in the city's historic downtown, was a bigger storm than Ike but only took thirteen. The other named storms were Debra and Jerry, both category ones – baby hurricanes, really. The National Hurricane Center didn't start naming the storms until 1953, and they only used female names until 1979. That was the year I was born, but this story starts around 1984, when I was five years old.

The neighborhood my grandmother lived in was called Sea Isle, a sort of working-class beach community where insurance salesmen took their families for vacation. The houses were elevated, the ground level of them just car ports – the exterior walls painted Easter-egg colors – and the grass of the lawns was burr-filled and the roads were caliche. Some folks call it hardpan, what the roads were. A sort of natural cement of sediment and oyster gravel, white the way chalk's white when it's been left out to weather. Underfed dogs roamed wild, and you had to chuck caliche gravel at them or they'd bite.

My grandmother had severe emphysema, and she spent most of the time in her bedroom huffing nebulizer air and playing crosswords. She'd send my brother and me down to the marina with dollar bills for the cantina, and we'd buy colas and PayDays and sit with our legs dangling down into vacant boat slips, and it was in one of those empty boat slips that I became, for a blindingly-short time, the best fisherman who ever lived.

The retaining walls of the marina were filthy with barnacles and algae, and piggy perch fed on the walls, could be seen working for food so long as the sun was up, and we always had our poles with us. I can't remember what we'd use for bait, but it might've been something as silly as lunch meat. We had treble hooks on our lines and we dropped them at the perch, pulled up whatever bit. The fish were the size of my five-year-old palms, and it was hard to unhook the perch without killing them. The way I remember it, there were a few dead piggies bobbing in the boat slip, and this hermit of a man staggered toward us as if drunk.

'What you got there?' he asked. His eyes seemed wacky and I remember his clothes like rags – some wild outfit he'd reclaimed from a beached hurricane victim.

My brother, two years older than me, manned up, bucked his chin, said, 'Fishing poles. Who's asking?'

If the man said his name, I've long since forgotten, and my brother just fished on, watching his baited hook dangle at the retainer wall, but the stranger had my attention, though I admit he spooked me deeply.

'And you, son?'

I shook my head.

He came in close, like he had a secret. 'Let me see your hook,' he said.

I shrugged and reeled up, and he reached for my wet line, contemplated the hook on it.

'No, sir,' he told me. 'It won't do, that.' He shook his head, stumbled off somewhere, and I figured it was the end of it.

'Who is that?' I asked my brother.

'Some drunk,' my brother said.

I didn't really know what that meant, but, after a time, the drunk reappeared. 'I got you something,' he told me, and he opened his hand, and a golden J hook, the kind some folks call 'limericks,' rested against his palm. 'For you,' he told me, then, 'Know how to tie it?'

I didn't. My brother, up until he died, always tied my hooks for me when we were fishing together.

I shook my head and the drunk smiled. He bit the treble from my line, spat it into his hand, and tied the golden limerick as I watched in silence. 'This is the hook for you,' he said. 'The right one for the job.'

Now, listen: all of this happened. The hurricanes and the underfed dogs and the PayDay candy bars and the drunk with the hook.

And when the golden thing had been tied to my line, it shimmered the way golden things do, and the man baited it for me – shit, maybe it was ham from my grandmother's fridge – and I dropped the line in the empty boat slip and damn if my line didn't tug.

But it wasn't a perch. Couldn't be. My rod bent, and that had never happened before, and I mean this was instantaneous. My brother shot wild-shocked eyes at me, as though he'd just witnessed some magic, but I'd frozen in the rapidity of it all, and my brother screamed, 'Reel!'

I started cranking and the line zipped out, and the drunk was hopping up and down and clapping, smiling oyster-colored teeth at me and hollering, 'I get half! I get half!'

In my mind, I saw him taking the head-end half, and my eyes were glued on the dark, shadowed water of the boat slip, and it took a while longer than I figured it should have before the fish's color showed below the surface.

See, magical things happen sometimes when you're fishing. Once, with five friends, I got into a run of whiting and caught a few dozen as my buddies, throwing tackle the same as my own, came away with nothing. On a deep sea trip off the coast of Costa Rica, I pointed at a rod and said 'Bang,' and the thing immediately bent under the weight of a marlin that I boated in less than fifteen minutes – no shitting you. But this was the first magic I'd known as a fisherman. It was wild, the feeling of it.

Beneath the surface of the water, back and forth like a golden ticket on the wind, a fish shimmied with despair, surely the fear of death coursing through it, and beside me, wrapped in the smells of the homeless, my drunk acquaintance cawed goofily at me to reel.

I reeled. I reeled.

But first, I have to tell you something that I have learned since then: the Great Red Spot of Jupiter is a storm, just like a hurricane. If you've forgotten the sight of it, go look it up. Makes that planet look like a Cyclops. A deep red eye on the surface of the thing, raging. The storm's the size of three Earths. It's lasted 400 years. Every six days, it makes a counterclockwise rotation. If it hit Galveston, Texas, the whole world would be dead.

I only bring it up, because you can't catch Jupiter on a limerick, but maybe I caught something just as good. When I hoisted the fish from the slip, I swelled with pride as though I'd nabbed the biggest planet in the solar system, and, as I said before, I was, for a faint sliver of time, the greatest fisherman who'd ever walked any world known to God. It was my first red fish, the first fish I'd ever caught that you could order off a restaurant menu. I remember the eye mark on its tail just staring back at me, colorfully, as the fish dangled, floundering wetly, beads of water shimmying off it and raining back down in the shadowed water.

My brother and the drunkard were elated, and I was in deep shock, paused permanently with my eyes on the dangling fish. I was a hero, for a minute.

Now, when you're young, everything seems bigger. My father was a giant to me, when I was five, and now I look down on him with saddened eyes.

And so it was with this fish. I don't remember specifics – size and weight – but I remember my brother throwing him back in the water because he was too small to keep.

This saddened the drunk. 'Let the kid keep it,' he kept saying. 'Who's gonna bother a kid?'

I would love to tell you that this birthed in me some great love for fishing, but that would be a lie. In the years that passed, when I'd go fishing with my brother, it seemed everything but the fishing was important to me.

Once, in Corpus Christi, Texas, skipping school and going down to Corpus Christi Bay, where we fished the shallow water on the far side of the barrier islands, my brother and I chanced into another drunk who was fishing beside us. He was a vacationer, he told us, and he was drinking Milwaukee's Best and driving some ludicrous car – a banged-up maroon thing patched with Bondo and duct tape.

'What kind of car is that?' my brother asked him.

'A summah car,' the man said.

We looked at him, puzzled.

'Summah this,' he said. 'Summah that.'

He gave my brother and me each a beer, and maybe I was fifteen then, and he told us how he'd flown in from Michigan, or some other northern state, and he had bought the car for $700 off an ad in a *Penny Saver*, and he told us that was the only way to go. 'Shit, when I'm done with this thing. I'm just gonna leave it behind.'

I think he may have even offered to leave it somewhere for us to have, and that got my brother suspicious of him and he wouldn't let me drink any more of his beer, and I can't remember if we caught anything that day, but I did look at the stranger at a point in time and ask, 'You don't by any chance have a magical hook do you?'

But he just smiled, said, 'Shit, I wish.'

My brother and I often talked about magical hooks.

Once, in the surf off North Padre Island, my brother and I got into some trout, but I wasn't catching shit. I've never been a big fan of beach fishing, because it's a struggle if you're not bringing in fish. The waves and wind just pummel you, and your bait gets churned off your hook, and I've always had a phobia of sharks, so I was just casting and reeling with dread in my heart, thinking any minute a mako would take one of my arms, but my brother was pulling in keepers, and he got pissed when I told him I was through.

'Just give it a minute,' my brother said. 'Pay your dues.'

'I don't wanna pay my dues,' I told him. 'I wanna go sit by the pool.'

My brother looked back at me, smiled. The waves were crashing. We stood on the back edge of the shallow lip of the second sand bar. He called back to me over the sound of the breakers, kinda singingly. 'I gotta magic hook,' he said.

'Fuck you,' I told him.

He came walking into me from his spot. 'I gotta magic hook,' he sang again.

'I'd rather you had a beer.'

He twirled his finger, 'Reel in,' he said.

I rolled my eyes and cranked in my set-up. I can't remember for sure what we had going. Bobbers and a couple feet of leader and live shrimp is my guess.

My brother fiddled something from his tackle box, and I made to reach for it.

'Hell no,' he told me. 'I don't trust you to tie my hooks.'

And I just shook my head at him, watching as he traded out whatever I had for whatever he was pretending was magic.

I think I loved my brother most when he was like that.

And I don't remember if I caught anything that day.

And the last time I went fishing with my brother in the surf, there was a rash of man o'wars bobbing on the water, and it didn't matter if he had any magic or not, I wasn't going to wade into any of that poison.

But let me tell you something you might already know: a man o'war is a colony of critters called zooids. If you've never seen one, they look like lost condoms filled with breath on the water. Some call them floating terrors, on account of this. Mostly, off the Texas coast, they're blue, and beneath their gas-filled bodies, which perch on the water's surface, dangle poisonous tentacles that can grow up to fifty meters long. The poison parts are zooids. The sack part is zooids. There are fucking zooids and feeding zooids, all somehow working together to become a thing that messes you up if you let it. See, it's a sedentary creature, for the most part. It only bobs around. It only waits for you to get caught in it.

My mind is made up of parts too, and sometimes those parts are poisonous.

Mostly, when my brother asked me to fish with him, I'd say no. He'd go out alone and come back with fish that I'd help him cook, or he'd come back with nothing and I'd say, 'You needed a magic hook.'

The last time I saw him he had killed and butchered a deer. It was the day after Thanksgiving and it was warm out, and he was streaked with blood down his shoulders and chest, and he had jumped into my mother's swimming pool to wash the blood off him, was standing waist-deep and rubbing pool water down his forearms.

'What'd you get?' I asked him.

'A doe.'

'What'd you use?'

'Use?' he asked. 'A magic hook, you fucking idiot.' Then he raised his hands like he was holding his rifle and he pretended to shoot me.

I pretended to die. Then I smiled. 'My ride's here,' I told him. At the time, he was living in Houston and I was living in Austin and we only saw each other from time to time. 'I'd hug you, but you're bloody,' I told him.

They found his body before Christmas.

When he was twenty or so, my brother caught the biggest red I'd ever seen. He brought it home in a white ice chest and had me stand in front of the thing with the lid closed and said, 'You're not gonna believe this,' and he waited dramatically for tension to build before flipping it open. The thing was over thirty inches. I have no idea what it weighed. But, in the picture that we took of my brother holding it to his chest, his face is straining, and his arms are clenched.

Three years later, at his funeral service, we had that picture blown up to poster size. And when people were coming through to pay respects, a man my brother worked with for a short time at Texas Parks and Wildlife came up to me smiling softly. He pointed at my brother's poster.

'He didn't catch that fish,' he said.

I was confused. 'No?'

'We were doing a survey for the service,' he told me. 'We had out nets. Catching and counting. That kind of thing. He asked me if he could keep it. I didn't see the harm.'

I looked at my brother's poster. At his eyes, so proud.

I looked at the man he'd worked with, and he seemed so proud too.

I don't know why they call it a limerick hook, but I do know what a limerick is.

It's a five-line poem, usually humorous.

Here's one I wrote for you:

> I once had a brother who lied.
> But before I could catch him he died.
> Said he caught a big red.
> But once he was dead
> I'd learned he'd took me for a ride.

For a while, I was mad at the guy who ruined the lie for my brother, but now, it just makes me love my brother more.

On 24 August 1947 a category-one hurricane made landfall in Galveston, Texas. Records show it killed one person. This was before storms were given names. It's known as Hurricane Number Three. Three hundred and sixty-five million miles away, the Great Red Spot of Jupiter did its devastating six-day turn. Millions of years from now, that storm may rage on still.

I can't remember the last time I went fishing. Last year, I bought a new rod and reel, and I think the price tag is still on it. When I bought it, I asked the guy where he kept the magic hooks.

'Magic hooks?' he told me. 'We've been out of those for years.'

Somehow I knew exactly what he meant.

They've All Got That Old Jitterbug Spirit:
In Conversation with Bill Dance

INTERVIEW CONDUCTED BY CAMERON PIERCE

IN MY FATHER's house growing up, we rarely watched college football on Saturdays. Instead, we watched cartoons and fishing shows, and there was no bigger name in televised fishing than Bill Dance. As a child in love with fishing, I saw him as an amiable, mythic Tennessean who could coax big bass out of any water.

There is no other fish in American angling pursued more in organized competition than the black bass. Territorial, cunning, and aggressive fish, largemouth and smallmouth bass represent the zenith of freshwater fishing as a sport. Since 1967, the year of the first official bass tournament, the world of bass fishing has exploded into a multi-billion-dollar industry. Back then, however, none of the hundred or so fishermen in that first tournament knew how far it would go, and few could have predicted that Bill Dance, the young man who caught the first ever bass in a tournament setting, would go on to become one of the greatest bass fishermen of all time.

Winner of twenty-three national bass fishing titles and seven B.A.S.S. titles, and an inductee in both the International Game Fish Association's Hall of Fame and the National Freshwater Hall of Fame, Bill Dance is best known for his show, *Bill Dance Outdoors*, which has run for over 2000 episodes and spanned nearly five decades. Recently I spoke with Bill on the phone, and incredibly, my boyhood vision of him holds up. Even after all these years, off-camera and unfiltered, Bill Dance is still the same old legend.

Cameron Pierce: What's your earliest memory associated with fishing?

Bill Dance: You know, I was really blessed as a youngster. Growing up, I had a daddy and a granddaddy who loved to hunt and fish. My daddy was a doctor and he shot all over the world. He was a big hunter. He hunted more than he fished. My granddaddy was my idol. I liked to hunt, but I loved to fish. I hunted a long time, up until after I got married. I've done a little big game hunting, but it never turned me on as much as smaller game, and then finally I lost interest in it, and I fell back on what my granddaddy taught me. What he taught me, Cameron, he taught me more about moving water. Fishing creeks and rivers.

To this day, I'll grab a spinning rod and wade three or four miles in these clear creeks in Middle Tennessee and catch smallmouth. I still love to drift fish the Mississippi River for catfish. My granddaddy gave me the greatest gift of all and that was teaching me how to fish, but he taught me a lot more. He taught me fish anatomy, and how fish see. He taught me the importance of sound, the importance of smell. I guess he got that from being a doctor.

I remember when I was little, even when I was real little, I'd go to Mulberry Creek up in Lynchburg, where Jack Daniel's Distillery is. I remember on Wednesday afternoons in Lynchburg, the town would close down, half day. Small towns, they do that a lot. My grandmother and granddaddy and I would go to the creek and my grandmother would put a big quilt out and crochet and my granddaddy would fish in the creek and I would wade and catch crawfish and swim. The older I got, I learned more about fishing and spent more time beside my granddaddy.

When I was eight years old, I had seventy-five cents, and I went to Connor Motlow's hardware store. Connor owned the bank in Lynchburg and also the hardware store. I bought my first lure. Arbogast Jitterbug. You'll find that bait still sells. Nearly every bait store still sells that lure. They've all got the old Jitterbug. All sell that old original. It's got a metal lip on it and it wobbles. This particular day I had my old metal rod with my old metal reel. Braided line, Cortland braided line. We went to a lake about ten miles outside Lynchburg called Cumberland Springs, a crystal-clear lake. I'd caught perch in the creek and catfish, but I'd never caught a largemouth bass. Grandma had the quilt set out. Granddaddy was fishing for red-ears. He'd catch big red-ears on red worms.

I walked about fifty yards from him down through some bushes to a point. When I looked off the point I saw two largemouth bass swimming side by side. One weighed one and a half pounds and the other two. I couldn't believe what I saw. I made a pretty accurate cast. When the bait hit the water, both fish stopped swimming. I realized both fish heard that. I remembered my grandfather talking to me about sound. And then I started reeling the bait. Both fish turned and started swimming toward the bait. I realized those fish could see the bait. I was overwhelmed. I was so excited. I reeled a little further. And all of a sudden I stopped the bait and they stopped. I started and they started. I stopped and they stopped. That move started the Bill Dance move. That's what started my career, when I saw that bass blow into a piece of plastic that had metal on it and two treble hooks. That bait, that artificial nothing, I went, 'My gosh, what just happened here?'

I got so excited, that fish blew water everywhere. I couldn't hear the bait wobbling because my heart was pounding so loud. I reeled and could feel the tug of the fish, and the fish jumped what seemed like six feet in the air – more like two – I got so excited I well-roped him in. I ran back to my granddaddy and grandmother. I've got a picture of that fish to this day. The most impressive thing to see was those two fish swimming, and to work them right up to the bait. That right there was what kickstarted . . . that was the deal right there, brother. I've relived that moment a million times.

You originally intended to become a doctor. How did your family initially feel about your decision to leave the medical field to pursue fishing?

For five generations back they all were [doctors]. I gave it some thought. I was young at the time. I was driving and I was behind a gal on a motorcycle in my early teens. Then I see all this metal and glass all in front of me. Just a terrible accident. I was the first one on the scene. I jumped out of the car and ran up there to it, and what I saw and what I experienced, I thought there was no way I could ever do this. It was the most grotesque sight I've ever seen.

Two nurses pulled up in another car and they got on the scene. I couldn't even look at what I saw. I walked away from it and said there's no way I could ever be a doctor. Worst thing I ever saw in my life. I wondered how in the world a man could take a body and try to save it and put it all back together after it's mangled like this. My parents never tried to force me into doing that. I went another route. I'm glad I did. As a result of that, I met the greatest person in the world. My wife. We've been married over fifty years. We have four great children, seven grandchildren.

How has the fishing world evolved since you first came into it?

It's absolutely . . . you know, when it first really exploded, I've seen major changes but, when I first started, it probably centered around the tournaments. June '67. When I started seeing from the competitive side all these fishermen from around the country get together, seeing all the rods and lures and boats that they used. We were fishing all over the country, from lowland lakes to midland lakes to highland lakes, meeting new fishermen at every tournament, learning from each other. Then I got to watch the industry, seeing the new equipment they were introducing. After five years I thought, 'Boy, it just can't get any bigger than this.' Then ten years later the payout in tournaments was so much bigger. Twenty years passed and I said, 'My goodness, look at the braided lines we're using now. Look at the fluorocarbons. Look at the GPS stuff.' Now in the present time, I'm holding a rod in my hand that weighs three ounces. It's so sensitive, so lightweight, yet so strong. I'm fishing thirty-pound test braid that's got the diameter of eight-pound test mono.

How much we have learned about reading water. How we've learned to fish summer, fall, winter, spring, cold water, hot water, clear water, muddy water. How we've adapted. How we've become so much more versatile. To look at a body of water at any given time and just know. We've learned so much about their habits and habitats.

We learn from writers. We learn from people on TV. We learn from each other. Every few years we have a new crop of fishermen come up. It's an ongoing thing. This industry just changes. I guess five years from now, we're gonna say, 'My goodness, where are we now?' Five years ago we thought, 'It can't get any better.'

Here's one thing, though. For years, I've been fooled about secretions. There's no scientific evidence that bass react negatively to any scent from the human body. I've been preaching for years that you've got to spray your hands with these chemicals to mask human sweat.

Are there any fish species left that you still hope to someday catch?

There's a couple saltwater species that I've made several attempts to catch, but the time wasn't right. Tripletails. I've tried time and time again. Cobia. I've been at the prime place, the prime spot, off Pensacola in mid-May, when they're abundant. I've been there three times and just never hit it right. I'd be there ahead of time, or a week too early, a week too late. I'd hear, 'You're here at the right time, Bill,' but I just don't understand it. Last year we tried it. I was there the 14th, 15th, and 16th, and when I left, three days after I left, they killed 'em. The times that I've caught cobia, I wasn't fishing for them for the show. To go out and do a show strictly on tripletail and cobia, I've failed. My other on the bucket list would be a big sturgeon.

You're one of the most accomplished and respected bass fishermen of all time. What are some of the hardships of being a professional fisherman?

Well, there's a lot. You've got to have a lot of support. I had my family. They were highly supportive. I could have never done it without my wife's support. She always believed you could do anything you wanted if you put your mind to it. I always wanted to get into this business. I didn't know how I was ever going to do it. Eventually it worked out and I did get into it. It was a result of the tournaments. Back in '67, when Ray Scott held the first tournament, it was invitation only and I got an invitation. I had hardly any money. I had a family. We had three children and it was hard to make ends meet. This national tournament came along and I got an invitation. Tournament at Beaver Lake in north-west Arkansas, and I said, 'Dianne, I don't think my boss would dare let me get time off.' I didn't have money for the entry fee [$100] and the money to go, all the expenses of going. Dianne said, 'You oughta try it.' First place wasn't but $2,000.

So I met Ray Scott. He came to Memphis and I met him. He said, 'We'd love to have you.'

I said, 'I don't know if I'll ever be able to make it or not.'

I got a phone call from a guy by the name of Oscar Oakley. Oscar Oakley owned what at the time was the biggest Ford dealership in the United States. He said, 'Bill, this is Oscar Oakley. I'd like for you to come by. I'd like to meet with you. Would you come by and see me?'

I said, 'Yes sir, I will.' I went down there and the carpet was three inches thick. He had a big walnut desk. He got up and came halfway across the office and met me and shook my hand. He said he'd been following my career. He said he had a proposition. He offered me a Coke and we sat down.

He said, 'I understand there's going to be a big bass tournament. I want to sponsor you in that event.'

'What do you mean *sponsor*, Mr. Oakley?' I asked.

'We want to pay your entry fee, all your expenses. It won't cost you a dime to go.'

'Well, I really don't know what to say.'

'You can say yes,' he said. 'Go over there and just do your best.'

I did and I finished second. I went back and offered to pay Oscar Oakley for the money he'd put up and he said, 'You don't pay me nothing. That's all yours.'

I said, 'Well, I owe you.'

He said, 'You don't owe me nothing. When's the next one?'

So they sponsored me in the next one, about two months later. I went to it and finished second in it. And then the third one, at Smith Lake in Alabama, early the next year, and I finished second in it. And then I came home from that tournament and within the next two weeks I had three job offers. One to work for Jim Bagley Bait Company, who made the first five-dollar lure, out of balsa wood. The next was Creme Lure Company in Tyler, Texas. They invented and originated the plastic worm, made in Akron, Ohio in Nick Creme's basement. He was the inventor of the plastic worm. The third was Heddon Lure Company in Dow Jack, MI.

Anyway, I accepted the job with Creme. Fifty per cent of the fish I was catching in those days were on plastic worms. We flew down to Texas and stayed with them. Eventually I got to thinking, if I could do it for them I could do it for myself. Nick told me, 'You try it and if it doesn't work out, you can come back.' That's when the show started. That was forty-five years ago. We're now doing thirty-nine original shows every year – twenty-six fresh-water shows on NBC Sports, thirteen salt-water shows on the Outdoor Channel – and we're in the process of putting a show together for Discovery, their channel Destination America.

The whole thing started by being able to work with a good woman like Dianne, who believed, who made a lot of sacrifices, who believed if you set goals in life and worked toward those goals, you could do anything you wanted to do. She believed through all of this. All the days away from home, building a career, that someday it would pay off. She was mother and a daddy to our children. I guess my success has always been to surround myself with people a whole lot smarter than me, more talented than me. People like Dianne.

Our strength for all these years is not how many fish we can catch in thirty minutes of television. It's how you go about doing it. It's in education. When you can entertain and educate at the same time, you've got the best of both worlds. It's been a good ride for us for a long, long time. I just hope to do it forever and then a little bit more.

Bass Fishing on Rideau Lake

J. W. LONGLEY

I HAD REACHED FORTY without having cast a line, an unusual experience in this country among men who have any means of leisure. When a boy, armed with hook and line and limber rod, cut from the bushes, and with a worm for bait, I essayed to lure the trout and other small fishes from a stream near my paternal home. I would angle for hours, noting in the clear water whole swarms of little fish surrounding my hook and nibbling the bait at will. Terrible jerks made I, but to no purpose. Weary and vexed at ill luck I was induced to surrender my rod to a boy about half my size, who would forthwith begin pulling up the fishes by the dozen. I took a violent dislike for fishing. It was clearly not an intellectual diversion. It seemed unworthy of a man possessing any mental endowments.

Then came college life, the study for a profession and its pursuit. Laborious literary labors were interlarded, and thus the years passed. Boyhood gradually merged into manhood and youth crept along until the gray hairs and thin patch and the rude awakening of the fortieth birthday gave solemn warning that the vernal equinox was passed and life would know no more the odors of its first spring. During all these busy years, entirely absorbed in the pursuit of knowledge, fame and fortune, I looked with pity upon the deluded mortals who were wasting their time and energies on any such paltry and purposeless pastime as fishing. Among the mere pleasure-loving crowd I regarded these excursions as the fitting complement of an aimless life; but when I saw strong-minded men, possessing brains and ability and advancing rapidly in business, professional practice and public life, deliberately collecting together an elaborate kit and gear and starting out on a fishing excursion, I could not help feeling that they were the victims of a mild form of insanity.

This bit of very unimportant autobiography is given merely as a prelude to a narrative – a sort of quiet and somber background for the little picture that is to follow.

During the summer of 1889 I was urged by a friend residing near Brockville, Ont., to come for a visit, and among other inducements offered was a week's fishing on the Rideau Lakes. He had just discovered the beauties of this region and its merits, and had erected a hotel on one of the numerous islands, with the intention of making the place a favorite summer resort. If my dear friend could have known of the good-natured contempt that such a proposition awakened in my mind I fear his invitation would not have been given. But, to shorten matters, I was finally induced to go to Brockville for a little visit, but with many misgivings and painful anticipation of boredom. Out of good nature, and to avoid the appearance of churlishness, I also consented to go to the lake one Tuesday afternoon, spend the night at the hotel, and the next day start for home. With secret cunning I inwardly reflected that this would preclude the possibility of protracted boredom.

Off we started one Tuesday afternoon late in August. The day was beautiful. We took the new line of railway from Brockville – the Brockville, Westport and Sault Ste. Martie – and in a short time were at Westport, a little town situated at the head waters of the Rideau system of lakes. It was now dusk, and entering one of those charming little steam yachts that are so common along the St. Lawrence and its tributary waters we had a pleasant sail of ten miles, and then landed at Long Island, and were soon made comfortable in the hotel – one of the model summer structures of the period, built, as usual, of boards nailed to a frail framework – no shingles without and no plaster within. As you lie on a very comfortable bed, moonlight or sunlight works away in through apertures in the wooden walls, and your fellow guest in the room above makes his presence felt on the board floor over your head a trifle more distinctly than if he were in your own room. Broad verandas of course surround the house, and it is altogether an ideal summer lodging. I spent my first night in the deliberate pursuit of absolute rest and pleasure, it having been determined before retiring that we were to be up at 5:30 in order to indulge in one fishing tour before I took my departure. I accepted this as a compromise, and felt an inward sense of pride and self-complacency at this tribute to my good nature and self-sacrifice.

The morning broke radiantly clear, as only an August morning in Ontario can break. There was not a cloud in the sky, but the sun's brilliant rays were tempered by a thin, dreamy haze, which so often lends a subdued charm to the beauties of an early autumn morning. I did not need to be awakened; and, taking a hasty bath and throwing on my clothes, I stepped out upon the veranda. The scene was truly superb. Long Island stands in the center of the lake, and all about and in every direction are smaller islands covered with rich foliage, and here and there are newly-built summer cottages that wealthy persons have erected. These are the advance guard of numbers which will appear when the beauties and advantages of place become better known. My host soon appeared, together with the genial Dr. M., who accompanied us on the tour. Turning to the water's edge, I saw the boatmen already at work making the preparations necessary for the fishing excursion. Presently the rods were brought forth, the reels adjusted, the lines prepared and the hooks attached.

I was presented with the gear that I was to use and started with the rest of the part for the boats, feeling certain every moment that I would either break the rod by some blundering or contrive to get the hook neatly embedded either in my clothes or my flesh; but we got safely on board the boats. My host and I occupied one, the doctor and his friend the other. Each boat was admirably fitted up with all conveniences. Two heavily-cushioned seats were prepared for the fishers, while the boatman sat in the bow and rowed, and had, in addition, the care of a kettle of live minnows, our bait, and a landing net, which was to contain the many trophies of our prowess. Thus it was that for the first time in my life I started on a fishing excursion. The boatman gave his first pull at the oars. 'What a piece of hopeless idiocy,' thought I, 'and for grown-up men!' My self-respect was well-nigh extinguished and the minutes were counted until it should be safely over and I once more back to sensible pursuits and among rational beings.

We soon reached the 'fishing ground.' Massie – that was our boatman's name, and he was a thorough expert – dropped his oars. The tin can was opened, a bright and lively minnow was fastened to the end of my hook, and, following the example of my host, with a sigh of self-contempt I threw the line out. I saw it sink into the water, and as Massie said it was deep and we should require thirty or forty feet of line, I began mechanically to pay it out. The click of the revolving reel was the only sound that broke the impressive silence of the sun-illumined waters. Thus sat we, my friend's line on one side of the boat, my own on the other, and I smiled to myself as I recalled the epigrammatic definition of fishing by some cynic: 'A fish at one end of the line and a fool at the other,' the only thing wanting, in my thought, being the fish.

Aye! What was that? Heigho! Something tugging at my hook. Quick as a flash I was upon my feet. 'You've struck him,' cries Massie, perfectly cool. How could a person be cool in such a case was the thought that darted through my brain. How can I describe everything that was crowded into that one moment? The little rod in an instant was bent and the whole hidden depths of the lake seemed to be in commotion. Instinct instantly taught me to keep the line taut, and so I began furiously to wind up the reel. I had at least forty feet out, a few feet had been wound in, when the enemy made a plunge, and to save my rod the line was paid out again. Then I began to reel in once more. I just held him and slowly wound in the line. Soon, at a little distance from the boat, I saw him – a perfect beauty! His next move was toward the surface, and with a sudden dash he leaped out of the water and into the air. My! Now I feared I should lose him. I kept a steady grip and he passed through the acrobatic ordeal without escaping me.

I resumed my work of taking in line. He tugged away gallantly and then made a dive under the boat; but, with an instinct which years of education could not have instilled, I instantly adjusted the rod to the changed conditions. My foe was evidently getting tired of the struggle. Click! went the winding reel. He was drawing near the surface. Again I could see him at a nearer view.

'A beauty!' exclaimed Massie, as he seized the landing net. Click! went the reel, but who could repeat the wild monologue I kept up during this intoxicating performance. Every second was bringing him nearer the surface. The landing net was already in the water and near to the struggling beauty. I gave him a little tip and Massie dexterously got beneath him. In a flash I saw him safely landed, and gave forth a shout that echoed to the remotest recesses of this isle-studded lake.

Thus was landed my first fish – a beautiful, fat black bass weighing four pounds! Oh, what a revolution! How life had changed in five short minutes! The cold cynic of forty winters – where was he? Gone! and in his place stood an enthusiast, his eyes beaming, his heart palpitating with delight, his pulse dancing, and his whole soul alive with rapture. What cared he for law or politics? What mattered it that constituents might grumble, newspapers rave, and opponents inveigh? Begone, vain world! What are all the dreams of ambition, the yearnings for power, the thirst for fame? Did he not recall the well-worn lines of – I think – Oliver Wendell Holmes?

> Ah, what are the treasures we perish to win
> Compared with the trout we first caught
> with a pin?

To veteran fishermen all this will, no doubt, seem turgid and ridiculous; but, perchance, memory will enable them to go back to the sunny hours of childhood when they first felt the ecstasy of the first fish. Multiply these sensations in a man of forty and then be charitable.

The morning wore quickly away, and this bass was not my sole trophy. Again and again the delightful sensation of a tug at the end of the line was repeated, and, one after another, a fine collection of black bass was safely deposited in the tin drawer which was fitted up as a receptacle in our boat. My host is an experienced fisherman, an enthusiast, and has always been regarded as both expert and lucky. But, by one of those concatenations of events that no fellow can understand, though he diligently dangled his line, he got nothing, while I was keeping Massie continually employed with his landing net and the fastening of fresh minnows on my hooks.

Eight o'clock came and we started for home and breakfast. We reached the little landing cove almost simultaneously with the doctor and his companion. They had had some luck, and got a few small ones, but nothing compared to mine; and as we walked up to the hotel, Massie bearing before us my pan of stunning big fish, there was not a prouder or happier man in the Dominion of Canada.

And what an appetite for breakfast! How delightful the fresh air of the morning; how uplifting was the beautiful scenery; how exhilarating the captivating sport! All the cares and worries of life seemed to have been thrown aside and a complete rejuvenation taken place. My heart was light, my spirits were buoyant. Ah, Mr. Brown-Séquard, methinks your elixir of life will prove an ephemeral renewer of youth beside the never-failing joy of a summer holiday, heightened by the exhilarating charms of fishing sport.

After a satisfactory breakfast and a composing pipe, seated on the veranda, in the most comfortable of chairs, my host reminded me that the time was approaching when we should have to take the steam yacht for Smith's Falls in order to catch the train for Halifax.

'I am afraid it will be inconvenient for you to leave today,' I timidly and insinuatingly suggested. 'I know you do not want to lose the whole day's sport.'

I thought I saw a wicked smile pass around as I glanced at the faces of the company.

'I see it,' said my genial host. 'You want to stay another day! By all means. You have not half seen the place. Stop until tomorrow.'

He had hit the idea completely. The individual who once counted the minutes that should bring an escape from boredom was now enthusiastically looking forward with consuming eagerness to more of the unspeakable delights of the rod and line. And let it be said here that not the next day nor the day following saw my departure from this interesting spot. Once the sweets of sporting life were tasted, no few hours would suffice to satisfy my growing appetite for more.

I rapidly overcame my long-cherished belief that to abandon my post of duty in the thick of business affairs for a single day would unhinge the whole machinery of the universe. Indeed, one morning's success with rod and reel converted me from an elderly, serious, plodding worldly worker into a modified savage, content to let men come and go at their own sweet will, while I enjoyed the keen thrill of playing a frisky black bass through the clear waters of that Canadian lake. How many men – and among them men of wealth – there are, who live devoid of a true knowledge of the real joys of existence, and probably shorten their days by reason of an inexorable sense of the supreme necessity of their personal attention to all the details of their affairs. If once the door could be opened and they could be induced to look in upon the feast that nature spreads for the weary and overworn in so many places on this great continent of ours, with its lakes and rivers, its forests and its streams, they would soon begin to partake, life would be sweeter as well as longer, and they would presently discover how marvelously well the world manages to wag along without the personal superintendence of any of us.

The trip to Smith's Falls having been abandoned by unanimous consent, of course another fishing excursion was in order. Other grounds were visited. My host and I were companions as before, and once more luck perched upon my rod. My friend managed to secure one fish while I succeeded in getting a half dozen, and back we came to luncheon. We fished with excellent luck in the afternoon until the shades of night began to fall. At last we wound up our reels and prepared to return to the hotel. The sun was down. The day had been clear

TAUT LINES: EXTRAORDINARY TRUE FISHING STORIES

and warm. As the sun departed and the twilight began to deepen into dusk came the delicious coolness of an August evening. There was scarce a breath of wind and the whole surface of the lake was like one vast mirror. Far as the eye could see were lovely vistas of island and water in every direction, the foliage reaching to the very edge of the lake.

As I lay back in the cushioned seat, the whole scene seemed the most beautiful and uplifting I had ever beheld. Supreme quiet and peace rested over the whole lake, save when broken by the weird echoes of the distant loon. Long Island is divided by an inlet on both sides. Entering either north or south by a narrow passage, one presently opens out into a beautiful little lake within the island completely overshadowed with a luxuriant growth of hardwood. Once upon the bosom of this little inland lake in the gloaming of a summer twilight the scene is beyond description. The mirror-like surface is darkened by the shades of night, and from its unruffled surface is reflected everything near of earth and sky with such perfection that it is impossible, even on the most intent observation of material objects, to determine whether you are gliding through water or sky. Everything is unreal and mystic, and all the early dreams of fairyland seem realized.

Suddenly from the tall maples above our heads came the plaintive notes of a whippoorwill. It was the first time I had ever heard the strains of this love-fabled bird, and amid such surroundings and under such influences, is it any wonder that rooms of the heart, long closed and locked with rusty keys, were opened, and the soft and delicious impulses known only when love plays upon the tender chord of youth came back for the moment in great torrents of sentiment? I could not but recall then and there one especially suggestive verse of the old song of the whippoorwill, that I had always cherished, but which now filled me with its meaning as never before:

> It is said that whatever sweet feelings
> May be throbbing within a fond heart,
> When listening to whippoorwill's singing
> For a twelvemonth will never depart.
> Oh, then we will meet in the woodland,
> Far away from the hurrying throng,
> And whisper our love to each other
> When we hear the first whippoorwill's song.

But let me not drift into sentiment. It is well sometimes to have the soul stirred up a bit, and these reflections were the wholesome results of a first day's fishing. Amid these happy dreams the boat glided along, and soon we were at the landing place. With an appetite not etherealized by the beauties and glories of the scene we were soon partaking of a substantial dinner. Not, indeed, a formal affair, with courses of dainties designed to tempt a cloyed appetite, but a toothsome collection of substantials, fresh bass caught by our own hand, served hot and sweetened by that most effective of sauces – a healthy appetite, born of outdoor exercise, freedom from care and the uplifting influences of nature. This, indeed, was living! This was getting out of one's self – out of the ruts of monotonous routine and restoring tone to body and mind.

After dinner how delightful the pipe tasted as we again seated ourselves on the veranda to enliven an hour with tale and gossip, and how soon, nature having free scope to assert herself, we felt a sweet drowsiness which told us that bed was the place for us all. Not after midnight and with nightcaps and other noxious inventions, but early in the evening, the system all aglow with health. We arranged for another tour at half past five next morning, and soon we were all in bed, and with a delightful sense of healthy exhaustion the world and consciousness began to fade out of sight.

That sleep was undisturbed by restless dreams; but in the balmy slumbers of the night came to me pleasant sensations of a tug at the line. In visions I was holding the rod once more, and felt what the fisherman so longs for and starts with delight in finding – the rapturous tug at the hook which indicates a bite, and, in many cases, a capture. Here was the enthusiast of a day completely carried away with the sport, and continuing the happy exercise in dreams. But what sportsman who has whipped a stream all day for salmon, and been rewarded by landing a thirty-pounder before the day was over, has not gone over the exciting scenes in the silent watches of the night? It was as the scarred veteran of a hundred fights recalls the stirring incidents of some infantry charge when the enemy's stronghold was stormed, and the old flag was planted on the deserted battlements of the foe amid the battle's roar and his comrades' cheers.

Day after day passed, each filled with its quota of sport and pleasure. My exceptional luck continued, and though the party was increased by fresh arrivals I still remained each day *facile princeps* – the new meteor in the piscatorial heavens. The longer I remained the more indifferent I became to all that was occurring in the outer world. Rest and renewed health were the guerdons of each day's experience. But all things must come to an end, and the time necessarily arrived when I was to take my last look at Rideau Lake and go back to newspapers, letters, telegrams and business. Thus endeth the story of my first – but I hope not last – fishing expedition, which had been postponed by the accidents of fate for forty years. Once more I am in the old routine, but with renewed vigor and energy. The prosaic now surrounds and prevails. But amid the din of duty it is pleasant to go back to such scenes as I have been describing. They brighten up one's life, and some other unfortunate old boy who like myself has not indulged in sport, because it was undignified, may be roused from his lethargy while reading these pages and become what I now am, an enthusiastic, though I hope a sensible, sportsman.

A New Hand at the Rod

C.R.C.

A ll summer long I have waited my opportunity. I have seen the male members of the camp, encased in rubber boots and armed with bamboo rods, go striding off down the gulch, while conversational fragments relating to reels, flies and 'leaders' were wafted to my envious ears. I have frequently seen them come back wet, torn and triumphant, sometimes loaded with fish, and sometimes not, as luck favored them; but always with stories. I have heard all about the big one that fell back into the water; about the bigger one that got caught in the bushes and jerked off the hook, and about the biggest one of all, 'regular Jumbo, by George!' that gave one flop just as he was being dropped into the bag and – vanished!

Why should I not have the privilege of shaping some of these romances?

The camp is deserted.

The brothers and husbands and visiting cousins have all gone to town.

The fish poles lean invitingly against a pine.

'Woman's hour has struck.'

I will go fishing.

The selection of a pole becomes the first difficulty and that arises not from the superiority of one pole over another, but from the question as to which man's wrath I can most safely provoke. Lose his knife, break his pipe, mislay his papers, slander his wife, but keep his jointed rod holy, is the eleventh commandment of the amateur fisherman. This smaller rod seems the least elaborate; it is also light and easy to hold – besides, it belongs to a cousin's friend who, if anything happens, will have to look pleasant whether he feels so or not. So, Mr. Jones, by your leave, while you are in town getting the mail or ordering provisions, or going to the circus, or whatever it is that takes the men off in a body, leaving the camp to the women and children and chipmunks – by your leave, I say, I will borrow your rod. So that matter is settled, only it would be simpler and pleasanter if you had not put two hooks on the line; one at a time is enough to catch in one's hair.

Now for something in which to bring home the fish. The game bag, to be sure, and here it hangs on a branch. Ugh! how it smells! I really cannot hang that thing around my neck. Strange how impervious men's faculties are to disagreeable odors. A basket would answer the purpose, but in this benighted valley of the Arkansas there is no such thing as a splint basket, the want of which we have discovered to be one of the small housekeeping difficulties of this region. A tin pail would answer the purpose, but it would not be sportsmanlike, look at it in any light you please. The kitchen tent offers nothing else in the way of a receptacle except a deal cracker box with a picture of Pike's Peak on the end; clearly unavailable. Nor will I degrade to such uses my burnt alligator satchel or the case to my camera.

Ah! a handkerchief. Silk, and a large one; I hope it is not Mr. Jones'; but he will forgive me if I bring it home full of trout. A knot in each corner and it will hold a dozen easily. See! And yet they say that women have no adaptability.

What a steep path it is down into this gulch! I say path, but there is not a sign of one except a foothold here and there on a pine root or a bunch of soap weed; elsewhere boulders and long steep stretches of loose gravel. As I dig my heels into the soil, sliding frantically downward, grazing my elbows and peeling the leather in strips from my best shoes, I long unspeakably for an old pair bestowed weeks ago on an ungrateful washerwoman. My scramble comes to an end at the brink of the Cottonwood River, foaming among the rocks at the bottom of the gulch. Steep, chalky cliffs rise on either side, and all around the stately pines keeping guard over the solemn fastnesses of a Rocky Mountain canyon. Ah! this lovely river. How it rushes and swirls and quarrels with the boulders! See that smooth, green slant of water, curving over a granite shelf and breaking into foam below like a Kodak view of Niagara. The color is entrancing; it is not emerald (there is too much ochre in the rocks), but a restful brownish green with an unexpected touch of blue at intervals which can only be a reflection of the Colorado sky. Surely a reflection, for here, in the only quiet portion of the troubled surface, I see the inverted outline of Sheep Mountain as it stands blocking the view toward the head of the canyon.

I will paraphrase Wordsworth:

> *Three* voices are these: one is of the sea,
> One is of the mountains, another of a trout stream,

which, if you don't vex yourself unduly about the meter, is a very good version. This pool has a bass voice, a double diapason; the one above, where I can see the pebbles on the bottom, gives out a shallow soprano tinkle as the water ripples lazily along. The silence of this hushed auditorium is further broken only by the wind in the pines and the occasional hoarse call of a magpie or a blue jay. Song birds do not venture above the valleys when the valleys themselves are 8,000 feet above sea level.

However, all this is not fishing, and what will the camp say to an empty game bag at supper time? As soon as I have unhooked the brown fly from my hat and the white fly from my hair I will begin.

Now, let me see; what are the rules of the game? I must stand 'up stream' and 'cast' down, letting the fly lie as near as possible on the surface, then draw it slowly toward me, so. Then repeat the operation.

This is called 'whipping' the stream. One learns a great deal in this world by careful observation, and the camp talk is bearing fruit. Yes, trout fishing is delightful and not at all difficult if only this rock would not tip so. It destroys my equanimity as well as my equilibrium, and one needs both in a trout stream.

It seems as though I ought to have a bite by this time. I have been 'repeating the operation' for fully twenty minutes; the sun is hot, and the rapid water makes my head dizzy. I wonder what the men do at this stage?

Ah! I remember. According to the professional lingo the fish are not 'rising' in this pool, and I must go farther upstream, which I proceed to do as soon as my skirts are tucked up a little more securely. How I regret my incapacity to wear those big rubber boots that fasten around the waist! They would be just the thing for this swampy place.

There! One foot is wet – the other also! Dear me! It would have been wiser to go out on the road and come back to the stream farther on. Still, let me be philosophical. One can no more have trout than fame or riches without some accompanying disadvantages. Emerson says in his essay on compensation –

Is that a fish? Surely – there – to the right, just under the shade of that rock! See him, with his head up stream, his tail lazily waving in rhythm with the water, his pink-spotted sides flashing in the sunlight! Oh, you beauty! how delicious you will taste, served up in bread crumbs with a dash of lemon (or Worcestershire sauce?) and a garnish of watercresses! Do have this nice little brown fly, or the nicer white one at the end. See, I drop them just over your nose and dangle them invitingly. 'Will you walk into my parlor?'

Ah! he is gone, and strange to say I did not see him go, though my eyes were on him. That is too bad, but not an uncommon experience if I may judge from our dinner-table talk. Our authoritative angler (alias the Camp Liar) says if you 'whip' a pool and the fish sees you there is no use staying in that place any longer.

Now, who would give a trout credit for so much discernment? This one saw my hat and my general get-up and, like a sensible fish, he took himself off directly.

I must now try my luck farther upstream. This trout fishing is a perpetual 'movin' on;' as arduous as poor Jo's peregrinations, and with as little result.

Oh, for one more safety pin! That last jump loosened my dress skirt, and now there is an appalling rent in the front breadth, the result of the interference of a dead branch. What is to be done? Ah, of course – a hairpin!

There, that will last a little time, and in the meanwhile I will see what is in this pool; it looks trout-full. Or, on second thoughts, I will not. Just on the opposite side of the bank is a cow, and she is looking this way. If it was just an ordinary Ohio cow I would pay no attention to her, but these range cattle have a gaze that would freeze the blood in one's veins.

Shoo! I will move on.

Here at last is the place. A glassy sheet of water surrounded by lichenous purple rocks; a volume of foam pouring in from above and spreading out into ripples below; a dead pine spanning the stream from bank to bank, and cushions of moss meeting the placid water on all sides. Could there be a more ideal spot for fishing or meditation? All around is a grove of quaking asp (first cousin to poplar). A refined, gentle tree with whispering leaves and lady-like attitudes.

The change is refreshing, for pines, be they ever so poetical, are grim and monotonous, and their blackened trunks covering the side of the mountain speak of fire and storms, snowslides and the roar of beasts in the night. That they should be succeeded in Nature's plan by these clean, white-stemmed trees is a silent allegory. *Post tenebras lux.*

Beneath the trees and among the rocks grow the vivid Colorado wild flowers; not such pale beauties as we find in April in New England and the Middle States, but gorgeous, scarlet, yellow and rose pink blossoms, like dabs of pigment on a palette. I really would not care to carry this bit of scenery home in a water color, except to show to people who have been here. It would seem like an attempt to improve on one's subject.

Now I am going to do something that will show great strength of nerve and will. I am going out on that log. You can see it is directly over the pool, and I can throw the fly just where it ought to go. The case is perfectly clear; heretofore I have not been in the proper position. Those men who wear big boots, climb right into the water up to their knees, and, of course, they catch trout – who couldn't?

Well, here I am, safe and sound, looking down into the very depths of the stream, where I am confident there is a whole panful of trout waiting yearningly for my flies. Not in the least difficult getting out, either, and if one of the gentlemen had been here he would have thought it necessary to help me.

What's the matter now? I can't move my pole; the hook is fast in that tree. Dear, dear, how stupid of me to carry it over my shoulder as Mr. Winkle did his gun! Come off there! I do not wish to be slangy, but really –

No, it won't stir; neither this way nor that! Now, I don't wonder that men 'say things' when they have such provocation as this. What do they say, anyway, and when they say it how does it work? I would like to make any kind of a remark that I thought would loosen that hook. I have heard Mr. Jones in the remote seclusion of his own tent say, 'Gee whang it!' but that is his own particular property, and to borrow a man's jointed rod and his expletive, too, is stretching a privilege in a way my conscience won't allow.

Am I to sit here all day?

I wonder what a steady pull would do – like *that*. I don't dare to be very forcible for this log is quite round and – I'll try a series of coaxing jerks with an emphatic yank to finish with.

Ah! there it comes, with the air of saying, 'I was not caught at all, only fooling.'

Nevertheless the brown fly is left up in the tree, where, it is to be hoped, he will lead a useful and prosperous career. Now, if the trout will only be persuaded that the flavor of this white fly is as fine as that of the brown one, I'll catch a string of fish that will prove me entitled to a rod of my own. No hurry, however. The camp timepiece is Mt. Harvard. When the sun drops behind that wall of granite which towers above us to the West we know it is a quarter to five. Long before that time chilly shadows fill the gulch and creep up the cliff, and the South Park Range takes on a cold gray, then deepens to purple, while the three snow peaks of Mt. Princeton glow with rosy pink against the evening sky.

According, then, to signs and omens, it must be about half past three o'clock, and as long as the sun continues to warm up this particular nook I am going to sit and swing my feet over the water. It is comfortable and romantic, and I don't care so much about fish after all. To tell the truth we have had salmon trout for dinner every day for the past two weeks and are thinking of sending to Buena Vista for ham and bacon or some such delicacy for a change. So why should I cast flies?

What are those beautiful lines of Whittier's addressed to Monadnock? They begin with something about a painter and 'for her sake.' I do not quote readily. I wish I did. Let me see.

> First a lake
> Tinted with sunset; next the wavy lines
> Of far receding hills, and yet more far
> Monadnock.

Shades of Izaak Walton, was *that* a bite? That earthquake, that cyclone, that terrific tug that is bending the pole into a letter C and lashing the water into suds. It is never a trout; it is nothing less than a sturgeon, or perhaps a sea serpent, and it is pulling me off the –

* * * * *

Something must always be left to the imagination of the reader. When the Russian poet Pushkin is carried beyond the force of language his emotions explode into a shower of stars. So I find nothing but asterisks will express my situation. Up to my waist in the Cottonwood; the water sweeping my skirts around me; my head dizzy and my hat floating rapidly off toward the Arkansas! But the trout? Ah, yes! Here he is; I seized him with both hands as I took my plunge and he shall *not* get away. He is not so large as I expected. Indeed, quite inside the law; hardly worth cooking for a camp of nine people. Still, he is my first trout, and I'll not surrender him to any fish commissioner.

I steal up to camp the back way, and after leaving the rod with its fellows against the tree I seek my own tent.

As the six o'clock horn sounds I hear Mr. Jones' footsteps going supperward. Will he stop at the pine tree?

He does.

I hear the click of the metal reel and then a growl –

'What in thunder!'

The Fishes of Our Boyhood

ED. W. SANDYS

THERE WAS NOT a trout in our country. The region of rock ended miles to the eastward, and with it the laughing brooklets and tumbling falls, the ripples and shadowed pools beloved of the speckled fellows. We had waters a-plenty – deep, calm, slow-moving rivers and creeks, which took their own time in reaching the big lakes which half-surrounded our territory. The country had few slopes, except the banks of its waterways. For miles one would not find a stone. The great levels of fat land bore alternate growths of ancient forest and bountiful crops. It was not a trout country.

Of all the old crowd of boys, who knew the ways of every beast, bird, and fish indigenous to their stamping-ground, possibly not one ever set eyes upon a trout, until after he had traveled considerably beyond the confines of his native district. What the eye does not see the heart does not crave after, so we troubled ourselves not at all about the trout.

Our waters teemed with other fish. We had fishing in plenty and good fishing at that, and perhaps, after all, we were better off without the trout. In a trout region, as a general rule, one fishes for trout and nothing else; quite frequently the trout is the only fish available, hence the youth of that region, while they may know all about trout, remain in ignorance of a dozen other varieties of interesting fish.

In our country things were different. In order to be a successful angler and so to command the respect of one's associates, one had to know more or less about a dozen kinds of fish, at least as many kinds of baits, and also the methods by which the fish and baits might best be brought into close relationship. The old boys knew these things, and many other things not to be found in books. They could tell you when, where, and why to try at a certain place for a certain fish, and what bait to use. Then, if you did not catch the fish, they'd take the tackle and prove that their knowledge was correct.

Those were indeed glorious days: from sunrise to sunset, care-free; at night, a dreamless sleep. We were for ever busy, on, in, or about the water. To rise, feed, and flee to the river; back, feed, off to the river, was the daily program. We knew every foot of bank and shallow, and most of the depths; where the turtles buried their eggs, when the muskellunge might be expected, when the pike followed the overflows; in fact the waters had no secrets. When a new boy came into our midst, as he sometimes did, with tales of the trout and trout-fishing of distant parts, we hearkened not to him. Instead we took him fishing, and speedily convinced him that what he knew about trout was not a circumstance to what we knew about fish.

And such fish as they were, too! With the thought arise mental pictures of strings upon strings of captives, large and small; of happy, sun-browned, barefooted boys, forever wading, perching, prying along the banks; stealing marches upon each other, using every resource which practical knowledge and ready adaptability could command, in order to finish high hook at the close of the day. The boys were no minnow-fishers, and few indeed were the blank days. Fine fish, up to five pounds in weight, rewarded those youthful toilers; indeed, a few plump bass sometimes stopped awkward questions concerning truancy and other trifling lapses from rectitude.

Let us glance at the fish which afforded such unbounded enjoyment, for many of them are worthy of an expert's attention.

As a course before the fish two forms of life may be discussed. Neither may be considered a fish, but both were very interesting to the boys – the one as a bait and the other as an unfathomable mystery. Let us first take the bait.

It is the crawfish, the miniature lobster of fresh water. These were very abundant in the shallow water at the river-banks, in the creeks, and in certain bush-ponds. At times crawfish are the best of baits for both varieties of black bass, and also for rock-bass. We always selected medium-sized crawfish, and instead of spitting them crosswise upon the hook, as is usually done, we forced the hook in at the mouth and out through the tail. So placed and allowed to sink freely, the bait gives an irresistible imitation of the crawfish's backward, wavering rush to shelter.

The best thing for securing such agile bait is a boy's deft brown paw; the nip of the large claws is only a trifling matter. The crawfish are found under stones and sunken rubbish in the streams, in the bush-ponds, under bits of sodden bark and sunken leaves. Their burrows, capped by curious little mud-towers, are familiar objects to those who go much afield. When not easily obtainable elsewhere, the crawfish may be taken from its burrow by overturning the mud-tower, lowering a bit of flesh fixed to a cord into the hole, and jerking the bait when a nibbling is felt. The boys had another method: 'Fuzz it and churn for 'um,' was a common expression, which meant to break a switch with a ragged end, and manipulate this into the hole until the outraged crawfish took a tight grip and was promptly jerked from its stronghold.

The creature referred to as a mystery is what is termed the 'horsehair snake,' in reality, a hairworm. It is found in all of our waters, and greatly resembles a hair from a horse's mane. The boys all swear that this hairworm really is a horsehair turned into a snake, and many grown persons will back up the claim. People have declared that they have taken a hair, placed it in a bottle of water, corked the bottle, and kept it so until the hair turned into a snake and swam about. Of course, science will accept no such testimony. The worm may be found in shallow water, perhaps lying upon the bottom like a snarl of black thread, or like a hair-spring of a watch, or closely twisted about a spear of grass. Where horses drink one may find genuine hairs and the hairworms in close proximity, which doubtless accounts for the hairsnake story. The hairworm is a gordioid nematode worm, which considering its structure and habit of snarling itself up is a good, if not very interesting description. The worm's first stage of life is as a parasite, the hairlike form representing the adult. It swims like a snake.

Now for the fish. Largest, most imposing and most difficult to take was that king of the pike family, the muskellunge. Just how large these chaps ran is an open question. About forty-five pounds might be the limit for trolling with the hand-line and spoon. Much heavier specimens were occasionally speared or shot. The largest fish were secured by spearing through the ice. The best I ever saw was one that had died from some unknown cause, and lay stranded upon a sand-bar. In prime condition this fish should have weighed fully sixty-five pounds.

During late May and early June the muskellunge made their way up the larger streams, two fish, male and female, usually traveling together. At such times fishing tackle proper was of little use, though now and again a troll attached to a very long line did tempt a strike. Much more reliable were the very long-handled spear and the rifle and shotgun. From gray dawn till an hour or two after sunrise was the best time for muskellunge, as the fish might be discovered swimming near shore, or playing over the bars. As a general thing the first intimation of their proximity was the sight of a strongly defined wake stretching far upon the placid water, as the fish moved a trifle below the surface. Then the important matter was to get to a commanding point ahead of the apex of that wake without alarming the fish. This was rather a difficult thing to accomplish, as it frequently demanded some lively skirmishing through the brush and up and down wooded banks. I have known gun and spear to chase the watery sign, losing it and finding it again for a good two miles, and then fail to obtain a fair chance.

Some of the old hands at this work had favorite points where they would post themselves like overgrown kingfishers and wait for fish to pass. This method demanded much patience, and it had a disadvantage in the fact that fish might be playing just beyond the bends above and below the stand, and the watcher not know it. As a rule the odds were in favor of the man who cautiously stole along the bank and kept a keen eye upon the water ahead. During the best part of a morning he could cover several miles of stream and, perhaps, have as many as three or four chances.

In practiced hands the long-handled spear did excellent service, but woe was the portion of the duffer who attempted to use one. Badly scared fish and a much surprised man were the almost certain results of clumsy work, and fish once scared seldom give another chance that day. Many of the country lads used cheap rifles, which were all right where the opposite bank was sufficiently high to stop glancing balls, but there was always the undesirable chance of a ball going somewhere upon a dangerous errand. A reliable shot-gun was as deadly to the fish, not dangerous in other directions, and much handier for quick work.

Our pike, small brother to the muskellunge, we did not hold in very great esteem. They ran from a pound to about fifteen pounds in weight, were full of bones, and the flesh was rather insipid. When the main streams overflowed their banks in the spring, the pike sometimes occupied the lesser tributaries and ditches in astonishing numbers. Then the short spears and guns were busy day and night, for the fun was great, though the fish were not prized. By the light of torches, lanterns and bonfires, many large pike were shot and speared during the warm, muggy nights when the run was at its height. Later in the season pike were taken by troll and hand-line, by whipping with rod and spoon, or other artificial lure, and by minnow-bait, the 'shiner' being the best of small live bait, the frog ranking next.

What we termed 'pickerel' (walleyed pike) were better table-fish, but could not be depended upon for a day's sport. There was a heavy run of them about spring freshet time, when tons of them fell victims to the seines. At this time, too, numbers were speared in the discolored eddies, but later, during the regular season for the rods, only one or two would be found among a day's catch of good fish. Specimens weighing five or six pounds were quite commonly taken, while the seines took much heavier ones.

Three curious fish found in our waters were taken solely for the fun of playing them, for none of the boys would ever carry one of them home. Most abundant of these was the 'sheepshead' (freshwater drum), a good-looking, silvery fish, somewhat like the lake shad. They ran large, ranging from one to ten pounds, took various sorts of baits freely, and fought pretty well upon light tackle. All of the upper parts were of a pretty, silvery blue, which below shaded off to a dead white. In the head of this fish are two enamel-like substances, roughly circular in shape, and about the size of a nickel in the larger specimens. These were termed 'lucky stones,' and the boy's first business, after landing a sheepshead, was to crush its head with his heel, or something as convenient, and extract these two precious affairs. One or more of them lurked in every boy's pockets, for were they not equal to the famed rabbit's foot of the South? No boy cared to hook and lose a sheepshead, and none would dream of casting away the dead fish without first 'gettin' his luckies.' The 'stones' were marked upon one side with a design which suggested a pollard willow with a badly bent stem, the rough resemblance of this bent stem to a letter L, being, presumably, the cause of the luck theory.

I have caught scores of these fish, yet never tasted one. I have heard that the flesh is astonishingly tough and flavorless, and that the sheepshead required a power of cooking before one could chew it at all. This may be so, yet the actual experimenter does not appear within my field of acquaintances. At certain points we used to kill from a dozen to twenty sheepshead in a day, the fish freely taking worms and crawfish, so freely of the latter that many a bait intended for a bass got into the wrong pew.

The second of our curious fish was the gar-pike, as a rule, very abundant. This fish was also voted 'pizen,' and none would touch it for food. To the boys they were 'swordfish,' and only good to have fun with. A big gar, with his round, tapering body, stiletto-like jaws, sharp teeth and wicked-looking eyes, was an unpromising customer who appeared to be full of bite. During warm weather gars floated for hours at the surface, and their trim lines someway suggested speed, power, and something of a relationship to marine torpedoes and things like that. The bony structure of their long, lean jaws frequently baffled efforts at hooking them, and, if hooked, their teeth were apt to cut anything but gimp. I have, however, taken them with minnows, the play afforded by them being poor. A specimen a yard long would be deemed a large fish in those waters.

While the adult gar is decidedly ugly, the young are very beautiful. The very small ones look like gold bodkins, while one of about the size of a lead-pencil, with his bronzy tinting, snow-white belly and gleaming gold eye, in modeling and coloration may well hold his own with the best. These smaller fish may be found floating among the bent water-grasses, and so closely do they match their surroundings that sharp eyes are required to locate them before they dart to shelter. One flick of the tail, which is always kept in a slightly curved position for instantaneous action, will cause the smooth, slim body to vanish in what is apparently a miraculous manner. We used to take the floating gars by stealthy work with a small landing-net made of mosquito-netting, the fish being interesting for aquariums.

The third of the freak fish was prized on account of his decided method of taking bait and his stubborn resistance when hooked. He was never eaten, everybody agreeing that he surely was 'pizen.' This fish, the bowfin (*Amia calva*), was always termed 'dogfish,' and he was an ugly-looking fellow. His greenish-yellow, snaky-looking body was not pleasant to contemplate, and there was an ugly expression about his big mouth and a glint in his lurid eye which suggested a disposition not sugary, to say the least. Careless fingers would get pinched when removing the hooks; indeed, some of the boys cut him loose and sacrificed hooks rather than have anything further to do with him beyond clubbing him to death.

Early in the spring we speared and hooked many mullet, which were also taken in large quantities by the seines. The red-finned, olive-backed, foolish-looking fish were held in fair esteem for the table, especially the large ones. When the water was very muddy from the freshet, the red fins were about all one could distinguish, as the fish rolled in the eddies, or struggled against the rapid current. At such times one had need to be quick with his spear, and at the same time to instantly estimate where to strike. With the mullet came the pallid-looking suckers – bony, worthless creatures, which were not deemed fit to carry home.

After the clouded waters had run clear and had regained their normal level, came the cream of our fishing. Then the bass were on the feed, and the sport they afforded was something never to be forgotten. There were plenty of bass – large and small-mouth black fighters, weighing from one to six pounds; square-built rock bass, sometimes over a pound in weight; shapely white bass, not much as fighters, even when a foot long, yet dainty for the pan; and lastly, the calico, or grass bass, a showy, mottled fellow, sometimes a foot long, and a quick, jerky fighter.

Upon many days a catch would include specimens of all of these varieties of bass, as they take the same baits and favor the same haunts. Most prized of the lot were the black bass, especially the small-mouth. His big-mouthed cousin ranked second, calico and silver were equally esteemed, while the rock-bass was by no means to be despised. Some of the boys had jointed rods and reels, but the majority favored a bamboo cane, or a springy pole, cut in the woods. For these the lines were made fast near the butt, then carried with a few turns round the pole to the tip, and there made fast, the free line being a trifle shorter than the pole. Floats were seldom used, the boys, as a rule, preferring to trust their hands to determine when to strike.

The bass were found in the greatest numbers about old piling, submerged trees, where trees hung far over deep water, and near lily-pads and dense grasses. The best baits were crawfish, minnows, white grubs, frogs, grasshoppers, larvae of bees and wasps, and worms; and they were esteemed about in the order as named. If one bait did not promptly tempt a fish some other was substituted. The boys knew where and how to secure all in their season.

The fishing was never confined to one spot for any great length of time, nor did the boys believe that silence was either golden or necessary; in fact, they chaffed each other and joked at will. The rule they followed was that one place was good only so long as bites were not too far apart; and when the water within reach had been once thoroughly tested a move was the proper thing.

A small-mouth black bass was the prize first tried for, say about a submerged tree. For him minnow, crawfish, frog or grub, as the case happened to be, was deftly cast a few yards from all about the supposed stronghold. If two or more of these baits failed to tempt the desired victim, the conclusion was that the black bass, if thereabouts, was not in a biting humor. Then a rock-bass was voted good enough, and the bait was sent down as close as possible to the submerged tree-trunk, and into all likely-looking dark holes. The rock-bass, all honor to him, was usually there and ready to make a fight. So one promising place after another would be tried, the sport for the day ending perhaps two or half a dozen miles from the starting point.

The rock-bass, for his size, was a good fighter, and also a very tasty morsel when properly cooked. He – also termed 'google-eye' and 'red-eye' – frequently turned up as black as one's boots, always blacker than the true black bass, which is of an olive-green tint above and lighter below. The boys called the rock bass the 'black bass,' while large and small-mouth black bass were known as 'green' bass. Now and then, great catches of white bass were made.

I remember once, after a heavy rain, taking (where the discolored water of a creek met the clear current of a large river) more than one hundred white bass within one and one-quarter hours. I fished standing in a small shooting-skiff, and dropped the fish behind me as fast as they could be removed from the artificial baits. The rod used was short and stiff, and there was hardly any playing. This happened about the middle of a town, a few yards from a bridge from which a crowd eagerly watched the fun. I might have taken more bass, but the weight of the catch, all in the stern, brought the little skiff so low behind that, before I knew it, the water was pouring in. A yell from the crowd warned me, and I got ashore with only my feet wet. That catch is, or was until two years ago, the record for white bass in that water. Presumably, the muddy water of the creek brought down so much feed that all the fish in the neighborhood were attracted to the common point. They took my bait before it was two yards below the surface, and just as it passed the line between the muddy and clear water.

Another reliable fish for sport and fairly good for the pan was the yellow perch. These handsome fellows frequently traveled in large schools; and, when once a school had been struck, some lively work was certain to follow. The fish would range from half a pound to three times that weight. The best bait for them was the worm, although other baits frequently proved attractive. On a good perch day and at a good perch place, the catch might number from twenty to nearly one hundred fish.

A very beautiful fish, excellent for the pan and dearly loved by the small boy, was the sunfish or pumpkinseed. A large one would weigh about three-quarters of a pound, but specimens of quarter that size are more commonly taken. They are greedy biters and game in their own way, but their mouths are too small for ordinary bass hooks and baits. A very small hook, bearing a portion of worm, will be at once taken by a sunfish, if he be there; and he *is* there in almost every stretch of our old waters. He delights in sunny shallows, in pools among the grasses, and he is also given to lying beside roots and rubbish near shore. It is a common sight to see these fish poised with wavering fins above their spawn, where the sand and gravel are only a foot or so below the surface. When a boy marks sunfish so engaged, those fish are as good as caught. They will not desert the spawn, and they will bite, in hunger or anger, at anything dropped too near their precious charge. This fish, with the shiner and young perch, ranks among the first victims of pin-hook wiles.

Among rarely taken specimens were the young whitefish and the herring. These were delicate-mouthed, yet most palatable dainties, but so small a part did they play in our sport that they are not properly included here. When they did take the hook the bait was a worm.

The catfish and bullheads, however, could always be depended upon – thirty, forty or more of them during an evening. What the boys called 'channel-cats' were taken from midstream by long hand-lines which had a sinker at the end and one or more hooks bent to short lengths of line above the sinker. Worms were deadly bait, and shortly after sunset was the best time. The catfish were of all sizes, from fingerlings with more horns than body, up to great whiskered varieties of twenty-odd pounds. With the exception of the head, repulsive with its huge mouth, small eyes, and long appendages, the smaller channel-cat is a handsomely modeled fish. The body is clean-cut, the fins are well-proportioned, while the silvery, scaleless, slippery skin is not unattractive. Fish of about one pound in weight were excellent eating, though many people would not touch them. At home, I had them prepared, half-a-dozen together, in a manner most acceptable. The process I do not understand, but the fish reached me entombed within a solid mass of transparent jelly, in which were also a few slices of hardboiled egg, some sprigs of parsley and a dash of vinegar – all ice-cold. Good? Say! The block of jelly would be as large as two brickbats, and I could get – but there! Those days have passed away.

These fish had to be very carefully removed from the hook! The long horns, or feelers, were perfectly harmless, but in the fins near the gills were awful serrated spikes which could inflict most painful wounds. If given a chance, the slippery fish would swing his head vigorously, whereupon his captor's hand or wrist was certain to suffer. The small 'mud-cat,' or bullhead, also had these weapons with a complete knowledge of their use. Quite frequently wounds from them caused a severe inflammation, which sometimes extended to the temper and the talk of the victim.

When fishing for channel-cats after dark, the boys often started a big bonfire. A lot of fun is mingled with the ashes of those old fires. A row of hand-lines stretched to the outer darkness, and the boys sat more or less patiently, each holding his cord. A whispered 'Got a bite,' would stop all conversation, and then would come the quick strike and the unerring snatch-snatch as dirty hands flew through their task of recovering the line. If the resistance told of a heavy prize, muttered grunts and inarticulate exclamations added tenseness to the situation, till the big fish threshed the surface within the fire's light. Then would go up such a yell of triumph, that our folks in nearby houses would not know whether we had merely caught a good one, or had all tumbled into the river. If we eventually turned up home, they knew that everything was all right, and they were, or they pretended to be, greatly pleased to see us. Sometimes a boy *did* fall in and elicit nearly as many yells as greeted the fish, though the yells lacked the ring of true enthusiasm. We were such water-dogs that nobody bothered about a little thing like that.

At intervals it happened that a boy got a bite which puzzled him, though those hands could feel and recognize, through thirty or forty yards of line, any fish that touched the bait. Upon these occasions the excitement was keen. The last heave would surely reveal either a mud-turtle or a mud-puppy. Both of these are awkward customers to handle. The turtles could bite like fury, and fingers had no business near their cutting jaws. The shortest way was to cut the hook free, and allow the turtle to keep it as a souvenir.

The mud-puppy was different. No power on earth would induce a boy to touch that slate-colored, slimy, writhing shape. Its fate was ever the same. The cord was cut, and into the fire went the puppy. This creature, by the way, is a repulsive-looking water-lizard. His heavy body, four stumpy legs, apparent lack of eyes, and bunches of external gills, were neither understood nor appreciated by his captors. He was 'pizen,' and no respect was owing to those who might claim that he was harmless. He would bite, or at least he would try to do so, for never to my knowledge was he allowed an opportunity to illustrate what he was capable of in that direction. Peace be to his ashes, for he suffered much!

The lamprey, too, could cause quite a commotion. This creature, the boys could never understand, and they were more or less afraid of it. I do not remember ever taking one upon the hook, but at rare intervals one was seen attached to a fish – I think, invariably, to a bass. The lamprey, or lamper-eel, may once have been considered a delicacy, but the boys would have none of him. He was from a foot to a foot and a half long, eel-like in form, and possessing a round, sucking mouth, with a palate well supplied with small teeth. Behind the mouth, upon either side, were seven small openings, which greatly puzzled the boys.

I have more than once seen bass walloping about with one of these suckers firmly attached, and the fish's actions indicated that it was either in pain, or in deadly fear of its comrade. One bass which I shot, and from which I detached the lamprey, showed an ugly-looking raw spot where the sucker had been; I have also seen many bass that bore similar scars. Once, when some boys were wading in a pool, left by high water, a lamprey fastened upon a bare leg. That boy did more 'stunts' in five minutes than he would attempt now for five thousand dollars! The thing finally let go, and only a slight mark remained.

So much for the fishes of boyhood and, incidentally, for the boys themselves. Of that happy party some have since learned about the fishes in the Shadow River. The others are scattered far and wide, some glad with human hopes, some gray with human griefs. Some have seen the great salmon-rivers and trout-pools of remotest wilds, and have learned the science of modern tools and perfected methods. Perchance their bare-foot training has oft times stood them in good stead. It may be that the survivors would gladly cast aside their modern improvements for the privilege of once again assembling the old bonfire; to see the lines leading into the darkness, the floating captives upon their separate tethers, the mud-puppy roasting upon his pyre, and some boy carving his initials upon a hapless, hissing turtle.

Quién sabe?

Fishing with a Worm

BLISS PERRY

'The last fish I caught was with a worm.'

– Izaak Walton

A DEFECTIVE LOGIC IS the born fisherman's portion. He is a pattern of inconsistency. He does the things which he ought not to do, and he leaves undone the things which other people think he ought to do. He observes the wind when he should be sowing, and he regards the clouds, with temptation tugging familiarly at his heartstrings, when he might be grasping the useful sickle. It is a wonder that there is so much health in him. A sorrowing political economist remarked to me in early boyhood, as a jolly red-bearded neighbor, followed by an abnormally fat dog, sauntered past us for his nooning: 'That man is the best carpenter in town, but he will leave the most important job whenever he wants to go fishing.' I stared at the sinful carpenter, who swung along leisurely in the May sunshine, keeping just ahead of his dog. To leave one's job in order to go fishing! How illogical!

Years bring the reconciling mind. The world grows big enough to include within its scheme both the instructive political economist and the truant mechanic. But that trick of truly logical behavior seems harder to the man than to the child. For example, I climbed up to my den under the eaves last night – a sour, black sea-fog lying all about, and the December sleet crackling against the window-panes – in order to varnish a certain fly-rod. Now rods ought to be put in order in September, when the fishing closes, or else in April, when it opens. To varnish a rod in December proves that one possesses either

159

a dilatory or a childishly anticipatory mind. But before uncorking the varnish bottle, it occurred to me to examine a dog-eared, water-stained fly-book, to guard against the ravages of possible moths. This interlude proved fatal to the varnishing. A half-hour went happily by in rearranging the flies. Then, with a fisherman's lack of sequence, as I picked out here and there a plain snell-hook from the gaudy feathered ones, I said to myself with a generous glow at the heart: 'Fly-fishing has had enough sacred poets celebrating it already. Isn't there a good deal to be said, after all, for fishing with a worm?'

Could there be a more illogical proceeding? And here follows the treatise – a Defense of Results, an Apology for Opportunism – conceived in agreeable procrastination, devoted to the praise of the inconsequential angleworm, and dedicated to a childish memory of a whistling carpenter and his fat dog.

Let us face the worst at the very beginning. It shall be a shameless example of fishing under conditions that make the fly a mockery. Take the Taylor Brook, 'between the roads,' on the headwaters of the Lamoille. The place is a jungle. The swamp maples and cedars were felled a generation ago, and the tops were trimmed into the brook. The alders and moosewood are higher than your head; on every tiny knoll the fir balsams have gained a footing, and creep down, impenetrable, to the edge of the water. In the open spaces the Joe-Pye weed swarms. In two minutes after leaving the upper road you have scared a mink or a rabbit, and you have probably lost the brook. Listen! It is only a gurgle here, droning along, smooth and dark, under the tangle of cedar-tops and the shadow of the balsams. Follow the sound cautiously. There, beyond the Joe-Pye weed, and between the stump and the cedar-top, is a hand's breadth of black water. Fly-casting is impossible in this maze of dead and living branches. Shorten your line to two feet, or even less, bait your hook with a worm, and drop it gingerly into that gurgling crevice of water. Before it has sunk six inches, if there is not one of those black-backed, orange-bellied, Taylor Brook trout fighting with it, something is wrong with your worm or with you. For the trout are always there, sheltered by the brushwood that makes this half mile of fishing 'not worth while.' Below the lower road the Taylor Brook becomes uncertain water. For half a mile it yields only fingerlings, for no explainable reason; then there are two miles of clean fishing through the deep woods, where the branches are so high that you can cast a fly again if you like, and there are long pools, where now and then a heavy fish will rise; then comes a final half mile through the alders, where you must wade, knee to waist deep, before you come to the bridge and the river. Glorious fishing is sometimes to be had here – especially if you work down the gorge at twilight, casting a white miller until it is too dark to see. But alas, there is a well-worn path along the brook, and often enough there are the very footprints of the 'fellow ahead of you,' signs as disheartening to the fisherman as ever were the footprints on the sand to Robinson Crusoe.

But 'between the roads' it is 'too much trouble to fish'; and there lies the salvation of the humble fisherman who disdains not to use the crawling worm, nor, for that matter, to crawl himself, if need be, in order to sneak under the boughs of some overhanging cedar that casts a perpetual shadow upon the sleepy brook. Lying here at full length, with no elbow-room to manage the rod, you must occasionally even unjoint your tip, and fish with that, using but a dozen inches of line, and not letting so much as your eyebrows show above the bank. Is it a becoming attitude for a middle-aged citizen of the world? That depends upon how the fish are biting. Holing a put looks rather ridiculous also, to the mere observer, but it requires, like brook-fishing with a tip only, a very delicate wrist, perfect tactile sense, and a fine disregard of appearances.

There are some fishermen who always fish as if they were being photographed. The Taylor Brook 'between the roads' is not for them. To fish it at all is back-breaking, trouser-tearing work; to see it thoroughly fished is to learn new lessons in the art of angling. To watch R., for example, steadily filling his six-pound creel from that unlikely stream, is like watching Sargent paint a portrait. R. weighs two hundred and ten. Twenty years ago he was a famous amateur pitcher, and among his present avocations are violin playing, which is good for the wrist, taxidermy, which is good for the eye, and shooting woodcock, which before the days of the new Nature Study used to be thought good for the whole man. R. began as a fly-fisherman, but by dint of passing his summers near brooks where fly-fishing is impossible, he has become a stout-hearted apologist for the worm. His apparatus is most singular. It consists of a very long, cheap rod, stout enough to smash through bushes, and with the stiffest tip obtainable. The lower end of the butt, below the reel, fits into the socket of a huge extra butt of bamboo, which R. carries unconcernedly. To reach a distant hole, or to fish the lower end of a ripple, R. simply locks his reel, slips on the extra butt, and there is a fourteen-foot rod ready for action. He fishes with a line unbelievably short, and a Kendal hook far too big; and when a trout jumps for that hook, R. wastes no time in manoeuvring for position. The unlucky fish is simply 'derricked' – to borrow a word from Theodore, most saturnine and profane of Moosehead guides.

'Shall I play him awhile?' shouted an excited sportsman to Theodore, after hooking his first big trout.

'—— no!' growled Theodore in disgust. 'Just derrick him right into the canoe!' A heroic method, surely; though it once cost me the best square-tail I ever hooked, for Theodore had forgotten the landing-net, and the gut broke in his fingers as he tried to swing the fish aboard. But with these lively quarter-pounders of the Taylor Brook, derricking is a safer procedure. Indeed, I have sat dejectedly on the far end of a log, after fishing the hole under it in vain, and seen the mighty R. wade downstream close behind me, adjust that comical extra butt, and jerk a couple of half-pound trout from under the very log on which I was sitting. His device on this occasion, as I well remember, was to pass his hook but once through the middle of a big worm, let the worm sink to the bottom, and crawl along it at his leisure. The trout could not resist.

Once, and once only, have I come near equaling R.'s record, and the way he beat me then is the justification for a whole philosophy of worm-fishing. We were on this very Taylor Brook, and at five in the afternoon both baskets were two thirds full. By count I had just one more fish than he. It was raining hard. 'You fish down through the alders,' said R. magnanimously. 'I'll cut across and wait for you at the sawmill. I don't want to get any wetter, on account of my rheumatism.'

This was rather barefaced kindness – for whose rheumatism was ever the worse for another hour's fishing? But I weakly accepted it. I coveted three or four good trout to top off with – that was all. So I tied on a couple of flies, and began to fish the alders, wading waist deep in the rapidly rising water, down the long green tunnel under the curving boughs. The brook fairly smoked with the rain, by this time, but when did one fail to get at least three or four trout out of this best half mile of the lower brook? Yet I had no luck. I tried one fly after another, and then, as a forlorn hope – though it sometimes has a magic of its own – I combined a brown hackle for the tail fly with a twisting worm on the dropper. Not a rise! I thought of E. sitting patiently in the saw mill, and I fished more conscientiously than ever.

> 'Venture as warily, use the same skill,
> Do your best, whether winning or losing it,
> If you choose to play! – is my principle.'

Even those lines, which by some subtle telepathy of the trout brook murmur themselves over and over to me in the waning hours of an unlucky day, brought now no consolation. There was simply not one fish to be had, to any fly in the book, out of that long, drenching, darkening tunnel. At last I climbed out of the brook, by the bridge. R. was sitting on the fence, his neck and ears carefully turtled under his coat collar, the smoke rising and the rain dripping from the inverted bowl of his pipe. He did not seem to be worrying about his rheumatism.

'What luck?' he asked.

'None at all,' I answered morosely. 'Sorry to keep you waiting.'

'That's all right,' remarked R. 'What do you think I've been doing? I've been fishing out of the saw-mill window just to kill time. There was a patch of floating sawdust there – kind of unlikely place for trout, anyway – but I thought I'd put on a worm and let him crawl around a little.' He opened his creel as he spoke. 'But I didn't look for a pair of 'em,' he added. And there, on top of his smaller fish, were as pretty a pair of three-quarter-pound brook trout as were ever basketed.

'I'm afraid you got pretty wet,' said R. kindly.

'I don't mind that,' I replied. And I didn't. What I minded was the thought of an hour's vain wading in that roaring stream, whipping it with fly after fly, while R., the foreordained fisherman, was sitting comfortably in a sawmill, and derricking that pair of three-quarter-pounders in through the window! I had ventured more warily than he, and used, if not the same skill, at least the best skill at my command. My conscience was clear, but so was his; and he had had the drier skin and the greater magnanimity and the biggest fish besides. There is much to be said, in a world like ours, for taking the world as you find it and for fishing with a worm.

One's memories of such fishing, however agreeable they may be, are not to be identified with a defense of the practice. Yet, after all, the most effective defense of worm-fishing is the concrete recollection of some brook that could be fished best or only in that way, or the image of a particular trout that yielded to the temptation of an angleworm after you had flicked fly after fly over him in vain. Indeed, half the zest of brook fishing is in your campaign for 'individuals' – as the Salvation Army workers say – not merely for a basketful of fish *qua* fish, but for a series of individual trout which your instinct tells you ought to lurk under that log or be hovering in that ripple. How to get him, by some sportsmanlike process, is the question. If he will rise to some fly in your book, few fishermen will deny that the fly is the more pleasurable weapon. Dainty, luring, beautiful toy, light as thistle-down, falling where you will it to fall, holding when the leader tightens and sings like the string of a violin, the artificial fly represents the poetry of angling. Given the gleam of early morning on some wide water, a heavy trout breaking the surface as he curves and plunges, with the fly holding well, with the right sort of rod in your fingers, and the right man in the other end of the canoe, and you perceive how easy is that Emersonian trick of making the pomp of emperors ridiculous.

But angling's honest prose, as represented by the lowly worm, has also its exalted moments. 'The last fish I caught was with a worm,' says the honest Walton, and so say I. It was the last evening of last August. The dusk was settling deep upon a tiny meadow, scarcely ten rods from end to end. The rank bog grass, already drenched with dew, bent over the narrow, deep little brook so closely that it could not be fished except with a double-shotted, baited hook, dropped delicately between the heads of the long grasses. Underneath this canopy the trout were feeding, taking the hook with a straight downward tug, as they made for the hidden bank. It was already twilight when I began, and before I reached the black belt of woods that separated the meadow from the lake, the swift darkness of the North Country made it impossible to see the hook. A short half hour's fishing only, and behold nearly twenty good trout derricked into a basket until then sadly empty. Your rigorous fly-fisherman would have passed that grass-hidden brook in disdain, but it proved a treasure for the humble. Here, indeed, there was no question of individually-minded fish, but simply a neglected brook, full of trout which could be reached with the baited hook only. In more open brook-fishing it is always a fascinating problem to decide how to fish a favorite pool or ripple, for much depends upon the hour of the day, the light, the height of water, the precise period of the spring or summer. But after one has decided upon the best theoretical procedure, how often the stupid trout prefers some other plan! And when you have missed a fish that you counted upon landing, what solid satisfaction is still possible for you, if you are philosopher enough to sit down then and there, eat your lunch, smoke a meditative pipe, and devise a new campaign against that particular fish! To get another rise from him after lunch is a triumph of diplomacy, to land him is nothing short of statesmanship. For sometimes he will jump furiously at a fly, for very devilishness, without ever meaning to take it, and then, wearying suddenly of his gymnastics, he will snatch sulkily at a grasshopper, beetle, or worm. Trout feed upon an extraordinary variety of crawling things, as all fishermen know who practice the useful habit of opening the first two or three fish they catch, to see what food is that day the favorite. But here, as elsewhere in this world, the best things lie nearest, and there is no bait so killing, week in and week out, as your plain garden or golf-green angleworm.

Walton's list of possible worms is impressive, and his directions for placing them upon the hook have the placid completeness that belonged to his character. Yet in such matters a little nonconformity may be encouraged. No two men or boys dig bait in quite the same way, though all share, no doubt, the singular elation which gilds that grimy occupation with the spirit of romance. The mind is really occupied, not with the wriggling red creatures in the lumps of earth, but with the stout fish which each worm may capture, just as a saint might rejoice in the squalor of this world as a preparation for the glories of the world to come. Nor do any two experienced fishermen hold quite the same theory as to the best mode of baiting the hook. There are a hundred ways, each of them good. As to the best hook for worm-fishing, you will find dicta in every catalogue of fishing tackle, but size and shape and tempering are qualities that should vary with the brook, the season, and the fisherman. Should one use a three-foot leader, or none at all? Whose rods are best for bait-fishing, granted that all of them should be stiff enough in the tip to lift a good fish by dead strain from a tangle of brush or logs? Such questions, like those pertaining to the boots or coat which one should wear, the style of bait-box one should carry, or the brand of tobacco best suited for smoking in the wind, are topics for unending discussion among the serious-minded around the camp-fire. Much edification is in them, and yet they are but prudential maxims after all. They are mere moralities of the Franklin or Chesterfield variety, counsels of worldly wisdom, but they leave the soul untouched. A man may have them at his finger's ends and be no better fisherman at bottom; or he may, like R., ignore most of the admitted rules and come home with a full basket. It is a sufficient defense of fishing with a worm to pronounce the truism that no man is a *complete* angler until he has mastered all the modes of angling. Lovely streams, lonely and enticing, but impossible to fish with a fly, await the fisherman who is not too proud to use, with a man's skill, the same unpretentious tackle which he began with as a boy.

But ah, to fish with a worm, and then not catch your fish! To fail with a fly is no disgrace: your art may have been impeccable, your patience faultless to the end. But the philosophy of worm-fishing is that of Results, of having something tangible in your basket when the day's work is done. It is a plea for Compromise, for cutting the coat according to the cloth, for taking the world as it actually is. The fly-fisherman is a natural Foe of Compromise. He throws to the trout a certain kind of lure; and they will take it, so; if not, adieu. He knows no middle path.

> 'This high man, aiming at a million,
> Misses an unit.'

The raptures and the tragedies of consistency are his. He is a scorner of the ground. All honor to him! When he comes back at nightfall and says happily, 'I have never cast a line more perfectly than I have to-day,' it is almost indecent to peek into his creel. It is like rating Colonel Newcome by his bank account.

But the worm-fisherman is no such proud and isolated soul. He is a 'low man' rather than a high one; he honestly cares what his friends will think when they look into his basket to see what he has to show for his day's sport. He watches the Foe of Compromise men go stumbling forward and superbly falling, while he, with less inflexible courage, manages to keep his feet. He wants to score, and not merely to give a pretty exhibition of base-running. At the Harvard-Yale football game of 1903 the Harvard team showed superior strength in rushing the ball; they carried it almost to the Yale goal line repeatedly, but they could not, for some reason, take it over. In the instant of absolute need, the Yale line held, and when the Yale team had to score in order to win, they scored. As the crowd streamed out of the Stadium, a veteran Harvard alumnus said: 'This news will cause great sorrow in one home I know of, until they learn by to-morrow's papers that the Harvard team *acquitted itself creditably*.' Exactly. Given one team bent upon acquitting itself creditably, and another team determined to win, which will be victorious? The stay-at-homes on the Yale campus that day were not curious to know whether their team was acquitting itself creditably, but whether it was winning the game. Every other question than that was to those young Philistines merely a fine-spun irrelevance. They took the Cash and let the Credit go.

There is much to be said, no doubt, for the Harvard veteran's point of view. The proper kind of credit may be a better asset for eleven boys than any championship; and to fish a bit of water consistently and skillfully, with your best flies and in your best manner, is perhaps achievement enough. So says the Foe of Compromise, at least. But the Yale spirit will be prying into the basket in search of fish; it prefers concrete results. If all men are by nature either Platonists or Aristotelians, fly-fishermen or worm-fishermen, how difficult it is for us to do one another justice! Differing in mind, in aim and method, how shall we say infallibly that this man or that is wrong? To fail with Plato for companion may be better than to succeed with Aristotle. But one thing is perfectly clear: there is no warrant for Compromise but in Success. Use a worm if you will, but you must have fish to show for it, if you would escape the finger of scorn. If you find yourself camping by an unknown brook, and are deputed to catch the necessary trout for breakfast, it is wiser to choose the surest bait. The crackle of the fish in the frying-pan will atone for any theoretical defect in your method. But to choose the surest bait, and then to bring back no fish, is unforgivable. Forsake Plato if you must – but you may do so only at the price of justifying yourself in the terms of Aristotelian arithmetic. The college president who abandoned his college in order to run a cotton mill was free to make his own choice of a calling; but he was never pardoned for bankrupting the mill. If one is bound to be a low man rather than an impractical idealist, he should at least make sure of his vulgar success.

Is all this but a disguised defense of pot-hunting? No. There is no possible defense of pot-hunting, whether it be upon a trout brook or in the stock market. Against fish or men, one should play the game fairly. Yet for that matter some of the most skilful fly-fishermen I have known were pot-hunters at heart, and some of the most prosaic-looking merchants were idealists compared to whom Shelley was but a dreaming boy. All depends upon the spirit with which one makes his venture. I recall a boy of five who gravely watched his father tramp off after rabbits – gun on shoulder and beagle in leash. Thereupon he shouldered a wooden sword, and dragging his reluctant black kitten by a string, sallied forth upon the dusty Vermont road 'to get a lion for breakfast.' That is the true sporting temper! Let there be but a fine idealism in the quest, and the particular object is unessential. 'A true fisherman's happiness,' says Mr. Cleveland, 'is not dependent upon his luck.' It depends upon his heart.

No doubt all amateur fishing is but 'play'– as the psychologists soberly term it: not a necessary, but a freely assumed activity, born of surplusage of vitality. Nobody, not even a carpenter wearied of his job, has to go fishing unless he wants to. He may indeed find himself breakfast-less in camp, and obliged to betake himself to the brook – but then he need not have gone into the woods at all. Yet if he does decide to fish, let him

> 'Venture as warily, use the same skill,
> Do his best ...'

whatever variety of tackle he may choose. He can be a whole-souled sportsman with the poorest equipment, or a mean 'trout-hog' with the most elaborate.

Only, in the name of gentle Izaak himself, let him be a *complete* angler; and let the man be a passionate amateur of all the arts of life, despising none of them, and using all of them for his soul's good and for the joy of his fellows. If he be, so to speak, but a worm-fisherman – a follower of humble occupations, and pledged to unromantic duties – let him still thrill with the pleasures of the true sportsman. To make the most of dull hours, to make the best of dull people, to like a poor jest better than none, to wear the threadbare coat like a gentleman, to be outvoted with a smile, to hitch your wagon to the old horse if no star is handy – this is the wholesome philosophy taught by fishing with a worm. The fun of it depends upon the heart. There may be as much zest in saving as in spending, in working for small wages as for great, in avoiding the snapshots of publicity as in being invariably first 'among those present.' But a man should be honest. If he catches most of his fish with a worm, secures the larger portion of his success by commonplace industry, let him glory in it, for this, too, is part of the great game. Yet he ought not in that case to pose as a fly-fisherman only – to carry himself as one aware of the immortalizing camera – to pretend that life is easy, if one but knows how to drop a fly into the right ripple. For life is not easy, after all is said. It is a long brook to fish, and it needs a stout heart and a wise patience. All the flies there are in the book, and all the bait that can be carried in the box, are likely to be needed ere the day is over. But, like the Psalmist's 'river of God,' this brook is 'full of water,' and there is plenty of good fishing to be had in it if one is neither afraid nor ashamed of fishing sometimes with a worm.

Trophies

CAMERON PIERCE

I WAS BORN A collector. From the ages of seven until about twelve, the heart of my angling fixation boiled down to one question: *Can it be mounted?* I wanted to hang a trophy on the wall beside my father's ten-pound largemouth bass and his pair of deep red Kern River rainbows. I collected action figures, football cards (at age ten, a list of mine was published in *Beckett Football Monthly*), *Goosebumps* books, and nearly anything else with the remotest collectability, so naturally I was also inclined to collect the fish kingdom as well. Sometimes my old collecting habit paid off. I convinced my father to drop thirty dollars on a hand-painted, hand-carved nine-inch Castaic Lure Co. trout. That model, which ceased to be produced by hand in 1996, now goes for as much as $300. Mine remains in mint condition. My card collection, primarily consisting of rookie cards from the sixties through the early nineties, might be valued at several thousand dollars. And yet there was nothing I wanted to collect more than a trophy fish of my own to mount on the wall. In 1996, the same year as the value of my Castaic Lure Co. trout skyrocketed, my father made a promise he would soon regret.

We were fishing Buena Vista Lakes outside Bakersfield, California. Even though Lake Webb, the larger of the two lakes, was primarily known as a boating and jet ski lake, we tended to fish there instead because fishing pressure was lighter and the fish tended to be bigger and more plentiful. We spent innumerable days catching crappie and bluegill, brown trout and rainbow trout, largemouth bass and striped bass, blue catfish and channel catfish, with hardly anyone else fishing on Lake Webb. If we hiked around to the reed-lined far shore, we were pretty much guaranteed to have the shoreline to ourselves. We were doing just that one May evening in 1996. We walked along the bank, throwing six-inch white curly tail grubs between the reeds for largemouth bass. As daylight ran down, I pitched my grub out into the water and began retrieving it with subtle twitches. During the retrieval, a big fish boiled on top of it. The fish didn't take, but that hardly mattered. I had its number now. I cast back out and almost as soon as the grub hit the water, the fish exploded on it. My rod buckled. The fight was on. I'd finally nailed it, a monster bass worth hanging beside my father's bass. There was no way he could resist mounting it. The fish peeled line, making several impressive runs. We didn't have a net, so my father stripped down to his underwear and waded out to his thighs. After several minutes, the fish tired out and resigned. My father stood in the water, ready to snatch up the bass of a lifetime. But when the fish finally surfaced, it flashed gold. It was a ten-pound carp, not a ten-pound bass. A beautiful fish, a hell of a fighter, and my first carp, but to a bass lover like my father, that's the equivalent of catching a ten-pound bag of dog shit.

'It's just a big ol' carp,' my father said.

'Can we mount it?' I said, hopeful.

'No, son. You can't mount a carp.'

I pleaded. Look at the *size* of it. Look at the golden scales. Do fish get any prettier?

He'd always had a hard time telling me no, so he made me a deal.

'We'll come out this weekend,' he said. 'If you catch a bigger one, we'll take it to the taxidermist.'

That sounded like a sweet deal to me, so we let my ten-pound carp swim free. My father was a little pissed that he'd taken off his pants and waded out into the lake over a carp, but at least he'd avoided taking one home for the wall.

A couple days later, we returned with my stepbrother and my dad's friend Harry, a diabetic with the flowing white hair of Gandalf. This time around, we fished with whole kernel sweet corn. We were getting serious about carp.

My stepbrother caught the first fish of the day. A five-pound goldfish. After that, we caught a couple four- to six-pound carp, but nothing came close to dethroning the fish from the previous trip. Eventually, my dad grew bored of carp fishing and he and Harry wandered along the back shoreline to throw for bass, leaving my stepbrother and me alone in the pursuit of carp. We drank Pepsi and sat there sweating under the hot Central Valley sun. At some point, my pole popped out of the rod holder and smacked against the rocky shore, half in the water and half out. I ran over and started reeling. Something on the other end pulled back, something heavier than I'd ever felt. A minor population of sturgeon existed in Buena Vista Lakes, but I had never caught one, and I didn't think they ate corn. All I knew was I had something big on.

I shouted for my father. He and Harry took their time returning, and by the time they arrived, whatever was on the other end of my line had stopped moving. My father took the rod from me and gave it a short, sharp jerk. 'You're snagged up,' he said.

'It's a big one,' I said.

'Naw, it's just a snag.' He attempted to free the rig from whatever rock or weed he believed it was caught on, and that's when the fish made its first big run, burning off fifty yards in mere seconds.

He couldn't believe it, and for a moment, neither could I. The fish was already halfway to the island in the middle of the lake. My father handed the rod back to me and rushed to clear the other lines to give me room to fight the Goliath. A crowd gathered as the battle stretched beyond five minutes, then ten. A younger kid asked if he could net the fish if I landed it. We'd once again failed to bring a net, so we agreed. He ran off to borrow a net from some other fishermen, returning a short time later.

'Remember you said we'd get it mounted,' I told my father, confident that I was going to land this fish, and that it was bigger than my last.

'We'll see,' he said.

Finally, twenty minutes after the fight began, we got a first look at what was on the other end.

A thirty-five-pound carp, three and a half feet long.

The fish was netted and brought ashore. My father, my stepbrother, Harry and I all took pictures with the big carp. I don't think we caught another fish that day, but it didn't matter. I'd gotten the fish I came for, the fish I could mount on the wall.

As we left the lake that day, a man offered me twenty dollars for the fish. He and his wife and three kids were out fishing for their dinner but they'd caught nothing. My father told him sorry, that I insisted on keeping it. 'We're getting it mounted,' I said.

That evening my father promised to call the taxidermist who'd mounted his bass and trout. The next time I was over at his house, I asked about the fish. 'I sent it off to the taxidermist,' he said. 'It'll be a few months.'

I asked for updates every time I visited my father. I was relentless. Finally, after six months had passed, I received some news. 'He's having trouble with the eyes. Not many people mount carp, so he had to special order the eyes,' my father told me. That sounded plausible enough. Carp do have beautiful eyes.

Eventually a year passed. Then two. Sometimes my father said the carp was on its way, but it never came. I caught other big fish. Nice channel cats, monster crappie, fat rainbow trout, and yet I never gave much thought to mounting them because I knew my carp lay in a taxidermist's workshop somewhere, and that if only I was patient, my fish would return to me, preserved to last a lifetime.

Years passed and we ceased speaking of the carp even though I still believed. Last year, while visiting my father, I finally asked him what really happened to the carp.

'I threw it in a field,' he said, with a laugh and a sheepish grin. 'That was a big-ass fish. It was a shame to kill it. But you can't mount a carp.'

Somewhere over the years, I lost my desire to mount a trophy on the wall. A hundred yards behind where I live now, a creek runs through the forest. Native cutthroats live there. I'm fine just watching them. I like to eat fish and nothing beats what you've caught yourself, yet many of the fish I catch are released without ever leaving the water. Sometimes, though, I think about that thirty-five pound carp and what it would've looked like above the fireplace. They say you can't mount a carp, but someday, I think I will.

Observations of the Carp

FROM *THE COMPLEAT ANGLER* BY IZAAK WALTON

Pꜱᴄ. ᴛʜᴇ ᴄᴀʀᴘ is the Queen of Rivers, a stately, a good, and a very subtle fish, that was not at first bred, nor hath been long in England, but is now naturalized. It is said, they were brought hither by one Mr. Mascal, a gentleman that then lived at Plumsted in Sussex, a county that abounds more with this fish than any in this nation.

You may remember that I told you, Gesner says, there are no Pikes in Spain; and doubtless, there was a time, about a hundred or a few more years ago, when there were no Carps in England, as may seem to be affirmed by S. Richard Baker, in whose Chronicle you may find these verses.

Hops and Turkies, Carps and Beer
Came into England all in a year.

And doubtless as of sea-fish the Herring dies soonest out of the water, and of fresh-water-fish the Trout, so (except the Eel) the Carp endures most hardness, and lives longest out of his own proper element. And therefore the report of the Carps being brought out of a foreign country into this nation is the more probable.

Carps and Loaches are observed to breed several months in one year, which Pikes and most other fish do not. And this is partly proved by tame and wild Rabbits, as also by some Ducks, which will lay eggs nine of the twelve months, and yet there be other Ducks that lay not longer than about one month. And it is the rather believed, because you shall scarce or never take a Male Carp without a Melt, or a Female without a Roe or Spawn, and for the most part very much; and especially all the Summer season; and it is observed, that they breed more naturally in ponds than in running waters (if they breed there at all); and that those that live in rivers are taken by men of the best palates to be much the better meat.

And it is observed, that in some ponds Carps will not breed, especially in cold ponds; but where they will breed, they breed innumerably; Aristotle and Pliny say, six times in a year, if there be no Pikes nor Perch to devour their Spawn, when it is cast upon grass, or flags or weeds, where it lies ten or twelve days before it be enlivened.

The Carp, if he have water-room and good feed, will grow to a very great bigness and length: I have heard, to be much above a yard long. 'Tis said (by Jovius, who hath writ of fishes) that in the Lake Lurian in Italy, Carps have thriven to be more then fifty pound weight, which is the more probable, for as the Bear is conceiv'd and born suddenly; and being born is but short-liv'd: So on the contrary, the Elephant is said to be two years in his dams belly (some think he is ten years in it) and being born grows in bigness twenty years; and 'tis observ'd too that he lives to the age of a hundred years. And 'tis also observ'd that the Crocodile is very long-liv'd, and more than that, that all that long life he thrives in bigness, and so I think some Carps do, especially in some places; though I never saw one above twenty-three inches, which was a great and a goodly fish: But have been assured there are of a far greater size, and in England too.

Now, as the increase of Carps is wonderful for their number; so there is not a reason found out, I think by any, why they should breed in some ponds, and not in others of the same nature, for soil and all other circumstances: and as their breeding, so are their decays also very mysterious: I have both read it, and been told by a gentleman of tried honesty, that he has known sixty or more large Carps put into several ponds near to a house, where by reason of the stakes in the ponds, and the owners constant being near to them, it was impossible they should be stole away from him: and that when he has after three or four years emptied the pond, and expected an increase from them by breeding young ones (for that they might do so he had, as the rule is, put in three Melters for one Spawner) he has, I say, after three or four years, found neither a young nor old Carp remaining. And the like I have known of one that has almost watched the pond, and at a like distance of time, at the fishing of a pond, found of seventy or eighty large Carps not above five or six: and that he had forborne longer to fish the said pond, but that he saw in a hot day in Summer, a large Carp swim near to the top of the water with a Frog upon his head, and that he upon that occasion caused his pond to be let dry: and I say, of seventy or eighty Carps, only found five or six in the said pond, and those very sick and lean, and with every one a Frog sticking so fast on the head of the said Carps, that the Frog would not be got off without extreme force or killing: and the gentleman that did affirm this to me, told me he saw it, and did declare his belief to be (and I also believe the same) that he thought the other Carps that were so strangely lost, were so killed by frogs, and then devoured.

But I am fallen into this discourse by accident, of which I might say more, but it has proved longer than I intended, and possibly may not to you be considerable; I shall therefore give you three or four more short observations of the Carp, and then fall upon some directions how you shall fish for him.

The age of Carps is by Sir Francis Bacon (in his *History of Life and Death*) observed to be but ten years; yet others think they live longer. Gesner says a Carp has been known to live in the Palatinate above a hundred years: But most conclude, that (contrary to the Pike or Luce) all Carps are the better for age and bigness, the tongues of Carps are noted to be choice and costly meat, especially to them that buy them: but Gesner says, Carps have no tongue like other fish, but a piece of flesh like fish in their mouth like to a tongue, and should be called a palate: But it is certain it is choicely good, and that the Carp is to be reckoned amongst those leather-mouthed fish, which I told you have their teeth in their throat, and for that reason he is very seldom lost by breaking his hold, if your hook be once stuck into his chaps.

I told you, that Sir Francis Bacon thinks that the Carp lives but ten years, but Janus Dubravius has writ a book of Fish and Fish-ponds, in which he says, that Carps begin to spawn at the age of three years, and continue to do so till thirty: he says also, that in the time of their breeding, which is in Summer, when the sun hath warmed both the earth and water, and so apted them also for generation, that then three or four Male-Carps will follow a Female, and that then she putting on a seeming coyness, they force her through weeds and flags, where she lets fall her Eggs or Spawn, which sticks fast to the weeds, and then they let fall their Melt upon it, and so it becomes in a short time to be a living fish; and as I told you, it is thought the Carp does this several months in the year, and most believe that most fish breed after this manner, except the Eel: and it has been observed, that when the Spawner has weakened her self by doing that natural office, that two or three Melters have helped her from off the weeds, by bearing her up on both sides, and guarding her into the deep. And you may note, that though this may seem a curiosity not worth observing, yet others have judged it worth their time and costs to make glass hives, and order them in such a manner as to see how Bees have bred and made their honey-combs, and how they have obeyed their king, and governed their commonwealth. But it is thought that all Carps are not bred by generation, but that some breed other ways, as some Pikes do.

The physicians make the galls and stones in the heads of Carps to be very medicinable; but 'tis not to be doubted but that in Italy they make great profit of the spawn of Carps, by selling it to the Jews, who make it into red caviar, the Jews not being by their Law admitted to eat of caviar made of the Sturgeon, that being a fish that wants scales, and (as may appear in Levit. 11) by them to be reputed unclean.

Much more might be said out of him, and out of Aristotle, which Dubravius often quotes in his *Discourse of Fishes*; but it might rather perplex than satisfy you, and therefore I shall rather choose to direct you how to catch, than spend more time in discoursing either of the nature or the breeding of this Carp, or of any more circumstances concerning him, but yet I shall remember you of what I told you before, that he is a very subtle fish, and hard to be caught.

And my first direction is, that if you will fish for a Carp, you must put on a very large measure of patience; especially to fish for a River Carp: I have known a very good fisher angle diligently four or six hours in a day, for three or four days together for a River Carp, and not have a bite: and you are to note, that in some ponds it is as hard to catch a Carp as in a river; that is to say, where they have store of feed, and the water is of a clayish colour: But you are to remember, that I have told you there is no rule without an exception, and therefore being possessed with that hope and patience which I wish to all fishers, especially to the Carp Angler, I shall tell you with what bait to fish for him. But first you are to know, that it must be either early or late; and let me tell you, that in hot weather (for he will seldom bite in cold) you cannot be too early or too late at it. And some have been so curious as to say, the 10 of April is a fatal day for Carps.

The Carp bites either at worms or at paste, and of worms I think the bluish Marsh or Meadow worm is best, but possibly another worm not too big may do as well, and so may a green Gentle; And as for pastes, there are almost as many sorts as there are medicines for the toothache, but doubtless sweet pastes are best; I mean, pastes made with honey or with sugar: which, that you may the better beguile this crafty fish, should be thrown into the pond or place in which you fish for him some hours before you undertake your trial of skill with the angle-rod: and doubtless if it be thrown into the water a day or two before, at several times and in small pellets, you are the likelier when you fish for the Carp to obtain your desired sport: or in a large pond to draw them to any certain place, that they may the better and with more hope be fished for, you are to throw into it in some certain place, either grains or blood mixed with Cow-dung, or with bran; or any garbage, as Chicken guts or the like, and then some of your small sweet pellets with which you purpose to angle: and these small pellets being a few of them also thrown in as you are angling.

And your paste must be thus made: Take the flesh of a Rabbit or Cat cut small, and bean flour, and if that may not be easily got, get other flour, and then mix these together, and put to them either sugar, or honey, which I think better, and then beat these together in a mortar, or sometimes work them in your hands (your hands being very clean) and then make it into a ball, or two, or three, as you like best for your use: but you must work or pound it so long in the mortar, as to make it so tough as to hang upon your hook without washing from it, yet not too hard: or that you may the better keep it on your hook, you may knead with your paste a little (and not much) white or yellowish wool.

And if you would have this paste keep all the year for any other fish, then mix with it virgin wax and clarified honey, and work them together with your hands before the Fire, then make these in to balls, and they will keep all the year.

And if you fish for a Carp with Gentles, then put upon your hook a small piece of scarlet about this bigness [__], it being soaked in, or anointed with Oil of Peter, called by some Oil of the Rock, and if your Gentles be put two or three days before into a box or horn anointed with honey, and so put upon your hook, as to preserve them to be living, you are as like to kill this crafty fish this way as any other: But still as you are fishing chaw a little white or brown bread in your mouth, and cast it into the pond about the place where your float swims. Other baits there be, but these with diligence, and patient watchfulness, will do it better than any that I have ever practiced, or heard of: And yet I shall tell you, that the crumbs of white bread and honey made into a paste is a good bait for a Carp, and you know it is more easily made. And having said thus much of the Carp, my next discourse shall be of the Bream, which shall not prove so tedious, and therefore I desire the continuance of your attention.

But first I will tell you how to make this Carp that is so curious to be caught, so curious a dish of meat as shall make him worth all your labour; and though it is not without some trouble and charges, yet it will recompence both.

Take a Carp (alive if possible), scour him, and rub him clean with water and salt, but scale him not, then open him, and put him with his blood and his liver (which you must save when you open him) into a small pot or kettle; then take sweet marjoram, thyme and parsley, of each half a handful, a sprig of rosemary, and another of Savory, bind them into two or three small bundles, and put them to your Carp, with four or five whole onions, twenty pickled Oysters, and three Anchovies. Then pour upon your Carp as much claret wine as will only cover him; and season your claret well with salt, cloves and mace, and the rinds of oranges and lemons, cover your pot and set it on a quick fire, till it be sufficiently boiled; then take out the Carp and lay it with the broth into the dish, and pour upon it a quarter of a pound of fresh butter melted and beaten, with half a dozen spoonfuls of the broth, the yolks of two or three eggs, and some of the herbs shred, garnish your dish with lemons and so serve it up.

Fishing for a Cat

FRANCIS W. MATHER

THERE IS A great deal written as to how to catch trout and bass, with all their cousins and aunts of game fish included within a Highland Scotch relationship, and epicures have frenzies of anticipation over the delights of fried crokers, broiled pompano and baked red-fish, while all pass by with scorn an humble fish of our Southern waters, which for gameness in fight, toothsomeness and general all around qualities of fryer, baker and broiler, is hard to be surpassed – the catfish.

Don't laugh, for that displays ignorance of his excellent qualities, but seriously incline thine ear and learn of the wisdom of cat fishing and how to cook after having caught – of the variety of his tribes, and then hie with pole and pan to the streams that flow into Lake Maurepas, and if you have learned your lesson in fishing, and have made due and acceptable sacrifice to the gods of palate and appetite – you shall sit down to a feast of fish that will last long ere satiety come.

The catfish that inhabit the waters of Amite, Tickfaw, Blood, Natalbany and Ponchatoula rivers are in their order of inferiority, the small yellow and black 'mud cats,' the slender-built, quick-striking, hard-fighting blue, or 'channel' cats, and the broad-headed, big-mouthed, heavy-bodied and rather sullen 'Opelousas,' or 'tabby cats;' last so called on account of the peculiar marks and spots which give it a resemblance to a tortoise-shell house cat. These fish are found in all of the streams of the southland, but in greater quantity, and of infinitely more edibility, in those streams that empty into land-locked salt lakes, such as Lakes Pontchartrain and Maurepas. There is no doubt that their alternate sojourning in the saline lake waters and the cold spring waters of the upper portion of these streams, vastly improves their flesh, and when they are eaten with hot corn bread and strong black coffee – gourmandizing becomes almost a virtue. The natives of these parts do not as a rule fish for the mere sport; it's fish to eat they are after, but if the most ardent rod and reel man who has killed pike, pickerel, salmon or trout would be lucky to hook a ten- or twelve-pound 'blue cat,' he'd have a fight on his hands that would amply satisfy his sporting blood.

In Tickfaw River the blue cats are the fattest, finest and gamiest; and where the stream narrows naturally, or where saw logs have been thrown in to await the down-rushing flood that will bear them to the boom at tidewater – in these swift waters the catfish, especially the blue cats, gather to the feast of little fishes who try to run the gauntlet of their swift striking jaws. Almost any kind of bait will tempt them, but in the full green leaf of spring there is a peculiar, large caterpillar, found only on the Catalpa trees (where it feeds on its large, juicy leaves that resemble the mulberry leaves) and so is known as the 'Catalpa worm,' and the catfish never has been hatched yet that could resist taking a snap at this bait. The big red earth worms, large as lead-pencils, and found in old stables, offer plenty inducement to a hungry catfish, and the intestines and white stomach of perch are a tidbit with which to tempt a partly gorged 'tabby cat.' The last are not often hooked, for the very good reason that the blue cats are too swift in striking, but when one takes hold, the experienced fisherman knows at once what kind of a fish is at the end of his line. There is a rush, a swift dart for the bottom, one or two plunges, and, except for a sullen backward pull, the fight is all over and one is sure of his fish if the line holds. Not so with the blue cat – he fights to the last, flops like mad when he is landed on the bank, and the fisherman is never sure of his game until he has him on a string, back from the water. And beware of those sharp side fins when the hook is being extracted!

On the Tickfaw River at the big 'cut-off,' a few miles before Centerville, in Livingston Parish, the writer fought a sixteen-pound blue cat for nearly two hours. The pool was at the foot of a steep bank twelve feet high, and as there were several old sunken saw logs in the pool, Mr. Blue had the fight in waters of his own choosing. He made rushes to right and left, with sudden dashes at the bottom to get under one of the logs and snap the line, with occasional leaps out of the water like a salmon, when he would savagely shake his head in an endeavor to get free of the hook. That was his undoing, for it wrapped the line round and round his gills and each struggle drew it tighter and seemed to choke the very life and spirit out of him – until finally he rolled over and lay gasping. A companion of the fisher climbed down the steep bank and with a long hooked stick drew his blue majesty out of the water.

But when you are out for meat, there are two preferred methods of taking the cat, one with the 'trot line,' and the other with set hooks. The trouble with the former is, that after it has been baited for a few days the gars find the place and take off the bait almost as fast as the fisher can put it on. So the location has to be changed frequently. If a spot cannot be readily found where the line can reach across the stream, a good plan (and one which the writer has found successful and prefers) is to fasten one end of the line high up on a tree on the bank, then weight the other end of the line heavily and carry it in a boat diagonally down, not up stream, and drop the weighted end in deep water. With hooks strung on short lines and baited with small perch, there is something to tempt the fish at every depth of water, from a few inches below the surface to the bottom, where the gars seldom hunt. They seek their prey nearer the surface, and for this reason are so troublesome about a straight-across trot line.

And a word just here about the gar – the shark of fresh waters – is very apropos. He is an ugly brute, sly and cruel, but if he runs all the catfish away from your line and gets caught himself, eat him out of revenge, and the next time you catch one of his brethren you'll fry and eat the second one because the first was so succulent. The meat is snow-white, firm and deliciously toothsome, and it is surprising that the meat of this fish – though he be of monstrous ugliness – has not yet found its way to the tables of epicures.

The most catfish are taken on set lines tied to swinging limbs, which give play to the fish that are hooked. Choose a dark night, for catfish are shy of biting at baits that they can see distinctly, or better wait for a rain that has muddied the water and caused a slight rise in the river. Then the catfish begin to swim upstream, feeding along close to the banks in little bays and eddies where the smaller fish have taken refuge from the rush of waters. Set out your lines before dark so that you can see how to choose well the location of each hook, if they are to be visited during the night, and bait the hooks with small perch. Fasten the hook through the fleshy part of the perch's back, just in front of the dorsal fin. This will not hurt him, and a perch so fastened will swim and play around for hours, and proportionally offer a more attractive bait to the feeding catfish. Another excellent morsel is spring-frog, artistically put by being hooked through the back with his hind legs tied with a string to the shank of the hook, thus giving the frog the appearance of having just dived into the water. Catfish thinks so – makes a rush and a gobble, and – well, he's your meat if the line holds.

If one is hard put to it, woodpeckers, sparrows, any kind of birds, plucked and quartered, make good bait, but the intestines of a chicken strung on a hook during the 'fall rise' will break up catfish families in a surprising manner. It is well to visit your set hooks and swinging lines at least once during the night, and as soon after daylight as possible, as man is not alone in his love for its delicate flesh. Gars and turtles quickly find when a fish is helplessly hooked and tear it to pieces, and water snakes will also attack them. Only a few days since, the writer, while passing along the banks of a big ditch, tributary to one of the small streams of this section, witnessed a curious sight. A large moccasin had swallowed a little catfish, head first, until his mouth reached the side and back fins which the fish had erected in self-defense. There he lay, unable to swallow or to disgorge, while a small snapping turtle was busy at the tail of the unfortunate fish, biting lumps of flesh from its wriggling body. A stout stick broke up that dinner party, but the catfish was mutilated beyond hope of life.

Most lovers of catfish like it fried in corn meal and boiling lard, with adjuncts of corn bread and hot coffee, but stuffed and baked, *à la* red fish, the meat has hardly a superior among fresh-water fish. Sliced and broiled, with a basting of butter, black pepper and salt, and served with egg sauce, it is simply delicious; or if one's taste runs to court bouillon or stew, it is equally good. Catch a few and try them.

How big? How many? Well, this is a tale of veracity, but 'tabby cats' have been taken from the Tickfaw and its kindred streams, that weighed fifty-four pounds in one instance, and over seventy in another, while there are plenty of catfish of twenty and thirty pounds weight. But don't catch a big fish; catch some of his smaller brothers that pull down the scales to ten, twelve or fifteen pounds. Then fry, bake, or stew them – sit down and eat, and thank your gods for the feast.

Right There

J. DAVID OSBORNE

AFTER MY WIFE left and I set about to ruining myself as best I could, I took a job moving furniture up in the city. I still can't tell if it was what I needed at the time. It was hot work, perfect for sweating out the toxins I'd ingested the night before. I was surrounded by men all day, and we laughed and cut up and talked about all sorts of unsavory business.

Tommy drove the box truck. I wasn't allowed to get behind the wheel after I hit a low-hanging tree branch, which peeled the top back on the box like a can of sardines. Tommy never got into an accident, but I'm not sure how. He'd drive with his knees and smoke a Black & Mild and fumble with his phone, looking for either good spots to fish on his GPS or for naked pictures his recent girlfriend had sent him. Either way, when he found what he was looking for, he'd hold the picture out to me, eyes off the road, and wait for me to react. Whether it was a brown river bend or a spread-open vagina, I'd quickly nod and tell him that it looked good, anxious for him to look back at the oncoming traffic.

On the weekends, Tommy would take the information he'd gathered that week and go out in a little johnboat with his cousin Lawrence. Lawrence was fresh out of jail, having served one year of a ten-year bit for selling cocaine. Together, they'd stuff their arms into catfish holes.

Noodling is a popular pastime in Oklahoma. Originally, it was a matter of life and death: Native Americans fished for catfish with their hands because the government blocked access to their fishing tools. Over time, it became a part of the culture, with a yearly festival taking place in Paul's Valley, just south of Oklahoma City.

It works like this: in the spring and the summer, catfish lay their eggs. The male guards the nest. If one is so inclined, one can stick their arm into the hole and provoke the cat into biting. Once it swallows your hand, you hook your fingers out through the gills and yank that son of a bitch out of its hole. It's a dangerous sport. Tommy told me about a time that he snagged a fifty pound cat in a deep hole. He's a big guy, six feet and pushing 250, but he couldn't wrestle the thing out. He was losing air and beginning to panic. Luckily he had Lawrence there, pulling on his free arm for all it was worth. He laughed and told me that he thought he was going to die. He showed me a picture of the giant fish, then he showed me a picture of his girlfriend squeezing her breasts together.

We were in the cab of that truck for ten hours a day, sometimes five days a week. I learned a lot about Tommy. He lived with his mother on the south side of OKC. They liked to watch TV and smoke weed together. I'd crack up, him telling me about his mother attempting to eat an entire pot cookie, how she spent the rest of the day with a warm rag over her face, convinced she was going to die.

The two of us connected over music and our sense of humor, but mostly we connected through our mutual disdain for our former partners.

My wife had left me a few months prior. She'd told me that I was an 'angry person.' Mostly I knew why she split: I was a loser with no prospects, a man who managed to fuck up every opportunity that came his way. I knew that she had to have looked at me and thought *Surely there's something better out there.*

Tommy had it a lot worse. Where my situation was fixable and temporary, he found himself in something more of a pickle: his ex-girlfriend was also the mother of his two children. She got her money from him every month, but she asked for more. When he couldn't give, she threatened to keep the children away from him.

So we took our disdain and we over-compensated. We honked at women on their way to work. We told filthy jokes. We stayed a little longer in the homes of the women we found attractive. We reveled in our perceived masculinity. We were a couple of real assholes.

One day Tommy offered to take me noodling. The thought of sticking my hand in a catfish hole was terrifying. My entire body said no, but the culture we'd built between us said yes. Of course I'd like to go noodling with him. So he entered our date into his phone and told me to meet him at a certain spot at a certain time.

I tried not to think about what I had agreed to. I got off work and went to the bar and watched the silent TV. Tie-Dye, an old dude who wore a tie-dye sweat suit complete with tie-dye Kangol, had loaded up the jukebox. I listened to Marty Robbins and chatted up the bartender and told her that I was going noodling the next day. She told me I was dumb. I felt brave, sitting there after a few beers. Proud of my potentiality for manliness.

It had been a while since I had even fished the normal way. When I was a kid, my uncle would take me out on the Shenandoah every summer. His hippy friends had a place out in the woods and a trampoline and we'd fry up the catfish we'd caught that morning. I'd burn my fingers in the grease and climb a tree and swing out over the river on the rope someone had tied to the highest branch years before. I loved those times. My uncle would tell me dirty jokes and we'd wave at the women going by in canoes. Once, I caught a huge catfish, at least twenty pounds. I fought it for a long time. We tied it to the stringer and celebrated with root beer and pictures. We pulled the boat up to the dock and my uncle went to get his truck. I scraped the boat up the rocks and when he got back, all the fish had been pulled off the stringer. There was a look he gave me, then, not necessarily mean, but something that told me I was too boneheaded to ever orient myself to that way of life. It made me run towards situations like the one I was in now, never sure if I'd regret it.

I woke up the next morning and shook off my hangover and met up with Tommy at the spot. Lawrence was there, smoking a cigarette. They loaded their nets into the boat and backed it into the lake and we were off.

Lawrence hopped out of the johnboat, the red water up to his chest. He picked a broom handle out of the floor of the boat and disappeared under the water. When he came back up, he spit out some river and nodded his head. 'There's one in there.'

Tommy got his camera ready. 'All right,' he said. 'Do it, fucker.'

Lawrence got his arm in up to the shoulder. He said, 'Shy boy.' Then there was a thrashing in the water. He grit his teeth and cussed under his breath. He pulled the cat out. About five pounds. Tommy nodded and took the picture on his phone.

We rowed out across the lake. Lawrence pointed at some brush. 'Could be some in there,' he said.

Tommy shook his head. 'Beavers. You want them bitches to bite your fingers off, yeah.'

No clouds in the sky. I applied sunscreen. Lawrence and Tommy laughed at the white boy. 'Hey,' I said. 'I'm delicate.'

'Gay, is what you are,' Lawrence said.

'Super gay,' Tommy agreed.

Lawrence and Tommy traded stories. Lawrence talked about being in jail. How his roommate and him used to wrestle. How one time Lawrence had shit himself. I asked did anyone get raped in prison? They both looked at me like I asked something wrong. Lawrence said yes. But not as often as you'd think. 'I heard one boy getting it pretty good a few cells down.' He shrugged. 'Depends on who they put you with, I guess.'

Tommy told us about a bar fight he'd been in recently. Someone had stepped on his shoe. Whenever I heard stories like that, I never believed it. They seemed to play out too by the book. Too *Road House*. The stories always ended with Tommy coming out on top, kicking someone's ass for this reason or the other. His ass-kicking story transitioned into talk of his baby mamma. She'd moved in with some new guy. 'I think he's gay,' Tommy said. He lit a joint and passed it to me. 'Looks gay.'

He pulled the boat up to the next spot and hopped out. He repeated the process Lawrence had done earlier: check to make sure the hole isn't occupied by a turtle or a snake, then in goes the arm. The catfish bit, and Tommy struggled. His head disappeared under the water. He got his face to break the surface and he said, 'Help me, motherfuckers.'

Lawrence jumped in after him. I stayed in the boat and watched. Lawrence grabbed his cousin by the arm and put his feet up in the dirt and pulled. Tommy finally broke the surface, coughing and sputtering. The catfish was huge, maybe four feet long. He held it up, suddenly forgetting his near-death experience. He smiled crooked teeth. 'Right there. Big one right there.'

Lawrence took the picture. They let the fish go.

'You don't eat any of them?' I said.

Tommy shook his head. 'Them dudes is just protecting their babies. I don't know. It makes me feel bad. Leaving the nest like that.'

'Why even do it, though?'

Tommy shrugged. 'Because it's fun. You're up next.'

It took me a long time, but I finally convinced them that I was too high to do any fishing at all. The truth was I was scared. They gave me that look, the same look I remember my uncle giving me all those years ago. They weren't mad, not even disappointed. They had maybe just held out hope that I wasn't too much of a pussy to put my hand in the hole.

We drank beers and talked more shit, and when the sun started dipping we headed back for Tommy's truck.

I had a bad sunburn.

We went back to his place and played video games and talked about the day, and I got my fair share of shit. I went home.

I remember I felt particularly deflated that night.

The next morning, Tommy showed up to work with a black eye.

Halfway through the day, he told me about it: he'd gone over to his baby mother's house and found another man there. The two had shouted at each other. They'd fought on her lawn. He told me he kicked the guy's ass. But after the fight, he'd gone to his car and gotten his gun. The mother's boyfriend had hidden in the house. 'Definitely queer,' he said. He ended the story there.

We were quiet in the cab for a long time.

He was back on his phone. He held it out to me, open to his GPS app. 'Right there. There's a big one there.'

The oncoming traffic honked.

Fourteen Pounds Against the World

GABINO IGLESIAS

LUIS AND I were out on the water, paddling lazily and letting the current do most of the work. The Caribbean sun glinted off my line as we trolled around somewhere on the east side of the Guanica Bay inlet on an old red canoe we'd named Freedom. We had stories to trade, nowhere to go for a few days, and bellies full of alcohol. It was summer and we were on the move, trying hard to escape the scary limbo young people fall into when they graduate high school and find themselves on the verge of adulthood with nothing even remotely resembling a plan.

We hadn't thought about fishing on this trip. We were staying with an older friend of mine who owned a house about ten feet from the Guanica Bay and didn't mind sharing it with anyone who asked. We'd gone to his place with a simple plan: hit the beach as much as possible and drink until things started making sense or we stopped caring about them being senseless. Then we stumbled upon a black plastic hand reel. It was ready to go and prepped with a white lure that could be seen in the inlet's murky waters. We decided to give it a shot.

The line had been in the water for over an hour. The conversation had zigzagged its way across most of our usual themes, but something had crept into Luis's voice, turning it somber. He wasn't smiling as much as he usually did. Then, after one of those long silences that are only comfortable between great friends, he spoke.

'Laura's pregnant.'

Laura was a girl we all knew. She was the kind of girl who knew how to dress and use make-up to hide her imperfections. She was also a heroin addict. Her mom allegedly shared her love for opiates. Her dad was a ghost no one talked about whose drug of choice was violence. She lived with her grandparents, a couple of angels who took care of her despite the bag of trouble that comes with living with a junkie. Laura was part of our group, but more like a satellite that sometimes got too close rather than a regular. Everyone knew she embodied the broken doll metaphor and no one got too close for fear of getting hurt. Well, no one except Luis. We warned him, but you can't choose who you fall in love with.

I can't remember exactly what I said out there on the water after the big reveal. I probably asked if he was sure the baby was his or if they planned on getting an abortion. Those words didn't matter. They were inconsequential and the greenish water around us swallowed them the way it would swallow small boats during hurricanes. What mattered was that Luis had started crying and I didn't know what to do.

We were living a strange period of our lives; pregnant with a mix of hope and apprehension while floating around aimlessly in the interstitial space between youth and adulthood. Our faces had outgrown boyhood, but the deep lines of manhood were still hidden under our skin. We knew of the pain that made older men weep and drink by themselves at tiny kitchen tables, but didn't dare talk about it because our own psyches hadn't been through that much yet. We'd lost friends and family, but death was still a somewhat alien concept akin to the things explained in documentaries about outer space. We knew something bad made Laura fill her veins with warm dreams, but didn't want to know what. More importantly, we were at that point where friends were everything and real life was a faraway monster incapable of harming our powerful, young hearts.

I had to remind my friend that we were all indestructible.

I told Luis not to cry. They had options. This wasn't the end of the world. Plenty of couples had dealt with similar circumstances successfully. They'd be OK.

Then my right foot jerked. I had inserted it through what's known in some countries as a Cuban Yo-Yo. Our eyes went to the black piece of plastic and then to each other's faces. There was something on the line, and for anyone fishing, a bite presses the pause button of life and everything else is immediately stripped of relevance.

I grabbed the line and slowly pulled on it. At the first sign of resistance, I yanked it to set my hook in. A few seconds later, whatever had taken the lure was pulling us along, the canoe moving faster than it had while we were paddling.

After a decent fight, I pulled a horse-eye jack into the canoe. It thrashed around madly, blood flying out of its mouth, its thick body thumping against the canoe. Luis took care of it with a paddle and then we sat there, looking at our unexpected dinner. We had hoped for a bite, but never expected to land a fish we associated with reefs in the muddy waters of the inlet. The fish was far from an adult and still had a bit of yellow on its fins, but it was the largest thing we'd caught in a long time. The sun reflected off its metallic skin and the tips of its dorsal fin and tail were the most beautiful shade of yellow we'd ever seen. Years later I'd learn that horse-eye jacks regularly swim into brackish water and even ascend rivers, but at the time, that fish seemed to us like a small miracle.

The excitement had made Luis stop crying. We threw the line back in and started paddling again. We were happy.

Luis started talking about past fishing trips, but then the conversation drifted back to his situation. Laura had left him because his reply to the news about the unwanted pregnancy had been to suggest they move in together and have the baby. A few days later, she'd called and told him he could take care of her while pregnant. She would have the 'damn baby' and then 'he could have it.'

The fishing gods didn't give me a chance to say something stupid. My leg jerked again, harder this time. Between the setting sun, our fading buzz, and the thirst, the second fight felt like a beating on my hands and arms. The line danced on the water as our eyes converged on it. Once again, life had been reduced to a line making V's on the water.

After a few minutes, and against all odds, I pulled a second, much larger horse-eye jack into the canoe. Luis had to hit it twice to get it to stay still. We were done for the day. The air we greedily sucked into our lungs as we paddled to shore tasted like victory.

Back at the house, my friend had a food scale he used to weight meat. He allowed us to use it. The first fish was close to six pounds. The second was a touch over eight pounds. We all took pictures holding our catch.

'Fourteen pounds of fish,' Luis kept saying. 'We got ourselves fourteen pounds of fish.'

That night we cleaned and grilled the small one. A few cuts stuffed with lemon slices and plenty of salt and pepper. We dined like young, proud gods with cheap beer and plastic forks.

Over the next few days, Luis talked about the baby and what he planned on doing. He was going to become an engineer and marry Laura, break her out of the prison she didn't even know she was trapped in. He was positive about the whole thing. Finally telling someone about it had apparently made the ordeal easier to digest. The two horse-eye jacks also played a part. He kept talking about them. I mostly nodded and contemplated my own uncertain future, fearful of the cracks my friend's problems were making on my sense of invulnerability.

The trip ended and we went back home. A few weeks later, limping from a car accident and happy to stay near my parents, I started college. Luis became a father. Then, somehow, the better part of a decade wedged itself silently between that afternoon full of fishing magic and the next time we talked about it.

The bar was dark inside and we'd both had too many drinks. Luis was sad, drunk, forty pounds heavier, and with a collection of broken vessels mapping reddish tributaries across his nose and cheeks. I was about to leave the country forever and we wanted to hang out, remember better times, and give each other the kind of hugs that brothers give each other in airports, funeral homes, and train stations all over the globe.

Luis was by then a full-blown alcoholic working on and off at a company that repaired industrial air conditioning systems. Laura had managed to stay off heroin for the duration of the pregnancy. She'd delivered a healthy baby girl, handed it over to Luis, packed her things, and disappeared. The girl had lived with him for a while, then with his parents, and was now back with him. He loved his daughter, but he also loved her mother and dreamed of her coming back to them one day. In the meantime, he drank.

He talked about his girl while I remembered the picture my friend had taken of him, triumphantly holding our fish like the most amazing trophies he'd ever held. In that photo he was all skinny arms and smile. I'd lost the photo in one of my many moves, but it was tattooed on my brain, an indelible memory of a perfect moment.

I looked at the bloated bluish ribbons of pain under my friend's eyes and felt mine fill up with tears. It was time to go.

Time and distance do to friendships what eons do to continents. I saw Luis on my first few trips back home, but that was it. We never went fishing together again. I never caught another horse-eye jack. Strangely enough, I don't want to. We shouldn't try to return to where we've been happy before because that's a surefire way of achieving disappointment. I don't feel inclined to ever attempt to pull out a fish from that same inlet. Years ago, one of my best friends and I stepped into a red canoe barefoot and came back to shore with fourteen pounds of fish. That's the kind of experience that lives inside you long after the photos have been lost.

Bonefish

ZANE GREY

IN MY EXPERIENCE as a fisherman the greatest pleasure has been the certainty of something new to learn, to feel, to anticipate, to thrill over. An old proverb tells us that if you wish to bring back the wealth of the Indias you must go out with its equivalent. Surely the longer a man fishes the wealthier he becomes in experience, in reminiscence, in love of nature, if he goes out with the harvest of a quiet eye, free from the plague of himself.

As a boy, fishing was a passion with me, but no more for the conquest of golden sunfish and speckled chubs and horny catfish than for the haunting sound of the waterfall and the color and loneliness of the cliffs. As a man, and a writer who is forever learning, fishing is still a passion, stronger with all the years, but tempered by an understanding of the nature of primitive man, hidden in all of us, and by a keen reluctance to deal pain to any creature. The sea and the river and the mountain have almost taught me not to kill except for the urgent needs of life; and the time will come when I shall have grown up to that. When I read a naturalist or a biologist I am always ashamed of what I have called a sport. Yet one of the truths of evolution is that not to practise strife, not to use violence, not to fish or hunt – that is to say, not to fight – is to retrograde as a natural man. Spiritual and intellectual growth is attained at the expense of the physical. Always, then, when I am fishing I feel that the fish are incidental, and that the reward of effort and endurance, the incalculable and intangible knowledge, emanate from the swelling and infinite sea or from the shaded and murmuring stream. Thus I assuage my conscience and justify the fun, the joy, the excitement, and the violence.

Five years ago I had never heard of a bonefish. The first man who ever spoke to me about this species said to me, very quietly with serious intentness: 'Have you had any experience with bonefish?' I said no, and asked him what kind that was. His reply was enigmatical. 'Well, don't go after bonefish unless you can give up all other fishing.' I remember I laughed. But I never forgot that remark, and now it comes back to me clear in its significance. That fisherman read me as well as I misunderstood him.

Later that season I listened to talk of inexperienced bonefishermen telling what they had done and heard. To me it was absurd. So much fishing talk seems ridiculous, anyway. And the expert fishermen, wherever they were, received the expressive titles: 'Bonefish Bugs and Bonefish Nuts!' Again I heard arguments about tackle rigged for these mysterious fish and these arguments fixed my vague impression. By and by some bonefishermen came to Long Key, and the first sight of a bonefish made me curious. I think it weighed five pounds – a fair-sized specimen. Even to my prejudiced eye that fish showed class. So I began to question the bonefishermen.

At once I found this type of angler to be remarkably reticent as to experience and method. Moreover, the tackle used was amazing to me. Stiff rods and heavy lines for little fish! I gathered another impression, and it was that bonefish were related to dynamite and chain lightning. Everybody who would listen to my questions had different things to say. No two men agreed on tackle or bait or ground or anything. I enlisted the interest of my brother R. C., and we decided, just to satisfy curiosity, to go out and catch some bonefish. The complacent, smug conceit of fishermen! I can see now how funny ours was. Fortunately it is now past tense. If I am ever conceited again I hope no one will read my stories.

My brother and I could not bring ourselves to try for bonefish with heavy tackle. It was preposterous. Three – four – five-pound fish! We had seen no larger. Bass tackle was certainly heavy enough for us. So in the innocence of our hearts and the assurance of our vanity we sallied forth to catch bonefish.

That was four years ago. Did we have good luck? No! Luck has nothing to do with bonefishing. What happened? For one solid month each winter of those four years we had devoted ourselves to bonefishing with light tackle. We stuck to our colors. The space of this whole volume would not be half enough to tell our experience – the amaze, the difficulty, the perseverance, the defeat, the wonder, and at last the achievement. The season of 1918 we hooked about fifty bonefish on three-six tackle – that is, three-ounce tips and six-thread lines – and we landed fourteen of them. I caught nine and R. C. caught five. R. C.'s eight-pound fish justified our contention and crowned our efforts.

To date, in all my experience, I consider this bonefish achievement the most thrilling, fascinating, difficult, and instructive. That is a broad statement and I hope I can prove it. I am prepared to state that I feel almost certain, if I spent another month bonefishing, I would become obsessed and perhaps lose my enthusiasm for other kinds of fish.

Why?

There is a multiplicity of reasons. My reasons range from the exceedingly graceful beauty of a bonefish to the fact that he is the best food fish I ever ate. That is a wide range. He is the wisest, shyest, wariest, strangest fish I ever studied; and I am not excepting the great *Xiphias gladius* – the broadbill swordfish. As for the speed of a bonefish, I claim no salmon, no barracuda, no other fish celebrated for swiftness of motion, is in his class. A bonefish is so incredibly fast that it was a long time before I could believe the evidence of my own eyes. You see him; he is there perfectly still in the clear, shallow water, a creature of fish shape, pale green and silver, but crystal-like, a phantom shape, staring at you with strange black eyes; then he is gone. Vanished! Absolutely without your seeing a movement, even a faint streak! By peering keenly you may discern a little swirl in the water. As for the strength of a bonefish, I actually hesitate to give my impressions. No one will ever believe how powerful a bonefish is until he has tried to stop the rush and heard the line snap. As for his cunning, it is utterly baffling. As for his biting, it is almost imperceptible. As for his tactics, they are beyond conjecture.

I want to append here a few passages from my note-books, in the hope that a bare, bald statement of fact will help my argument.

First experience on a bonefish shoal. This wide area of coral mud was dry at low tide. When we arrived the tide was rising. Water scarcely a foot deep, very clear. Bottom white, with patches of brown grass. We saw bonefish everywhere and expected great sport. But no matter where we stopped we could not get any bites. Schools of bonefish swam up to the boat, only to dart away. Everywhere we saw thin white tails sticking out, as they swam along, feeding with noses in the mud. When we drew in our baits we invariably found them half gone, and it was our assumption that the blue crabs did this.

At sunset the wind quieted. It grew very still and beautiful. The water was rosy. Here and there we saw swirls and tails standing out, and we heard heavy thumps of plunging fish. But we could not get any bites.

When we returned to camp we were told that the half of our soldier-crab baits had been sucked off by bonefish. Did not believe that.

Tide bothered us again this morning. It seems exceedingly difficult to tell one night before what the tide is going to do the next morning. At ten o'clock we walked to the same place we were yesterday. It was a bright, warm day, with just enough breeze to ruffle the water and make fishing pleasant, and we certainly expected to have good luck. But we fished for about three hours without any sign of a fish. This was discouraging and we could not account for it.

So we moved. About half a mile down the beach I thought I caught a glimpse of a bonefish. It was a likely-looking contrast to the white marl all around. Here I made a long cast and sat down to wait. My brother lagged behind. Presently I spied two bonefish nosing along not ten feet from the shore. They saw me, so I made no attempt to drag the bait near them, but I called to my brother and told him to try to get a bait ahead of them. This was a little after flood-tide. It struck me then that these singular fish feed up the beach with one tide and down with another.

Just when my brother reached me I got a nibble. I called to him and then stood up, ready to strike. I caught a glimpse of the fish. He looked big and dark. He had his nose down, fooling with my bait. When I struck him he felt heavy. I put on the click of the reel, and when the bonefish started off he pulled the rod down hard, taking the line fast. He made one swirl on the surface and then started up-shore. He seemed exceedingly swift. I ran along the beach until presently the line slackened and I felt that the hook had torn out. This was disappointment. I could not figure that I had done anything wrong, but I decided in the future to use a smaller and sharper hook. We went on down the beach, seeing several bonefish on the way, and finally we ran into a big school of them. They were right alongshore, but when they saw us we could not induce them to bite.

Every day we learn something. It is necessary to keep out of sight of these fish. After they bite, everything depends upon the skilful hooking of the fish. Probably it will require a good deal of skill to land them after you have hooked them, but we have had little experience at that so far. When these fish are along the shore they certainly are feeding, and presumably they are feeding on crabs of some sort. Bonefish appear to be game worthy of any fisherman's best efforts.

It was a still, hot day, without any clouds. We went up the beach to a point opposite an old construction camp. To-day when we expected the tide to be doing one thing it was doing another. Ebb and flow and flood-tide have become as difficult as Sanskrit synonyms for me. My brother took an easy and comfortable chair and sat up the beach, and I, like an ambitious fisherman, laboriously and adventurously waded out 150 feet to an old platform that had been erected there. I climbed upon this, and found it a very precarious place to sit. Come to think about it, there is something very remarkable about the places a fisherman will pick out to sit down on. This place was a two-by-four plank full of nails, and I cheerfully availed myself of it and, casting my bait out as far as I could, I calmly sat down to wait for a bonefish. It has become a settled conviction in my mind that you have to wait for bonefish. But all at once I got a hard bite. It quite excited me. I jerked and pulled the bait away from the fish and he followed it and took it again. I saw this fish and several others in the white patch of ground where there were not any weeds. But in my excitement I did not have out a long enough line, and when I jerked the fish turned over and got away. This was all right, but the next two hours sitting in the sun on that seat with a nail sticking into me were not altogether pleasurable. When I thought I had endured it as long as I could I saw a flock of seven bonefish swimming past me, and one of them was a whopper. The sight revived me. I hardly breathed while that bunch of fish swam right for my bait, and for all I could see they did not know it was there. I waited another long time. The sun was hot – there was no breeze – the heat was reflected from the water. I could have stood all this well enough, but I could not stand the nails. So I climbed down off my perch, having forgotten that all this time the tide had been rising. And as I could not climb back I had to get wet, to the infinite amusement of my brother. After that I fished from the shore.

Presently my brother shouted and I looked up to see him pulling on a fish. There was a big splash in the water and then I saw his line running out. The fish was heading straight for the framework on which I had been seated and I knew if he ever did get there he would break the line. All of a sudden I saw the fish he had hooked. And he reached the framework all right!

I had one more strike this day, but did not hook the fish. It seems this bone-fishing takes infinite patience. For all we can tell, these fish come swimming along with the rising tide close in to shore and they are exceedingly shy and wary. My brother now has caught two small bonefish and each of them gave a good strong bite, at once starting off with the bait. We had been under the impression that it was almost impossible to feel the bonefish bite. It will take work to learn this game.

Yesterday we went up on the north side of the island to the place near the mangroves where we had seen some bonefish. Arriving there, we found the tide almost flood, with the water perfectly smooth and very clear and about a foot deep up at the mangrove roots. Here and there at a little distance we could see splashes. We separated, and I took the outside, while R. C. took the inside close to the mangroves. We waded along. Before I had time to make a cast I saw a three-pound bonefish come sneaking along, and when he saw me he darted away like an arrow. I made a long cast and composed myself to wait. Presently a yell from R. C. electrified me with the hope that he had hooked a fish. But it turned out that he had only seen one. He moved forward very cautiously in the water and presently made a cast. He then said that a big bonefish was right near his hook, and during the next few minutes this fish circled his bait twice, crossing his line. Then he counted out loud: one, two, three, four, five bonefish right in front of him, one of which was a whopper. I stood up myself and saw one over to my right, of about five pounds, sneaking along with his nose to the bottom. When I made a cast over in his direction he disappeared as suddenly as if he had dissolved in the water. Looking out to my left, I saw half a dozen bonefish swimming toward me, and they came quite close. When I moved they vanished. Then I made a cast over in this direction. The bonefish came back and swam all around my bait, apparently not noticing it. They were on the feed, and the reason they did not take our bait must have been that they saw us. We fished there for an hour without having a sign of a bite, and then we gave it up.

Today about flood-tide I had a little strike. I jerked hard, but failed to see the fish, and then when I reeled in I found he still had hold of it. Then I struck him, and in one little jerk he broke the leader.

I just had a talk with a fellow who claims to know a good deal about bonefishing. He said he had caught a good many ranging up to eight pounds. His claim was that soldier crabs were the best bait. He said he had fished with professional boatmen who knew the game thoroughly. They would pole the skiff alongshore and keep a sharp look-out for what he called bonefish mud. And I assume that he meant muddy places in the water that had been stirred up by bonefish. Of course, any place where these little swirls could be seen was very likely to be a bonefish bank. He claimed that it was necessary to hold the line near the reel between the forefingers, and to feel for the very slightest vibration. Bonefish have a sucker-like mouth. They draw the bait in, and smash it. Sometimes, of course, they move away, drawing out the line, but that kind of a bite is exceptional. It is imperative to strike the fish when this vibration is felt. Not one in five bonefish is hooked.

We have had two northers and the water grew so cold that it drove the fish out. The last two or three days have been warm and to-day it was hot. However, I did not expect the bonefish in yet, and when we went in bathing at flood-tide I was very glad to see two fish. I hurried out and got my rod and began to try. Presently I had a little strike. I waited and it was repeated; then I jerked and felt the fish. He made a wave and that was the last I knew of him.

Reeling in, I looked at my bait, to find that it had been pretty badly chewed, but I fastened it on again and made another cast. I set down the rod. Then I went back after the bucket for the rest of the bait. Upon my return I saw the line jerking and I ran to the rod. I saw a little splash, and a big white tail of a bonefish stick out of the water. I put my thumb on the reel and jerked hard. Instantly I felt the fish, heavy and powerful. He made a surge and then ran straight out. The line burned my thumb so I could not hold it. I put on the click and the fish made a swifter, harder run for at least a hundred yards, and he tore the hook out.

This makes a number of fish that have gotten away from me in this manner. It is exasperating and difficult to explain. I have to use a pretty heavy sinker in order to cast the bait out. I have arranged this sinker, which has a hole through it, so that the line will run freely. This seems to work all right on the bite, but I am afraid it does not work after the fish is hooked. That sinker drags on the bottom. This is the best rigging that I can plan at the present stage of the game. I have an idea now that a bonefish should be hooked hard and then very carefully handled.

I fished off the beach awhile in front of the cabin. We used both kinds of crabs, soldier and hermit. I fished two hours and a half, from the late rising tide to the first of the ebb, without a sign or sight of a fish. R. C. finally got tired and set his rod and went in bathing. Then it happened. I heard his reel singing and saw his rod nodding; then I made a dash for it. The fish was running straight out, heavy and fast, and he broke the line.

This may have been caused by the heavy sinker catching in the weeds. We must do more planning to get a suitable rig for these bonefish.

Day before yesterday R. C. and I went up to the Long Key point, and rowed in on the mangrove shoal where once before I saw so many bonefish. The tide was about one-quarter in, and there was a foot of water all over the flats. We anchored at the outer edge and began to fish. We had made elaborate preparations in the way of tackle, bait, canoe, etc., and it really would have been remarkable if we had had any luck. After a little while I distinctly felt something at my hook, and upon jerking I had one splendid surge out of a good, heavy bonefish. That was all that happened in that place.

It was near flood-tide when we went back. I stood up and kept a keen watch for little muddy places in the water, also bonefish. At last I saw several fish, and there we anchored. I fished on one side of the boat, and R. C. on the other. On two different occasions, feeling a nibble on his line, he jerked, all to no avail. The third time he yelled as he struck, and I turned in time to see the white thresh of a bonefish. He made a quick dash off to the side and then came in close to the boat, swimming around with short runs two or three times, and then, apparently tired, he came close. I made ready to lift him into the boat, when, lo and behold! he made a wonderful run of fully 300 feet before R. C. could stop him. Finally he was led to the boat, and turned out to be a fish of three and a half pounds. It simply made R. C. and me gasp to speak of what a really large bonefish might be able to do. There is something irresistible about the pursuit of these fish, and perhaps this is it. We changed places, and as a last try anchored in deeper water, fishing as before. This time I had a distinct tug at my line and I hooked a fish. He wiggled and jerked and threshed around so that I told R. C. that it was not a bonefish, but R. C. contended it was. Anyway, he came toward the boat rather easily until we saw him and he saw us, and then he made a dash similar to that of R. C.'s fish and he tore out the hook. This was the extent of our adventure that day, and we were very much pleased.

Next morning we started out with a high north-east trade-wind blowing. Nothing could dampen our ardor.

It was blowing so hard up at No. 2 viaduct that we decided to stay inside. There is a big flat there cut up by channels, and it is said to be a fine ground for bonefish. The tide was right and the water was clear, but even in the lee of the bank the wind blew pretty hard. We anchored in about three feet of water and began to fish.

After a while we moved. The water was about a foot deep, and the bottom clean white marl, with little patches of vegetation. Crabs and crab-holes were numerous. I saw a small shark and a couple of rays. When we got to the middle of a big flat I saw the big white glistening tails of bonefish sticking out of the water. We dropped anchor and, much excited, were about to make casts, when R. C. lost his hat. He swore. We had to pull up anchor and go get the hat. Unfortunately this scared the fish. Also it presaged a rather hard-luck afternoon. In fishing, as in many other things, if the beginning is tragedy all will be tragedy, growing worse all the time. We moved around up above where I had seen these bonefish, and there we dropped anchor. No sooner had we gotten our baits overboard than we began to see bonefish tails off at quite some distance. The thing to do, of course, was to sit right there and be patient, but this was almost impossible for us. We moved again and again, but we did not get any nearer to the fish. Finally I determined that we would stick in one place. This we did, and the bonefish began to come around. When they would swim close to the boat and see us they would give a tremendous surge and disappear, as if by magic. But they always left a muddy place in the water. The speed of these fish is beyond belief. I could not cast where I wanted to; I tried again and again. When I did get my bait off at a reasonable distance, I could feel crabs nibbling at it. These pests robbed us of many a good bait. One of them cut my line right in two. They seemed to be very plentiful, and that must be why the bonefish were plentiful, too. R. C. kept losing bait after bait, which he claimed was the work of crabs, but I rather believed it to be the work of bonefish. It was too windy for us to tell anything about the pressure of the line. It had to be quite a strong tug to be felt at all. Presently I felt one, and instead of striking at once I waited to see what would happen. After a while I reeled in to find my bait gone. Then I was consoled by the proof that a bonefish had taken the bait off for me. Another time three bonefish came along for my bait and stuck their tails up out of the water, and were evidently nosing around it, but I felt absolutely nothing on the line. When I reeled in the bait was gone.

We kept up this sort of thing for two hours. I knew that we were doing it wrong. R. C. said bad conditions, but I claimed that these were only partly responsible for our failure. I knew that we moved about too much, that we did not cast far enough and wait long enough, and that by all means we should not have cracked bait on the bottom of the boat, and particularly we did not know when we had a bite! But it is one thing to be sure of a fact and another to be able to practise it. At last we gave up in despair, and upon paddling back toward the launch we saw a school of bonefish with their tails in the air. We followed them around for a while, apparently very much to their amusement. At sunset we got back to the launch and started for camp.

This was a long, hard afternoon's work for nothing. However, it is my idea that experience is never too dearly bought. I will never do some things again, and the harder these fish are to catch, the more time and effort it takes – the more intelligence and cunning – all the more will I appreciate success if it ever does come. It is in the attainment of difficult tasks that we earn our reward. There are several old bonefish experts here in camp, and they laughed when I related some of our experiences. Bonefishermen are loath to tell anything about their methods. This must be a growth of the difficult game. I had an expert bonefisherman tell me that when he was surprised while fishing on one of the shoals, he always dropped his rod and pretended to be digging for shells. And it is a fact that the bonefish guides at Metacumbe did not let anyone get a line on their methods. They will avoid a bonefishing-ground while others are there, and if they are surprised there ahead of others, they will pull up anchor and go away. May I be preserved from any such personal selfishness and reticence as this! One of these bonefish experts at the camp told me that in all his years of experience he had never gotten a bonefish bite. If you feel a tug, it is when the bonefish is ejecting the hook. Then it is too late. The bonefish noses around the bait and sucks it in without any apparent movement of the line. And that can be detected first by a little sagging of the line or by a little strain upon it. That is the time to strike. He also said that he always broke his soldier crabs on a piece of lead to prevent the jar from frightening the fish.

Doctor B. tells a couple of interesting experiences with bonefish. On one occasion he was fishing near another boat in which was a friend. The water was very clear and still, and he could see his friend's bait lying upon the sand. An enormous bonefish swam up and took the bait, and Doctor B. was so thrilled and excited that he could not yell. When the man hooked the fish it shot off in a straightaway rush, raising a ridge upon the water. It ran the length of the line and freed itself. Later Doctor B.'s friend showed the hook, that had been straightened out. They measured the line and found it to be 555 feet. The bonefish had gone the length of this in one run, and they estimated that he would have weighed not less than fifteen pounds.

On another occasion Dr. B. saw a heavy bonefish hooked. It ran straight off shore, and turning, ran in with such speed that it came shooting out upon dry land and was easily captured. These two instances are cases in point of the incredible speed and strength of this strange fish.

R. C. had a splendid fight with a bonefish to-day. The wind was blowing hard and the canoe was not easy to fish out of. We had great difficulty in telling when we did have a bite. I had one that I know of. When R. C. hooked his fish it sheered off between the canoe and the beach and ran up-shore quite a long way. Then it headed out to sea and made a long run, and then circled. It made short, quick surges, each time jerking R. C.'s rod down and pulling the reel handle out of his fingers. He had to put on a glove. We were both excited and thrilled with the gameness of this fish. It circled the canoe three times, and tired out very slowly. When he got it close the very thing happened that I feared. It darted under the anchor rope and we lost it. This battle lasted about fifteen minutes, and afforded us an actual instance of the wonderful qualities of this fish.

Yesterday R. C. hooked a bonefish that made a tremendous rush straight offshore, and never stopped until he had pulled out the hook. This must have been a very heavy and powerful fish.

I had my taste of the same dose to-day. I felt a tiny little tug upon my line that electrified me and I jerked as hard as I dared. I realized that I had hooked some kind of fish, but, as it was wiggling and did not feel heavy, I concluded that I had hooked one of those pesky blowfish. But all of a sudden my line cut through the water and fairly whistled. I wound in the slack and then felt a heavy fish. He made a short plunge and then a longer one, straight out, making my reel scream. I was afraid to thumb the line, so I let him go. With these jerky plunges he ran about three hundred feet. Then I felt my line get fast, and, handing my rod to R. C., I slipped off my shoes and went overboard. I waded out, winding as I went, to find that the bonefish had fouled the line on a sponge on the bottom, and he had broken free just above the hook.

Yesterday the fag end of the north-east gale still held on, but we decided to try for bonefish. Low tide at two o'clock.

I waded up-shore with the canoe, and R. C. walked. It was a hard job to face the wind and waves and pull the canoe. It made me tired and wet.

When we got above the old camp the tide had started in. We saw bonefish tails standing up out of the water. Hurriedly baiting our hooks, we waded to get ahead of them. But we could not catch them wading, so went back to the canoe and paddled swiftly ahead, anchored, and got out to wade once more.

R. C. was above me. We saw the big tail of one bonefish and both of us waded to get ahead of him. At last I made a cast, but did not see him any more. The wind was across my line, making a big curve in it, and I was afraid I could not tell a bite if I had one. Was about to reel in when I felt the faint tug. I swept my rod up and back, hard as I dared. The line came tight, I felt a heavy weight; a quiver, and then my rod was pulled down. I had hooked him. The thrill was remarkable. He took a short dash, then turned. I thought I had lost him. But he was running in. Frantically I wound the reel, but could not get in the slack. I saw my line coming, heard it hiss in the water, then made out the dark shape of a bonefish. He ran right at me – almost hit my feet. When he saw me he darted off with incredible speed, making my reel scream. I feared the strain on the line, and I plunged through the water as fast as I could after him. He ran four hundred feet in that dash, and I ran fifty. Not often have I of late years tingled and thrilled and panted with such excitement. It was great. It brought back the days of boyhood. When he stopped that run I was tired and thoroughly wet. He sheered off as I waded and wound in. I got him back near me. He shot off in a shoal place of white mud where I saw him plainly, and he scared a school of bonefish that split and ran every way. My fish took to making short circles; I could not keep a tight line. Lost! I wound in fast, felt him again, then absolutely lost feel of him or sight of him. Lost again! My sensations were remarkable, considering it was only a fish of arm's-length at the end of the line. But these bonefish rouse an angler as no other fish can. All at once I felt the line come tight. He was still on, now running inshore.

The water was about a foot deep. I saw the bulge, or narrow wave, he made. He ran out a hundred feet, and had me dashing after him again. I could not trust that light line at the speed he swam, so I ran to release the strain. He led me inshore, then up-shore, and out toward sea again, all the time fighting with a couple of hundred feet of line out. Occasionally he would make a solid, thumping splash. He worked offshore some two hundred yards, where he led me in water half to my hips. I had to try to stop him here, and with fear and trepidation I thumbed the reel. The first pressure brought a savage rush, but it was short. He turned, and I wound him back and waded inshore.

From that moment I had him beaten, although I was afraid of his short thumps as he headed away and tugged. Finally I had him within twenty feet circling around me, tired and loggy, yet still strong enough to require careful handling.

He looked short and heavy, pale checked green and silver; and his staring black eye, set forward in his pointed white nose, could be plainly seen. This fish made a rare picture for an angler.

So I led him to the canoe and, ascertaining that I had him well hooked, I lifted him in.

Never have I seen so beautiful a fish. A golden trout, a white sea-bass, a dolphin, all are beautiful, but not so exquisite as this bonefish. He seemed all bars of dazzling silver. His tail had a blue margin and streaks of lilac. His lower (anal) fins were blazing with opal fire, and the pectoral fins were crystal white. His eye was a dead, piercing black, staring and deep. We estimated his weight. I held for six pounds, but R. C. shook his head. He did not believe that. But we agreed on the magnificent fight he had made.

Then we waded up-shore farther and began to fish. In just five minutes I had the same kind of strike, slight, almost imperceptible, vibrating, and I hooked a fish exactly as I had the first one. He was light of weight, but swift as a flash. I played him from where I stood. This time I essayed with all skill to keep a taut line. It was impossible. Now I felt his weight and again only a slack line. This fish, too, ran right to my feet, then in a boiling splash sheered away. But he could not go far. I reeled him back and led him to the canoe. He was small, and the smallness of him was such a surprise in contrast to what his fight had led me to imagine he was.

R. C. had one strike and broke his line on the jerk. We had to give up on account of sunset at hand.

There was another hard thunderstorm last night. The last few days have begun the vernal equinox. It rained torrents all night and stopped at dawn. The wind was north-east and cool. Cloudy overhead, with purple horizon all around – a forbidding day. But we decided to go fishing, anyhow. We had new, delicate three-six tackles to try. About seven the wind died away. There was a dead calm, and the sun tried to show. Then another breeze came out of the east.

We went up on the inside after bait, and had the luck to find some. Crossing the island, we came out at the old construction camp where we had left the canoe. By this time a stiff breeze was blowing and the tide was rising fast. We had our troubles paddling and poling up to the grove of coconuts. Opposite this we anchored and began to fish.

Conditions were not favorable. The water was choppy and roily, the canoe bobbed a good deal, the anchors dragged, and we did not see any fish. All the same, we persevered. At length I had a bite, but pulled too late. We tried again for a while, only to be disappointed. Then we moved.

We had to put the stern anchor down first and let it drag till it held and the canoe drifted around away from the wind, then we dropped the bow anchor. After a time I had a faint feeling at the end of my line – an indescribable feeling. I jerked and hooked a bonefish. He did not feel heavy. He ran off, and the wind bagged my line and the waves also helped to pull out the hook.

Following that we changed places several times, in one of which R. C. had a strike, but failed to hook the fish. Just opposite the old wreck on the shore I had another fish take hold, and, upon hooking him, had precisely the same thing happen as in the first instance. I think the bag of my line, which I could not avoid, allowed the lead to sag down and drag upon the bottom. Of course when it caught the bonefish pulled free.

In some places we found the water clearer than in others. Flood-tide had long come when we anchored opposite the old camp. R. C. cast out upon a brown patch of weeds where we have caught some fine fish, and I cast below. Perhaps in five minutes or less R. C. swept up his rod. I saw it bend forward, down toward the water. He had hooked a heavy fish. The line hissed away to the right, and almost at once picked up a good-sized piece of seaweed.

'It's a big fish!' I exclaimed, excitedly. 'Look at him go! That seaweed will make you lose him. Let me wade out and pull it off?'

'No! Let's take a chance . . . Too late, anyhow! Gee! He's going . . .! He's got two hundred yards out!'

Two-thirds of the line was off the reel, and the piece of seaweed seemed to be a drag on the fish. He slowed up. The line was tight, the rod bent. Suddenly the tip sprang back. We had seen that often before.

'Gone!' said R. C., dejectedly.

But I was not so sure of that, although I was hopeless. R. C. wound in, finding the line came slowly, as if weighted. I watched closely. We thought that was on account of the seaweed. But suddenly the reel began to screech.

'I've got him yet!' yelled R. C., with joy.

I was overjoyed, too, but I contained myself, for I expected dire results from that run.

Zee! Zee! Zee! went the reel, and the rod nodded in time.

'We must get rid of that seaweed or lose him . . . Pull up your anchor with one hand . . . Careful now.'

He did so, and quickly I got mine up. What ticklish business!

'Keep a tight line!' I cautioned, as I backed the canoe hard with all my power. It was not easy to go backward and keep head on to the wind. The waves broke over the end of the canoe, splashing me in the face so I could taste and smell the salt. I made half a dozen shoves with the paddle. Then, nearing the piece of seaweed, I dropped my anchor.

In a flash I got that dangerous piece of seaweed off R. C.'s line.

'Good work! ... Say, but that helps ... We'd never have gotten him,' said R. C., beaming. I saw him look then as he used to in our sunfish, bent-pin days.

'We've not got him yet,' I replied, grimly. 'Handle him as easily as you can.'

Then began a fight. The bonefish changed his swift, long runs, and took to slow sweeps to and fro, and whenever he was drawn a few yards closer he would give a solid jerk and get that much line back. There was much danger from other pieces of floating weed. R. C. maneuvered his line to miss them. All the time the bonefish was pulling doggedly. I had little hope we might capture him. At the end of fifteen minutes he was still a hundred yards from the canoe and neither of us had seen him. Our excitement grew tenser every moment. The fish sheered to and fro, and would not come into shallower water. He would not budge. He took one long run straight up the shore, in line with us, and then circled out. This alarmed me, but he did not increase his lead. He came slowly around, yard by yard. R. C. reeled carefully, not hard enough to antagonize him, and after what seemed a long time got him within a hundred feet, and I had a glimpse of green and silver. Then off he ran again. How unbelievably swift! He had been close – then almost the same instant he was far off.

'I saw him! On a wave!' yelled R. C. 'That's no bonefish! What can he be, anyhow? I believe I've got a barracuda!'

I looked and looked, but I could not see him.

'No matter what you think you saw, that fish is a bonefish,' I declared, positively. 'The runs he made! I saw silver and green! Careful now. I *know* he's a bonefish. And he must be big.'

'Maybe it's only the wind and waves that make him feel so strong,' replied R. C.

'No! You can't fool me! Play him for a big one. He's been on twenty-three minutes now. Stand up – I'll steady the canoe – and watch for that sudden rush when he sees the canoe. The finish is in sight.'

It was an indication of a tiring fish that he made his first circle of the canoe, but too far out for us to see him. This circling a boat is a remarkable feature, and I think it comes from the habit of a bonefish of pulling broadside. I cautioned R. C. to avoid the seaweed and to lead him a little more, but to be infinitely careful not to apply too much strain. He circled us again, a few yards closer. The third circle he did not gain a foot. Then he was on his fourth lap around the canoe, drawing closer. On his fifth lap clear round us he came near as fifty feet. I could not resist standing up to see. I got a glimpse of him and he looked long. But I did not say anything to R. C. We had both hooked too many big bonefish that got away immediately. This was another affair.

He circled us the sixth time. Six times! Then he came rather close. On this occasion he saw the canoe. He surged and sped out so swiftly that I was simply paralyzed. R. C. yelled something that had a note of admiration of sheer glory in the spirit of that fish.

'Here's where he leaves us!' I echoed.

But, as luck would have it, he stopped that run short of two hundred yards; and turned broadside to circle slowly back, allowing R. C. to get in line. He swam slower this time, and did not make the heavy tugs. He came easily, weaving to and fro. R. C. got him to within twenty-five feet of the boat, yet still could not see him. It was my job to think quick and sit still with ready hands on the anchor rope. He began to plunge, taking a little line each time. Then suddenly I saw R. C.'s line coming toward us. I knew that would happen.

'Now! Look out! Reel in fast!' I cried, tensely.

As I leaned over to heave up the anchor, I saw the bonefish flashing nearer. At that instant of thrilling excitement and suspense I could not trust my eyesight. There he was, swimming heavily, and he looked three feet long, thick and dark and heavy. I got the anchor up just as he passed under the canoe. Maybe I did not revel in pride of my quickness of thought and action!

'Oh! He's gone under the rope!' gasped R. C.

'No!' I yelled, sharply. 'Let your line run out! Put your tip down! We'll drift over your line.'

R. C. was dominated to do so, and presently the canoe drifted over where the line was stretched. That second ticklish moment passed. It had scared me. But I could not refrain from one sally.

'I got the anchor up. What did you think I'd do?'

R. C. passed by my remark. This was serious business for him. He looked quite earnest and pale.

'Say! Did you see him?' he ejaculated, looking at me.

'Wish I hadn't,' I replied.

We were drifting inshore, which was well, provided we did not drift too hard to suit the bonefish. He swam along in plain sight, and he seemed so big that I would not have gazed any longer if I could have helped it.

I kept the canoe headed in, and we were not long coming to shallow water. Here the bonefish made a final dash for freedom, but it was short and feeble, compared with his first runs. He got about twenty feet away, then sheered, showing his broad, silver side. R. C. wound him in close, and an instant later the bow of the canoe grated on shore.

'Now what?' asked R. C. as I stepped out into the water. 'Won't it be risky to lift him into the canoe?'

'Lift nothing! I have this all figured out. Lead him along.'

R. C. stepped out upon the beach while I was in the water. The bonefish lay on his side, a blaze of silver. I took hold of the line very gently and led the fish a little closer in. The water was about six inches deep. There were waves beating in – a miniature surf. And I calculated on the receding of a wave. Then with one quick pull I slid our beautiful quarry up on the coral sand. The instant he was out of the water the leader snapped. I was ready for this, too. But at that it was an awful instant! As the wave came back, almost deep enough to float the bonefish, I scooped him up.

'He's ours!' I said, consulting my watch. 'Thirty-three minutes! I give you my word that fight was comparable to ones I've had with a Pacific swordfish.'

'Look at him!' R. C. burst out. 'Look at him! When the leader broke I thought he was lost. I'm sick yet. Didn't you almost bungle that?'

'Not a chance, R. C.,' I replied. 'Had that all figured. I never put any strain on your line until the wave went back. Then I slid him out, the leader broke, and I scooped him up.'

R. C. stood gazing down at the glistening, opal-spotted fish. What a contrast he presented to any other kind of a fish! How many beautiful species have we seen lying on sand or moss or ferns, just come out of the water! But I could remember no other so rare as this bonefish. The exceeding difficulty of the capture of this, our first really large bonefish, had a great deal to do with our admiration and pride. For the hard work of any achievement is what makes it worthwhile. But this had nothing to do with the exquisite, indescribable beauty of the bonefish. He was long, thick, heavy, and round, with speed and power in every line; a sharp white nose and huge black eyes. The body of him was live, quivering silver, molten silver in the sunlight, crossed and barred with blazing stripes. The opal hues came out upon the anal fin, and the broad tail curled up, showing lavender tints on a background of brilliant blue. He weighed eight pounds. Symbolic of the mysterious life and beauty in the ocean! Wonderful and prolific as nature is on land, she is infinitely more so in the sea. By the sun and the sea we live; and I shall never tire of seeking and studying the manifold life of the deep.

Buoy 10: Salmon Fishing
in the Half Pipe

BILL MONROE

17 August 2014

ILWACO, WASHINGTON – We're on the 'firing line,' rods locked and loaded at the infamous Buoy 10 fishing deadline, where the world's largest ocean sweeps in across earth's most dangerous bar – under, around, over and across freshwater run-off draining seven states and Canada.

That the salmon beneath the boat are heading upriver into an area roughly the size of France is obscured by the more immediate challenges ... crossing rips ... 200 or 300 other boats necking into a six-knot tidal current while dodging each other ... the odd renegade newcomer wanting to troll against the crowd ... rolling whitecaps on nearby Clatsop Spit promising bitter consequences for strays ... and, of course, an approaching container ship honking five times from behind its escort posse of boats with flashing blue lights.

One can only imagine the tension on the bridge of an inbound foreign ship facing the sport armada. Last Saturday's official count from the buoy to Tongue Point was 804 boats – and that wasn't even a busy day.

Son Bill Jr. edges to an open slot in the fleet of aluminum, wood and fiberglass as the ship's passage compresses us like schooled herring into a ribbon between the red buoy line and Clatsop Spit's whitewater.

As its stern fades in the upriver journey to Portland, the fleet relaxes its accordion. Back to work.

Granddaughter Kayla's rod tip dives into the maelstrom, pumping wildly.

A large coho erupts from the surface, towing the pink flasher and heavy cannonball weight at breakneck speed in a dangerous arc. Kayla can't keep up as the salmon torpedoes straight to the boat, dives under the hull and turns west, toward the sea. A tornado of fish, teenager and son with flashing net dance around the bow; the angry fish oh-so-tantalizingly close to the net's rim . . . before it spits the hook.

Kayla smiles broadly, far from disappointed. She'll replace it moments later with a keeper in the box.

More than 200 years after Capt. William Clark wrote in his journal 'Ocian in view! O! The joy' his quote still sings in searing, orchestrated harmony with sea, ships, boats, sun and salmon.

Buoy 10 is the overture of fall salmon symphonies.

17 August 2008

WARRENTON – A new trip to Buoy 10 . . . same old, sad story.

'Let's get out over the bar, Dad! That's where the action is,' blurted my son, Bill Jr., after we launched Wednesday at the Hammond Boat Basin.

I thought about it – briefly. Then, given my sense of caution, I opted instead to stay close to the boat basin while I adjusted to all of the nuances of my wife's 'back-up IRA,' a 21-foot Arima. It's equipped to get me out of sight of land on my own ship for the first time since my days aboard a US Navy destroyer.

I named it *Tempest*, the radio call sign for the USS *George K. McKenzie*, DD 836. We even got permission from the Oregon Marine Board to use her hull number, OR 836 DDD. She has multiple electronics, VHF radio, trim tabs, a powerful outboard and automatic steering on the smaller trolling outboard. It all needed a lot of perusing on my first trip of the season to Buoy 10's storied fishery.

So did Val Perry, a friend and guide whose boat was canted sideways to the current, opposite the basin entrance; Val, net in hand, standing next to an excited angler.

'Let's work some of the kinks out of the boat,' I blurted to my son, pulling alongside Perry like a long-lost friend.

He told us to fish thirty-five feet deep with spinners or herring, and we fell in astern of his boatload of Missouri and Iowa vacationers as they hooked and netted two more Chinook to our none.

Well into the flooding tide, Perry often moves as far upriver as the 'green line' opposite Astoria and the Columbia Maritime Museum, trolling the ebb back toward the bridge.

He moved, in fact, as we debated whether to stick it out or try crossing the bar. Moments before I ordered the lines reeled in for the long trip outside, Jr.'s rod dived for the water. We landed his chunky Chinook and decided to stay put.

By afternoon, of course, as the bay's trademark north-west breeze frothed the bay into whitecaps, we still hadn't had another bite.

We heard later anglers in the ocean averaged nearly limits all around – mostly coho – a short distance beyond the river's mouth. They can thank me for that. Never would've happened if we'd shown up.

Unfortunately, though, catches were so good Wednesday, the ocean will close at 2 p.m. Sunday, which in turn will bring more boats into the bay and probably a conclusion to the inside Chinook quota of 6,500 before the end of the month.

Perry, who stands to lose repeat customers who have booked flights for late August, is willing to share these tips for salmon on both sides of the Columbia from Hammond and Chinook, Wash., upriver to Tongue Point:

- (Avoid the middle of the bay, by the way. It's very, very shallow on both sides of the bridge. Only knowledgeable locals and guides know how to cross, and that boat you're following may not belong to one of them.)

- Use divers to troll deep for Chinook, between thirty and forty feet. Coho, due in the next week or two, will be closer to the surface but will hit most of the same baits.

- Fish with large spinners (such as Toman Thumpers, T-spoons, etc.) or cutplug herring.

- Let the rear hook trail from a cutplug herring and thread it through the herring's severed head. 'Watch that spin and hold on,' Perry said. 'Works great when the bite is off a little.'

- Color herring with Pautzke's Yellow Nectar or a chartreuse dye. 'It will not stain and gives your bait a great color when you need something different,' he said.

- Use two severed herring heads hooked tip of the nose through the lower lip, one on each hook. Make sure they spin.

- Try using a herring head on a spinner hook.

22 August 2010

We fueled the boat and cleared the steel breakwater protecting the Port of Astoria's West Mooring Basin at the crack of 10 a.m. (stylishly late for devout salmon anglers), cutting into the choppy current and rippling roil of the Columbia River estuary to churn a course toward distant Clatsop Spit.

Few boats worked the green line, marking the north side of the shipping channel between the Astoria-Megler Bridge and Hammond, but I knew about where the fleet would be and pressed on to the west end of Desdemona Sands.

An armada of 200 to 300 boats, clustered tightly, was a sure sign we should have been there an hour earlier. In this day and age of cell phones and binoculars, it takes very little time for word to spread when the tide sweeps salmon in from the sea.

I moved well up-current, turned and began trolling toward the fleet. Most boats moved along the sixteen- to twenty-five-foot depth line, meandering and dodging one another as they hovered over imagined schools of coho and Chinook. Those reaching the end of the pack turned, ran back against the tide and began new down-current trolls.

It's the preferred tactic here: assume most of the salmon typically nose into the current, then troll down-current, toward them. More fish will see your bait.

But we were too late for this bite, and I was idly watching some of the guide boats pick up and race off toward the distant Megler area when a rod doubled over and throbbed wildly. Several wild minutes and spectacular jumps later, a very angry hatchery coho was in the net.

Hooked by the catch, I repeated my run instead of following the now fast-moving fleet down to Megler. Most other boats had picked up and raced off. As I should have.

We didn't get another bite, of course, and by the time I got to Megler, the tide carried most of the fleet far upriver, where the boats meandered at high slack tide.

We lingered for nearly an hour before seeing several guide boats pick up and race off again, this time crossing the bay's shallows east of the bridge, heading back for the Oregon side of the river. There are a few paths across at low tide, but high tide is relatively safe and the only shallow spot I found as I fell in behind one of the sleds still gave me a comfortable four feet beneath the keel.

The fleet now aligned itself with the ebb in a narrow band, fishing a ribbon north of the channel in twenty to thirty-five feet of water. Salmon, especially the coho dominating Thursday's catches, seem to cluster along the channel's deeper edge, from anchored freighters downriver to the green line to Hammond.

We had come full circle around the estuary, now fishing off Astoria, close to the mooring basin.

And, just before we had to leave we landed another coho, an even feistier wild fish. We carefully released it from the net to continue its way upriver as we beat back to harbor against the current.

The next day, son Bill Jr. took the same boat over the bar and scored forty-one- and forty-four-pound Chinook in the Pacific Ocean before 8:30 a.m., filling out their limits with coho by mid-afternoon.

'I guess we now know which Monroe is the best fisherman,' a friend on the boat the day before fired back after I e-mailed him photos of their fish.

28 August 2011

ASTORIA – 2010 may have been the year of the coho in the lower Columbia River estuary, but 2011 is the year of the Chinook. And the frenzy, if possible, is even more intense.

Fall Chinook salmon, all 750,000 of them, have a short arrival window between mid-August and Labor Day.

Some were even mine:

17 August: Jasmine Azpiri of Seattle, a friend since we met on a mission trip to Kenya in 2008, has scrimped and saved for a few chances on a church's fund-raising raffle to send another team to the AIDS-stricken nation. I donated two trips. Against the odds, she won one.

Her three-hour drive to Astoria was rewarded with a twenty-two-pound Chinook, the first salmon and largest fish she's ever caught. As excited as she, I was reminded of a faded black and white picture in one of my childhood albums.

It's of my mother, standing in front of our Navy housing above Tongue Point in about 1950. Like Jasmine, she's hoisting a chinook salmon nearly as tall as she is, a lunker caught in the same fishery on an old Lucky Louie plug.

The background vista is the estuary, minus the bridge (there was a ferry then). Six decades later, the smiles are identical.

19 August: Son-in-law Jarod Jebousek of Corvallis and his buddy Pete Dryden of Astoria join me trolling on the Washington side of the Astoria-Megler Bridge. Jarod has already caught his Chinook and Pete has just hooked a much larger fish.

But then it takes off madly toward distant Astoria, peeling line from the reel. A harbor seal has it in tow, so we give chase, Pete barely keeping up on the reel.

We finally gain enough to be on top of the seal, which lets go.

The salmon fights some more then the seal has it again ... more chase ... seal drops the fish ... seal picks up the fish ... more chase.

After the third dash, Pete pulls the salmon between the outboards and I get it into the net. The seal surfaces twenty yards off and delivers a barrage of marine mammal invective.

The Chinook is barely scratched.

20 August: Brother Jim (yes, a minister), Jeff Hamilton of Grand Junction, Colorado, myself and Owin Hays of Portland ('Outdoor GPS' host) are guests of Buzz Ramsey, product manager for Yakima Bait and a regional fishing icon.

I forget the herring, but the unflappable Ramsey just happens to have some tackle in his brightly signed and painted boat.

Dawn breaks over a calm bay, squadrons of pelicans skimming in formation across the golden horizon.

Hamilton, a retired US Coast Guard captain, C-130 pilot and former commandant of the Astoria district who lived in quarters on Tongue Point, is circumspect on a day in which he will release several wild coho, but only Hays and I go home with Chinook.

'This is an entirely different perspective for me,' he quips with a wry smile.

23 August: Pete and I are joined by Darrell Ehl of Happy Valley and troll helplessly on the Washington side of the bridge in the midst of the hottest fishing in my memory. Ours seems like the only boat without a fish in the box.

We try everything, even follow guide Bob Rees for a while, but can only watch him net fish.

Our last gasp finds us off Astoria, near the anchored ship line, when we suddenly can do no wrong. Inside of an hour, we hook and land three cookie-cutter upriver bright Chinook, twenty-pounders.

24 August: Marty Lindstrand of Beaverton and his dad Bud Lindstrand of Cornelius are winners of a donated trip for a silent auction by the Oregon Wildlife Heritage Foundation.

Despite my bad decisions leaving us at the tail end of several flurries of action, Marty lands a nice seventeen-pounder and his dad releases a few wild coho.

We make our way above Tongue Point, where Bud lands two jacks after I call another friend, Steve Nehl of Scappoose and his wife, Liz, to tell them there are fish being caught off Rice Island.

Steve calls back less than half an hour after arriving. He's landed a thirty-seven-pound monster.

26 August: I team with retired State Marine Board director Paul Donheffner and a friend, Dan Shipman of Silverdale, Washington, in a fundraiser for the Northwest Sportfishing Industry Association.

It's another skunk day, but no last-hour silver bullets this time. More than 200 anglers in the event land more than six dozen salmon, up to thirty-one pounds.

No one feels like a loser.

19 August 2012

ASTORIA – If I wasn't wearing it, at least I knew my auto-inflatable lifejacket was nestled next to my seat.

And, if the next wave over the bow didn't activate it, I mentally reviewed my chances of slipping at least one arm through the strap before we flipped beneath a crashing whitecap.

'HANG ON!' my son shouted over the wind, waves and roaring jet outboard.

He'd seen a clear passage in the sudden, unexpected melee of six-footers outside the entrance to the Port of Astoria's West Mooring Basin and gunned the engine, shooting cleanly across the face of an angry, pre-cresting wave.

The sled glided safely into calm water in the lee of the seawall.

Fishing Buoy 10 is no cakewalk.

Farther west, a popular and seasoned fishing guide had his own set of problems when the trademark afternoon 'Nor'wester' suddenly intensified across the Columbia's long reach. (The wind here was soundly criticized by Meriwether Lewis more than two centuries ago.)

Faced with a long, wet ride in an open sled from Chinook to Astoria, he took off in the maelstrom of whitecaps and following seas, but on the way back lost his automatic bilge pump and found himself in ankle-deep water.

Fortunately, he'd installed scuppers with plugs that make his open sled self-bailing. He pulled them and cleared the water enough to maneuver his way to port – just after we entered, by the way, behind a tug in tow that helped churn the water even higher in the main shipping channel outside the basin seawall.

Lessons learned?

- Prepare for the unexpected. It will eventually happen and you don't want to be unprepared.

- Wear your inflatable. I usually do, but over, not beneath, my raingear, which we'd put on for the typically wet (spray) ride in from the Washington side of the river. I inadvertently forgot to put it back on. Since inflatables appeared on the market, I've been pleased to see more than half of boaters wearing them at all times. It just makes sense.

- Fish with a boat handler you trust. From a childhood culminating in fast cars, son Bill Jr. has matured into marriage, fatherhood, a profession of daily emergencies – and sometimes-deadly medical situations – as an ambulance EMT, and extreme skill at the helm of a sled. I like to think I probably could have handled the boat just fine if I'd been on the tiller, but the fact is I'm glad he was there. His judgment and anticipation are every bit as good as mine once were.

- ... (But I'm still going to wear that inflatable; or at least tell someone to remind me.)

1 September 2013

Among my most treasured possessions is 'Killer,' a fishing rod so important to me I won't hand it to even my closest friends because I don't want to jeopardize our relationship should an accident happen.

I do let my wife catch fish with it because she seems to like being constantly hugged from behind.

The blank was given to me for my fortieth birthday (1984) and I built the rod myself, with red, white and blue wrappings tinged with gold. Killer has caught countless salmon, walleye, sturgeon, a halibut (incidental in Puget Sound while salmon fishing), albacore tuna and all the attendant incidentals.

He (yes, it's a family member) was miraculously overlooked during a burglary some years back. Horrified that Killer might have been taken too, relief engulfed me in a wave when I found and locked him up, before even calling the cops or my insurance agent.

Most of us have a 'Killer' in our rod rack.

Most of us except at least one, that is.

A couple weeks ago, son Bill Jr. was guiding friends when one of their rods bent over and stayed bent rather than pulsing with a salmon. The tackle caught on someone else's line, one end of it firmly attached to a fish and the other to a rod and reel that was also boated.

But it's not just any new rod and reel that took a dive overboard during the melee at Astoria this summer.

It's an older rod of a well-recognized brand, its sweat-worn cork handle dark with patina, pocked with missing chunks . . . and a few fish scales still stuck to its finish, even after the extended bath.

This rod is someone's 'Killer' and, having survived the horror of nearly losing mine, we'd all like to see it returned and hear some of its stories.

So please, if you lost your rod to a vicious salmon strike or know someone who did (hopefully not your or their former fishing partner), please contact me. I'll need a pretty accurate description of the set-up and then hope to share its storied history.

. . . Or else the boys will use it to create their own future memories.

8 September 2013

Destiny trumps Charity.

Charity Houston, that is, an eleven-year-old from New Plymouth, Idaho, who fished 15 August with her mother, Joyce Houston, and uncle, Tom Partin of Lake Oswego.

Partin let her use the family standby, a stiff, single-piece, thirty-year-old vintage Lamiglas rod with a newer red Ambassadeur reel. They boated a nice hatchery coho and let the lines back out. Almost immediately, Charity's rod took a dive as a Chinook salmon struck.

Charity, who doesn't see many salmon in Idaho, tried to reel but the fish fought back; so for help from her uncle, she began to hand it his way – just as the angry salmon made its savage 'boat run,' typical of a Chinook.

The rod shot from her fingers and Partin barely missed a game-saving catch.

'My sister said she wished she had a photo of the looks on our faces,' Partin said. 'Our jaws just dropped. I didn't want to make a big deal out of it for Charity's sake. We had a good laugh instead.'

Later that morning, my son and his crew snagged the line and recovered both the exhausted and still-hooked fish (a twenty-pounder) and the rod and reel.

Partin's destiny was fulfilled when he read about the incident and contacted me, describing the rig right down to the wrapping on the sliding hooks. We knew it was someone's treasure, encrusted with patina, fish scales and memories.

Partin and I met up Friday and the rod is back in the right boat.

Turns out there were numerous rods lost there this year and even in past years. (Had to tell one hopeful that not only was it not his favorite Eagle Claw/Penn reel combo pulled from its holder by a large salmon five years ago, but also that it was highly unlikely the Chinook would have survived.)

Long, rich stories unfolded in the anglers' losses: rods from deceased family members, others fresh off the store shelves (one the morning of the loss). There must be a virtual sporting goods store on the bottom of the Columbia River estuary.

Like those, this rod also has a history.

Partin's son, Nick, thirty-two, of Estacada, who got it for his sixth birthday, estimates it's caught about 650 various salmon and steelhead, more than a dozen sturgeon while trolling for salmon, a handful of sharks, 100 or so pikeminnows and even fought off a few sea lions, accidentally hooked after their trademark salmon thefts.

The best memory, he said, was off the south jetty at Tillamook Bay. Nick Partin was only eight but clearly remembers hooking what they believed to be a fifty-plus-pound Chinook salmon. 'All of a sudden, a 140-pound halibut surfaced at the end of the line,' he said. 'For many years it was the only salmon rod I owned. I've moved up to others, but it's been a great old standby.'

(For the record, his father believes the halibut they released was closer to 100 pounds, maybe the rod caught a good bit fewer than 100 pikeminnows and perhaps it hasn't filled quite that many salmon tags.)

It's nice to know in this day and age of soundbite journalism and instant gratification from smartphones and the Internet, people still participate in the ancient ritual of storytelling. And they do so through memories found in such simple inanimate objects that seamlessly become the keys to our family lore.

Tom Partin refused his sister's offer to replace the outfit.

'I figured it was just payback,' he said. 'I was pretty sure somebody would hook onto it. I mostly hoped they would get as much good use out of it as we have.'

9 August 2015

ASTORIA – The Steller sea lion made only one mistake.

Buzz Ramsey didn't.

Ramsey, an angling industry and salmon-fishing icon, was having an uncharacteristic, challenging day after losing three Chinook salmon during our busman's holiday at Buoy 10.

Son Bill Jr. hosted us, trolling above the Megler side of the bridge down across the edge of Desdemona Sands to the checkerboard, where salmon linger in swirling riptides as converging currents meet on the ebb and split on the flood.

Noon approached with only Ramsey lacking his one-fish Chinook limit as we pulled in front of the Hammond harbor entrance.

Within moments, a rod went off and Buzz fought yet another angry Chinook from the bow.

Behind his back, a large Steller sea lion surfaced astern to get his bearings on the flashing net in Bill Jr.'s hand.

His bad.

We shouted a warning, and salmon-expert Buzz Ramsey micro-morphed into trout mode.

Reeling madly (and in this sequence), Buzz manhandled the heavy salmon to the surface and almost literally into the net; Bill did a heave-ho into the boat ... and the sea lion popped to the surface in the middle of the still boiling water beside the boat, glaring at us.

We shouted like teenagers at a rock concert and headed happily to port.

The Man in the Fish Tote

TELE AADSEN

7 SEPTEMBER 2012 is a bad day on the ocean.

With the forecast calling for south-east winds of thirty-five knots and eleven-foot seas, the *Nerka* spends Friday morning trolling in the mouth of Gilmer Bay. We hadn't expected to be fishing at all today. If we catch anything, we reason, they'll be bonus fish, and we'll already be safe in the harbor's arms when the wind comes up. On Day Thirteen of a grueling trip, a relaxing afternoon on anchor sounds good.

We eat lunch on the pick shortly after the wind bares its teeth, but any further thought of relaxing whooshes overboard with the building gusts. By early afternoon, eight trollers cluster on the bay's southern shelf, straining taut anchor lines. Our companions are forty-eight-foot fiberglass and steel rigs, sturdy, seaworthy vessels. As seaworthy as any of us can be. With September's onslaught of fall weather, no one wants to push their luck. Winner of the tough guy award, the final arrival drops his anchor at 3.00.

Whitecaps slam-dance between boats as the wind holds steady at thirty-nine knots. The gusts are dragon's breath, visibly rip-snorting through the bay. An elderly wooden troller, located several hours away behind St. Lazaria Island, begins taking on water, and one of our harbor mates drags anchor. As the captain naps, his boat shoots clear across the anchorage as if sail-powered, pausing a quarter-mile from the rocks. Another troller is charging over to alert him, when he wakes in time to avert disaster.

Darkness brings a rare pardon. The man taking on water reports that he's safe for the night. The gusts let up and the whitecaps come down. The dragon goes to sleep, and so do Joel and I. Deep in relieved dreams, neither of us hears the Coast Guard's midnight call to any vessels anchored in Gilmer Bay.

Saturday begins at 4.30, when Joel pulls the anchor and we run into the pitch black. Out Gilmer Bay, past Point Amelia, to Beaver Point. Though dawn is an hour away, so is the spot we want to drop our hooks. After the previous day's frenzied conditions, the sea's remaining bounce feels gentle.

When our fishing partner Marlin joins us on the drag, his voice is grave. 'There's a boat missing. That's why they were calling all of us in the anchorage last night, to see if they'd made it in there.' He describes a twenty-eight-foot troller, 'landing-craft style' – an open vessel rigged with a couple of davits and outboard motors. 'I've passed it in the straits. Can't remember the name, but they always wave as they go by.'

Fishermen are never a stronger community than in times like this. When tragedy cuts one of us down, we all bleed. We throw judgment to staunch the flow of fear; our anxiety turns hot, acrid. Envisioning the worst as foregone conclusions, our anger is that of parents waiting for a teenager out long past curfew. We talk about the 'big boats' that holed up tight or headed for town, and curse, 'What the fuck were they *doing* out there?'

All morning, the Coast Guard's orange bird buzzes Kruzof Island. The usual fishing chatter is eerily absent from the VHF. Throughout the fleet, we all turn up the volume, lean in to follow the helicopter's search updates.

Midday, the Sitka Mountain Rescue reports debris at Shoal Point. Hearts seize. 'Debris' is code for an oil slick on the water, drifting buckets, maritime tombstones marking the site where a boat went down. But the helicopter quickly disputes this sighting. 'The debris is tsunami-related, we can see the Japanese writing.' The search goes on.

At 1.40, the State Trooper patrol vessel *Courage* calls the Coast Guard. 'We've got one survivor in sight on the beach at Point Amelia. He's waving, ambulatory, and appears to be OK. If you've got a helo you can send, landing's gonna be tough.'

The response is immediate. 'We're about four minutes out, eight miles away.'

'It's a very steep, cliff-y area,' the Trooper warns. 'You're gonna have to use a hoist.'

'Roger that. Thanks for the help.'

* * *

Though Joel and I are alone on the *Nerka*, I swear the cabin rings with every other troller's cries of relief when the pilot's voice comes through the speakers. 'We've got one survivor on board.'

Thanks to the alert man's explanations, the pilot relays previously unknown details. We learn they went down off Beaver Point at 2.30 on Friday afternoon. *The last troller came into Gilmer at 3.00,* I remember. *An hour's run . . . He would've been right in front of them.*

Joel interrupts my pensive thoughts with his own. 'Dude. When we smelled the gas . . .'

Trolling along Beaver Point several hours earlier, we'd gotten a sudden whiff of gas. Marlin had, too, and had asked his deckhand to check that their skiff motor wasn't leaking. But there'd been no rainbow sheen on the water. The ghostly vapors were gone almost as soon as we'd smelled them.

Now we stare at each other in too-late dawning horror. 'Holy shit. That was their boat we were smelling.'

'Shit. I didn't even think . . . We should've let them know, gotten them on the scene a few hours earlier.'

Guilt is a cold shroud, and I shudder.

Now, thanks to the located survivor, the Coast Guard issues a Pan Pan radio call with additional information.

'The Coast Guard has received a report of zero-one persons in the water in the vicinity of Gilmer Bay. The person is described as a male wearing an olive green float coat, dark blue fishing pants, located in or near a light blue fish tote. All vessels in the vicinity are requested to keep a sharp look-out, assist if possible, and report all sightings. This is Coast Guard Sector Juneau, out.'

Not a survival suit – a float coat. I glance at the clock. It's been almost twenty-four hours since they went down. Fear again spits forth as frustration. *Oh, for god's sake. An olive green float coat? Wear stuff that allows you to be found!* Ahead, the coastline lurks through south-east Alaska's omnipresent ocean mist. Dense dark forest meets a charcoal shore. I glance down at myself – black fleece pants, black thermal shirt – and make a silent vow. From here on out, I will select fish clothes as if my life depends on them.

By 2.00, forecasted 'light winds' have escalated to a snarling twenty-seven knots. With the wind comes sideways rain. The fish stopped biting after a few good tacks; now Joel and I loiter in the cabin's warmth, ignoring our empty lines. 'This is stupid,' he finally says. 'We've had a good trip. Let's stack 'em and get going to town.'

The logical route back to Sitka is to run south, around Cape Edgecumbe and into Sitka Sound. But it's gotten shitty, and we'd be bucking right into it. We opt to run up the coast instead, tacking an extra ten miles onto the journey, to duck into Salisbury Sound and double back down to Sitka by way of the blissful calm of Neva and Olga Straits.

The *Nerka* charges along at 6.5 knots as Joel and I follow the radio conversation between the Coast Guard and the Trooper vessel. They've combed the entirety of Gilmer Bay and the surrounding area. 'Have you looked off-shore?' one asks the other. They haven't yet, but will run five miles out and begin tacking up.

'If he went off-shore, that's like looking for a needle in a haystack.' Joel turns to me. 'You know, we're running this way, anyway. Let's angle out and keep an eye out.'

I nod. 'Sounds good.'

'Keeping an eye out' is easier said than done. With dense cloud cover sitting heavy on the water, visibility has deteriorated to less than a half-mile. The seas are battleship gray, punctuated with white curlers that smack the *Nerka*'s port hindquarter as we angle offshore. We take a couple nasty rolls, traveling in the trough. I'm ashamed of my relief when Joel clicks the autopilot to the starboard.

He studies the chart on the computer screen. 'The helicopter said they already flew at two miles and didn't see anything. We're at two miles now, so let's angle in and run the one-and-a-half mile line up to Salisbury.'

I perch at the starboard windows while Joel surveys the area to our port, binoculars snug against his eyes. The glasses twitch at every paddling seabird. We simultaneously gasp at a head bobbing towards us. It disappears under the surface, then slowly pops up for a closer look – a head of bull kelp.

He shakes his head. 'Amazing how something like this makes the ocean seem like such a huge, lonely place.'

For the next thirty-five minutes, we stare into the sea. Loud silence settles in the cabin, until Joel breaks it. 'Can you imagine what that guy must be going through? Bobbing around in this weather, no idea where he is or if anyone'll find him.'

I don't voice my terrible thought: *I don't expect he's going through anything anymore.* Adrift in these conditions all night and all day, no survival suit, totally dependent on a plastic tote that may or may not still be upright?

Moments later, Joel says what I didn't. 'If they haven't found him by now . . . I think that guy's a goner.'

'Yeah.'

Still we look. Everyone does.

When I leave the window, it feels like kneeling to defeat. I cut an apple, slice some cheese. Neither of us is hungry. The food sits on the table like an accusation.

'THERE!' Joel leaps up from the pilot seat, pointing out the window with one suddenly shaky hand, yanking the throttle down with the other. 'What's that?'

Immediately ahead, sixty feet to our port, a blue tote wallows among the waves. It lists heavily to one side. The opening faces away from us. Another dreadful thought pops into my mind. Is a body weighing it down?

Joel fumbles with the knotted coil of the radio mic. 'Coast Guard Juneau, this is the *Nerka*. We've got a blue tote in front of us. I can't see anyone in it, but –'

Our shrieks mingle. 'There's another one!'

Several hundred yards ahead bobs a second sky-blue vessel. This one sits upright – and a tiny dark spot peeks out of the top.

'He's in that one!' Words shrill with disbelief. 'He's waving – he's alive!'

While Joel relays our position to the Coast Guard, I run up to the bow. The man in the tote stretches his arms wide overhead, raising and lowering them without pause. I mirror his movements, waving wildly. *Holy shit, man – you're alive!*

Adrenaline makes me foolish. I'm scrambling for buoys, lines, wondering how we'll pull him out of the water, when Joel sticks his head out of the helm window. 'The helo's already almost here; they'll pick him up.' Even as he says the words, an enormous thrum reverberates through our bodies. Suddenly we're inside a blender; the waves flare in dense rotor wash as the helicopter descends through the cloud ceiling and hovers above.

We aren't close enough to shout to the man in the tote. Even if the sea didn't yawn between us, the wind and helicopter would drown our voices. So I stand on the bow and continue to wave, hoping he'll be able to translate the prayerful thoughts in these gestures. *You made it through, sweetie, they've got you. You're gonna be OK, they've got you. They've got you.*

Joel puts the boat back into gear and runs us away from the scene, wanting to be out of the way. Then we stand in the cockpit to watch. I hold my breath as the rescue swimmer descends into the water – so fast! – and leans into the tote. *What does that first moment of physical human contact feel like,* I wonder. Had the man in the tote wondered if he'd never feel touch other than the ocean's assault, the wind and rain's stinging slap? Or had he maintained hope through the night's darkest hours?

Forty-three seconds. That's how quickly the Coast Guard has the basket down to the water, the man fastened in, and back into the helicopter. They hoist the rescue swimmer back up next, and the helo rises. The abandoned tote shudders in the rotor wash.

Joel climbs out of the cockpit. 'OK. Let's get going.'

He ducks out of the sideways rain, back into the warmth of the *Nerka's* cabin, and the engine revs back up to traveling speed. I stay on deck for a moment longer. Tears I wasn't aware of mingle with the rain on my cheeks, and my arms open once more in that wide windmilling motion. Slow with gratitude now, I wave to the helicopter, wishing again that body language translated.

You guys are amazing. Thank you. Thank you. Thank you.

At 4.07, the pilot calls the Sitka Air Station. 'Be advised, we've got the survivor on board.' Asked if they'd need medical services on scene upon their arrival, the pilot replies that it'd be a good precaution, 'but his vitals are good.'

The man in the tote lands in Sitka at 4.31 p.m., Saturday, 8 September 2012.

Fish

JUDITH BARRINGTON

I AM STANDING AT the draining board in our rented apartment looking down at a neat row of fish. I don't know what they are, since the fish market in this small Andalusian village is too noisy for me to hear the names, which probably don't correspond, anyway, to the correct Castilian they taught me at school.

The fish are whole. Each one has a head, a tail and a body, all joined together. And inside, guts. Each head has two eyes, which stare as I wave the small, sharp knife around in the air and contemplate the removal of these guts – a job I have never had to do before, although I am forty-three years old. Something about this gives me pause. I am hearing my mother's voice. Memories of my father hover around too, although I never hear his voice; he visits me in a series of blurred images, always at a distance, and often with a fishing rod in his hand. There was one summer, I remember, when I tried to bridge that distance, a summer when my mother's voice temporarily faded out and my father's image grew sharper...

* * * * *

That summer – 1954 I think it was – I tried fishing. Really tried. Before that, I had often gone with my father to row the boat, and I knew how to dip the oars without splashing as we stalked the big trout off the island at Posingworth Lake. I knew, too, how it felt hunched in the bow of the motorboat two miles off Shoreham, as we trolled for mackerel, and how slowly time passed when

228

we sat with our lines out, bottom fishing, while the swell rolled under us with a corkscrew twist that left my stomach hanging. But I wasn't really committed.

My mother despised fishing. She refused to have anything to do with it, although sometimes she would come out to Posingworth late in the day with a picnic tea, and we'd all sprawl on damp needles, where pines stood guard in front of the rhododendron wall. Once, choosing a patch of sun-warmed bracken, I almost sat on two adders coiled like an anchor rope still gleaming from the water.

Even though I admired my mother's tirades against those fools who hung around all day waiting for fish to swallow their hooks, from time to time I would go off with the men – my father and brother, my brother-in-law (under duress) and occasionally our family doctor, a Scot with a deadly accurate cast. My mother had long since given up: she got seasick fishing and sometimes even on a mirror-smooth lake; she hated the smell of wet wool; and it was, she said, *quite dreadful* if you actually caught a fish. The final insult was that she had to clean the fish my father caught, so we could cook them on the campfire and eat them with blackened potatoes in tin foil.

'We're not all that poor,' she used to say. 'The fishmonger has nice fresh trout, and they come with the innards already out' – my mother would never say guts – 'and no heads either. I can't stand the way they look at you with those reproachful pop-eyes.'

It was my mother who pointed out every year that the trout season opened on 1 April, and what more fitting comment could there be than that? And it was she who turned every mishap into a family story, poking fun at the fishermen. For example, when the three men went out from Brighton beach one freezing Boxing Day and capsized in the surf on their way in again, my mother recounted the event with triumphant satisfaction to all her bridge friends. Could my father really have dived down over and over as she described, surfacing only to yell, 'The fish, the fish! Save the fish!' while my brother tried to prevent the boat from being swept out to France, and my brother-in-law staggered around the beach in confusion because he had lost his glasses? I do remember that night, in the dress circle of the Theatre Royal, my father and brother sneezing throughout the play, while my brother-in-law, who couldn't see where the stage was, snored loudly. My mother's expression conveyed her certainty that this was the final proof: fishing was either caused by, or led to, insanity.

More often than not in these early years, I threw my lot in with my mother and sister, who spent a good deal of time playing the piano, the viola and the record player. I joined them with my array of recorders and, later, my clarinet. Until the summer of '54, that is, when, at the age of ten, I temporarily abandoned the female stronghold and joined the hard-core anglers, which had the overtones of a significant choice in a family that was divided along gender lines into two camps: the sportsmen on one side, the musicians and artists on the other.

As usual, my father organized our holiday around fishing, and we went to Scotland, just the three of us, since my brother and sister were old enough to holiday by themselves. The hotel in the Highlands was a huge stone mansion, once the seat of some powerful clan with its own tartan, whose crest still adorned the plates and silverware. Seen from the long approach across a heather-covered moor, it made sense of that Scots word *dour*: it cried out for mist and howling dogs – but in vain. That summer the sun shone and the sky was blue, and I was enchanted.

We stayed at Craiglynne for three weeks and the first week was warm, though a cool breeze ruffled the surface of the belfry pool, where 'the old preacher,' a salmon reputed to weigh at least thirty-five pounds, was believed to live. Inside the hotel's two-foot-thick stone walls, it was cool and dark, and in the library there was always a blazing fire, which someone told us they lit every day, year in year out. For two or three days, I retreated to one of the chimney seats and read my way through numerous Agatha Christies and James Bonds. After lunch, my mother would insist that I join her in a brisk walk on the moors with the dogs.

As the weather got hotter and stiller in the second week, I took to wandering on the moors by myself. One day, I sat on a rock high above the river, which cut a path through purple heather and was flanked by bands of lush grass rapidly fading to brown. Two lines of silver birches sprouted from this grass, shading the banks. Down there below the bend, where the current swept wide into a pool, my father stood in his thigh-waders, casting upstream. I watched him for a long time as he moved slowly toward the pool, throwing the line rhythmically, his head shaded by a tweed hat that, I knew, was stuck full of flies, though I couldn't see them from my viewpoint. I watched him untangle his line from one of the birches, patiently clinging to a root with one hand while he worked the fly free with his other. If he muttered, I was too far away to hear; up there on the wide moor, I could hear only the cries of buzzards and the occasional chirp of a grasshopper. I watched for a very long time and then decided that this summer I would catch my first salmon.

My father was surprised by my sudden enthusiasm. I demanded use of the small rod, a supply of flies in a tackle box and my own permit. Waders didn't matter: I simply put on my very small pink shorts and some old tennis shoes that would allow me to clamber over the rocky river bottom. This was unorthodox and made my father uncomfortable, but he acquiesced, only too glad of some support in the family. Indeed his jubilation was such that I later wondered if he battled a few pangs of guilt at dragging my mother and me along on these fishing trips.

We strode off together in the early morning, laden with canvas bag and fish basket, landing net and tackle box. At the river we would separate, each to our own beat, which saved me the embarrassment of admitting how many flies I lost in the birch trees. I really wanted to catch a salmon. Surely, if I cast the fly just right and hit those deep pools under the tree roots, I'd feel the fish grab. But nothing happened. Morning after morning, in between the hours I spent hooking tussocks of grass, clusters of leaves and sometimes even my own clothes, I made several perfect casts. But not one of them enticed a salmon.

I was easily disheartened. It didn't seem fair that perfect casting did not result in fish. I could understand not catching one when the line was wound around a tree trunk or the fly was slapping the water with a huge leaf attached to it, but I couldn't accept that perfect skill should go unrewarded. It never had before: if I studied, I passed the exams – in fact, I often passed without studying; if I practised piano, I could play Bach preludes from memory. But here was something I wanted badly and was prepared to learn to do right, and it wasn't working. I couldn't make that large silver fish swirl to the surface and grab my fly.

My father said the river was too low. The hotel proprietor said it was the heat. The gillie said it was the laird over the hill, who had diverted too much water from his stream to irrigate a rock garden. The only consolation was that nobody else caught anything either. The stuffed fish in glass cases on each landing of the wide staircase seemed to be grinning with delight at all the disgruntled conversations. 'Terrible weather,' the guests agreed as they passed each other on the stairs in their plus fours or mid-calf tweed skirts, which never varied, despite the eighty-degree weather.

The third week was unprecedented as the thermometer crept towards ninety and the library fire went unlit. I stopped fishing altogether and found a spot where I could lie on the bank under the birch trees and look into one of the still pools. The water was clean and the pebbles on the bottom distinct. Their bluish gray tones reminded me of the beach and seemed incongruous here in this clear brown water flowing between peat banks. The sun pierced the shade like a small spotlight and gnawed into the small of my back till sweat began to run down towards my waist.

I had been lying like this for an hour or two one day, when I noticed what looked like some logs lying in the pool, but it seemed unlikely as the branches of the overhanging trees were much more slender than these hefty objects. Suddenly, one of the logs turned around – not fast, but not pushed by the current either. It turned quite deliberately and faced the other way. Immediately, I saw that the logs were salmon, six of them, basking in the tropical water.

'Only way anyone could catch salmon in that state of mind would be by dapping,' grunted my father, when I told him what I had seen. 'The river's probably full of the lazy beasts just lying there. You can see them easily in this weather.'

For the rest of our vacation, I wandered the river banks spotting salmon. Anywhere the current was not too fast, you could see them, fat and happy. A few fish fell to an illegally dapped fly upstream from the hotel, and the dining room buzzed with the news when the poacher was caught, but mostly they just lay around as if they, too, were on holiday, and I grew very fond of them. My mother and I and the dogs walked as usual, and the men, cooped up in the hotel with nothing better to do but boast of other years when the weather was better, fumed. And every day I went to look at the happy salmon, until I knew without a doubt that my mother was right: it would be *quite dreadful* if I caught one.

That was almost my last attempt at fishing and at infiltrating my father's world. My mother never said a word about it, though I'm sure she was glad to have me back. She enjoyed that holiday and always spoke of it with a certain fondness. I'm not sure if it was because the men were frustrated in their foolishness or if it was because of my obvious pleasure at the salmon's refusal to co-operate...

* * * * *

I am standing over the pink-gilled Spanish fish with a knife in my hand, and my mother's voice is complaining: 'I do wish they'd sell them with the innards *out*.' In my mind, the fishmonger becomes my father, imposing this messy task on us females. And my father ... where is he? Has he, as usual, deposited his fish and disappeared until they are cleaned, cooked and sitting on a plate? Why is he so damned invisible?

As I make a neat incision into the belly of the first fish, I remember that the summer at Craiglynne was not, in fact, my last attempt to make sense of my father's world. It must have been '66 or thereabouts, after both he and my mother were dead, when I found myself in Scotland again, touring for a few days with a friend. We stopped at a mill with a little shop. To my surprise, I purchased a tweed hat in soft heather tones. The next day I bought a fly rod and several boxes of flies, some of which I stuck into the hat. Then, armed with a permit and some boots, I strode over the moor to a small hill loch, where I fished in the mist for nine hours without seeing a single trout. My friend thought I was insane, and I hardly knew how to explain, driven by some urge I didn't understand myself. But that truly was my last attempt. To this day, the pleasures of fishing elude me, and my father has not yet emerged from the mist.

Still, slicing the undersides of these fish, scraping off the translucent scales and piling the reproachful heads into the garbage, I am astonished at how familiar it all seems. I know how my mother would have felt about it as the scales glisten on my hands and the knife cuts clean. But I am quite enjoying the task. Somewhere along the way I must have learned there were more than two camps.

The Trout Man

MATT LOVE

I WAS SITTING IN Hoover's, a dive bar in Newport, Oregon, on a dull summer afternoon, when Debbie the cook came out from the kitchen, walked over to my table, and said, 'Do you want some fresh trout?'

'What?' I said, dumbfounded. 'Trout?'

I'd never tasted it.

Debbie said that Garrid, a regular who ran Hoover's karaoke nights, liked to fish for trout but detested eating them.

Did I want some? Well ... maybe ... well ... why not?

'But I don't know how to clean them,' I said.

'He cleans them up and then I store them bagged in ice in the refrigerator,' said Debbie. 'Give me your phone number and he'll call.'

So I did, and never expected to hear anything.

Two days later I received a call in the afternoon from an unfamiliar number and answered it. It was Garrid, and he had fresh trout waiting for me at Hoover's. 'Come down and get them,' he said. 'I caught them today.'

I drove immediately to the bar, walked in, and was barely ten feet inside the door when Debbie greeted me holding a bag full of ice containing what I guess is called a 'mess' of trout. Garrid was nowhere around and that left me keenly disappointed. Who catches trout, cleans them, calls up a total stranger to meet him in a bar, and offers up his entire catch because he doesn't like the taste of trout? This is someone I must know.

Debbie handed over the bag and there I stood inside Hoover's on a weekday afternoon in April with absolutely no idea how to cook trout. I told Debbie to thank Garrid and I left, too embarrassed to ask her how to cook the fish.

Back home, I called my stepfather in Canby. He had caught a million trout in his Oregon life. I asked how to cook them and he described a half dozen allegedly delicious methods ranging from poaching to barbecuing. I listened to him, unconvinced, probably because staring at the trout in the plastic bag unnerved me in a way that reminded me of standing naked in the front of a mirror and feeling hung over to the roof. But an unusual Oregon story was in obvious play so I had to see it through.

It was sunny and hot and I didn't want to stink up the house so I lit a small fire in the burn barrel and watched it burn while sitting in a lawn chair, drinking a cheap beer, and reading the new Jim Harrison novel.

Twenty minutes later, after adding lemon, white wine, butter, black pepper and tarragon to the fish, I wrapped the experiment in foil and banked it in the coals. I watched it cook while the dogs, Sonny and Ray, rested on the grass a few feet away.

I burrowed into Harrison for another chapter and then unwrapped the foil, poked at the trout with a piece of kindling from the wood pile. The fish seemed ready. I picked some radishes, peas and strawberries from the garden and placed them alongside the trout on a paper plate. I looked at the meal for a moment and then began eating it with my hands.

It was indisputably the best meal I'd ever cooked and I ate it standing up in my back yard. The dogs finished the rest of the trout and licked the plate spotless. Then Sonny ate the plate. I reclined on the lawn, read more of Harrison, and dozed off.

Two days later I got another call from Garrid. More trout. Then a week later, more trout. Soon I was eating cold trout for breakfast and trout and tomato sandwiches for lunch.

Garrid intrigued me and I began investigating him. I learned that he lived nearby and washed cars at a car lot. I also learned that he was very serious about his karaoke duties. One afternoon I was sitting at the bar writing in my journal when a tall man wearing his black hair in a ponytail walked in. It had to be Garrid. He sat a few stools down and I got up, went over and introduced myself, and thanked him for the trout.

Almost a year later, my book about Newport had just come out and it proved a big hit in Hoover's because the regulars love hearing crazy stories about drinking almost as much as they love living crazy stories about drinking.

I had written about Hoover's in the book, including a piece about Garrid and his trout. He called me and said he liked the book and had more trout waiting for me at Hoover's.

A day later I picked up the trout and cooked it up. I still hadn't seen Garrid since the book's release and I wanted to thank him in person for being such a good sport, so I dropped by on a Friday evening before his karaoke shift started.

Sure enough, Garrid was there, with a couple of other regulars, sitting on stools out on the deck, smoking, bullshitting. He stood up when he saw me, came over, and we shook hands.

'I've got some more trout for you back at home. Let me go get it,' he said.

'That would be great,' I said.

Garrid then went over to the sound system and played a new *longer* version of Peter Frampton's 'Do You Feel Like We Do,' which clocked in at nearly fifteen minutes on *Frampton Comes Alive*. He exited Hoover's to go across the street where he lived to fetch the trout. He never once looked in a hurry.

He was back before Frampton got into it on the talk box.

After stashing the trout in the refrigerator, Garrid came over to me. I was alternately drinking a beer, reading a newspaper and writing a letter.

'Thank you,' I said. 'I want to buy you a whiskey. What do you drink?'

'Well, whiskey,' he said.

'Fuck that! What's your favorite brand?'

'I never drink on the job,' he said.

A pro.

'I'll buy you one after the show,' I said.

He agreed and I told the bartender to make sure he got a double of whatever he wanted. The good shit.

Garrid then started telling Hoover's stories. Naturally, they were all priceless, but one towered above the rest. A name: Stevie Nicks, as in *the* Stevie Nicks, who stopped into Hoover's one night a few years ago with her brother on a drive down 101 to a show in the Bay Area. Garrid had been there, with at least one sodden regular at the bar. He claimed he knew Stevie from way back from his stint in the celebrity business in Los Angeles. He was the Trout Man so I believed him.

So the Stevie story went, she sang *a couple of her songs* on the karaoke machine. After 'Stand Back,' Garrid joined her for a duet of 'Stop Draggin' My Heart Around.' When Stevie left, the sodden regular remarked that the woman who just sang sure sounded like Stevie Nicks.

It was time to go and Garrid went to retrieve the trout. I walked over to the bar and paid for the drink he would be enjoying five or six hours from now.

Garrid returned and handed me the trout. As I left, I turned to him and exclaimed, 'Who leaves Hoover's with a bag of trout in his hand?'

'You do!' he said.

Unsound

NICK MAMATAS

I AM EIGHT, MAYBE nine years old. This fishing trip isn't like the others. I'm with my grandfather. He's actually my maternal step-grandfather, but is a blood relative on my father's side: a great uncle. We're both Nicks, but everyone calls my grandfather 'Pop', including people who are older than he. He's that kind of guy. It's the mid-afternoon, and it's just him and me in his huge white Cadillac. We drive up to a beach I don't recognize. Long Island, true to its name, is a loooong island, and there's plenty I've never seen. It's a rocky shore, on a gray day, and we walk down a wooden pier. The only bait we have is some green seedless grapes. After about twelve minutes, I say, 'Παπού, I don't think there are any fish here.'

'You're right,' he says. It's starting to drizzle too, and it's cold. 'Let's go home.'

That was fishing with my family. I'm from a small town on Long Island's north shore called Port Jefferson. As the name suggests, it's a harbor town right on the Long Island Sound, a highly productive estuary, the so-called 'American Mediterranean.' It's a Greek-American enclave, or really, an Ikarian-American enclave, Ikaria being a fish-shaped island in the fish-rich Aegean that was in ancient times called Ιχθυόεσσα. *The island of fish*. My mother's side of the family is from a little town there called Καρκινάγρι – 'field of crabs.' Port Jefferson is like a little Ikaria: the local businesses feature family names like Proios and Caraftis – the Caraftis Fishing Station has been renting fishing boats for decades. I used to live for a time on a street named

238

for one of my maternal great-grandfathers: Fradelos. (The one from the field of crabs.) Clearly, the family had emigrated to the right place.

My extended family, which basically ran the town, considered ourselves a bunch of great fishermen. Every Christmas or birthday someone got a rod and reel. My great-grandfather's basement was festooned with decorative oars and fishing nets. My father spent several years building a boat on the weekends, carefully layering sheet after sheet of fiberglass on the wooden frame. We sanded it, him and me, without the benefit of masks or other protection. It took ten relatives to turn the hull over and pop out the frame, then another two years of steady work to get the steering, the motor, the pumps, the rest of the sanding, and the paint, together. The closer we got to finishing, the larger the number of ever-more-distant relatives who would appear to 'help for a day', i.e., put in some face time in the hope of getting invited to a fishing expedition on the Sound.

In Port Jefferson, they say, the fishing always used to be good. I am a kid, and my grandfather is the maître d' of the Elk Hotel and Restaurant. My mother, sister, and I are there all the time. Another cousin, Tommy, is a waiter. Various of my uncles work there as well. I'm sitting at a booth, under a huge lobster mounted on the wall. I'm sure it's fake, but every adult who stops by the table explains that, oh no, back in the old days, when 'the Indians' owned Long Island, all lobsters were thirty pounds and they crawled right up onto the beach to be collected and eaten. Well, the local lobsters used to be pretty big anyway.

They also tell me that the fishing on the Long Island Sound was once so good that my grandmother's kitchen sinks – she had a double – were full of the day's catch of porgies, bluefish, flounder. The fish species changed each time my grandmother told her horror story. So full of fish that one, near the top and with an uncommon will to survive, spasmed and flew at my grand-mother, smacking her right in the face with its tail and leaving a big purple bruise. 'Revenge!' was the anecdote's punctuation mark, shouted by some other relative every time my grandmother told the story.

Fishing used to be important too. My great-uncle John – a brother to 'Pop' – has a small boat. I'm there with him and mother and father, and two of John's three kids. It's early. We actually packed tuna fish sandwiches, made from the canned stuff, to eat for lunch. As it turns out I get seasickness when the Sound is choppy, and the fishy smell of the sandwiches is no help. My father laughs at me – he gets seasick too, and he got seasick every day he was in the Greek Navy, and later as a merchant marine. I puke over the side and there's some discussion as the utility of tuna vomit as bait. None of the kids are even willing to handle the live bait without a rag – John indulges his kids, my father makes me handle and impale the worms, which doesn't help my nausea. It hardly matters, as nothing is biting. My cousins Kelly and Peter start amusing themselves by having a race to see who can cast and reel the weighted hooks back in faster. Uncle John snaps at them. I groan and say I want to go back home, and my father snaps at me. Then Uncle John adds, 'You're lucky. When your father was a boy and he'd complain when out on the boat, his father would beat him with chains!' That's how important fishing is. I puke a second time. I catch nothing, and ultimately we have only a few porgies and a sizable bluefish to show for the day. We are people of the sea. We should be really good at this. But we were actually terrible. The family, or rather the network of three or four families (depending on how you count) I grew up with were cursed. None of us could bring home a decent catch of fish to save our lives.

It's not that my family was suffering from a single collective delusion. They knew their way around boats, the sea, fish. Confirmation: we're in a restaurant, and it's a special occasion of some sort because my father is there. It's a Chinese place called Diamonds, for the large geodesic dome in which it is housed. (There was a fashion for putting restaurants in these little domes for a while in Port Jefferson in the 1970s and 1980s. An uncle briefly owned a luncheonette in one called Teddy Bear's, named for his mother.) He orders the fish of the day; it's up to my mother, who is Greek-American and speaks with unaccented English, to make it clear that my father wants the head and tail intact.

When the fish arrives my father eats the eye and works his way through the body. Waiters, all Chinese immigrants, begin to gather around the table. They're not disgusted or bemused, but appreciative. When my father is done, the fish's skeletal system is revealed, like a cartoon cat had just swallowed it and pulled a complete skeleton out of its mouth with a smack of the lips. There's not a major bone out of place. Impressive stuff. Greeks are almost as good at eating fish as Chinese. Long Island is full of tribal politics based on dubious grounds.

Finally, after years, the boat is done. My sister and I have pitched dozens of names; my father has rejected them all. The boat – twenty feet, nearly a flat bottom, outboard motor – is white with blue trim, in honor of the Greek flag. There are eight or nine of us out there to push the boat into the Sound, though several will be staying on shore. My great-grandfather, who walks with a walker, is of course going to be part of the maiden voyage, and the extra hands are just to carry him onto the boat. We get the boat into the water, and wade up to our knees (the grown-ups) and/or waists (me, a cousin) to get the damn thing floating. We all climb on, my father starts the engine, and we're off into the Sound to do some serious fishing with the family patriarch.

Didn't catch a damn thing that day.

The boat was soon retired, as my father turned his energies instead to building a home. It went out all of three times – the last was a special treat for yet more cousins, these light-haired half-Irish boys from a long-lost and recently rediscovered branch of the clan. When one has a large family, one is never quite sure how one is related: their grandmothers and my grandmother – the one who got smacked by a flounder – were second cousins. The kids had a good time and actually caught a black fish! The boat never touched water again. Two decades later, a co-worker of my father's from his days as a longshoreman, recalled the boat and asked, 'So, is there a tree growing through it now?' A decade after that, I met the two-year-old son of the cousin I knew as an eight-year-old kid, and the little boy got to hear the story of My Father, Man Who Built His Own Boat, Which His Father Got To Ride On As A Boy. 'And after your daddy went fishing on it, the boat never touched the water again,' I told the kid. I didn't bother telling him that his family was cursed – he was a little redhead whose only Greek word was 'γάλα' (milk) and that he mispronounced with a hard G, so I was sure he'd be fine.

In the late 1980s, 'Pop' moved to Florida, and my great-grandfather passed on. I went to college at SUNY Stony Brook and got a student job in the campus television studio. There I played a minor role in the post-production of a documentary called *How Sound is the Long Island Sound?*, sorting U-matic tapes and logging footage. As it turns out, the Long Island Sound was not very fucking sound at all. We'd been fishing in a 'dead sea' for my entire lifetime. Forty-four sewage plants ring the Sound, dumping tons of filth, mostly from New York City, into the estuary, spiking nitrogen levels and pushing out the oxygen. Oxygen depletion killed the oyster beds, I found out, and drove away the fin fish. Lobstermen had been pulling up dead lobsters in their pots.

The western half of the Sound, closest to Manhattan and the outer boroughs, was the worst off. The tony eastern half, where celebrities boat and pretend to fish for paparazzi every summer, was reasonably OK. (It's a loooong island.) Port Jefferson? Right in the middle of the North Shore – sixty miles from Manhattan, fifty from Orient Point. The village slopes gently downward toward the shoreline, meaning that there was plenty of uncontrolled, poisonous street and agricultural run-off – more nitrogen! – flowing into the estuary as well.

The major obstacle to cleaning up the Sound is its value to New York – both the city and the two suburban counties – and Connecticut. Long Island is full of tribal politics based on dubious grounds. Right as the documentary was wrapping up in 1991, a historic meeting between elected officials in both states was held, and a plan to write a plan to save the Sound was declared. A second meeting was held, in Port Jefferson ... in 2011. What's half my lifetime between friends?

Near smack in the middle of those two historic almost-events: the great 1999 lobster disappearance. Somewhere between seventy and ninety percent of the lobster population died off; divers found a foot-high layer of dead lobsters at the bottom of the Sound. Was it global warming (lobsters can't handle water temperatures over 68°), pesticides designed to attack mosquitoes carrying the West Nile virus (Cheminova Inc., a pesticide manufacturer, settled with Long Island Sound lobstermen for $12.5 million), or just a final fatal tipping point after decades of environmental degradation?

I have a kid now. Like those long-lost cousins, he's a fair-haired white boy with Celtic blood. We visit Long Island occasionally. Will there ever be a fish for him to catch, if I can get the old boat working again? Is there enough ξένο blood in him to avoid the curse? Maybe. The Long Island Seaport and Eco Center (LISEC) was founded in Port Jefferson in 1995 in order to try to save the local waters. They've done some good work, like rehabilitating a rusted-out marine garage into a village center – I had my wedding reception there, after promising the booking agent that my Greek family wouldn't break plates on the carpeting. And they have a grassroots plan to clean the water. The Shellfish Restoration Project has, since the year 2000, released nearly a quarter of a million adult shellfish – oysters, bay scallops, and clams – into the waters of Port Jefferson. The oysters are 'nature's filtration system' according to LISEC; seeding the Sound with them both fights pollution and gives the population a chance at a rebound. At least a few oyster seasons, November to April, have been a success in the past few years.

Maybe my boy will one day be able to do what I never managed: drop a line into the water and come out with a reasonably sized, tasty, Long Island bluefish at will. Maybe I'll be an old man who everyone calls Pop by the time that happens, but I won't be able to do it without hearing a dozen chuckling, accented voices in my head saying: *Eh? Americans put fish into the water? Βρε, you're supposed to take them out!*

Chum Some of This: *Jaws* and its Legacy

ADAM CESARE

I F YOU WERE to see pictures of me as a child, maybe anything shot between the ages four to eleven, it's possible you'd think I was some kind of fisherman's son. Or at least a kid that had grown up to be a fisherman. Or an adult who fishes with some kind of regularity.

I am none of those things, but every time I visit my parents and look at the pictures they've set out for visitors, I'm always taken aback by how many involve the water.

And how many involve fishing. There's one of cute little me, *Sesame Street* T-shirt, petting a puffer fish's belly before he gets tossed back over the dock. One of me, a few years older and on a boat, holding up a rather large flounder by a line (that one didn't get tossed back, I'm sure: flounder are delicious). Then there's a final picture on the same shelf, that is similar but apart, it's one of me, dopey-looking, beginning adolescence and standing under the large, bloody jaws of a great white shark. It's impossibly large and strung up by a large wench. The shark's also fiberglass. We took that photo during a family trip to Universal Studios.

Let me back up.

I grew up on Amity Island.

Well. There is no such place. But Peter Benchley's 1974 novel *Jaws* describes Amity as a beach town on Long Island, New York (clearly taking its name from real-life Long Island town Amityville) and that's where I was raised.

When Spielberg made the film he moved Amity to Massachusetts, Martha's Vineyard to be precise, but as a child I had no concept of New England. I was told – by a father who had read the Benchley novel – that Amity was on Long Island.

Amity Island was less a real hometown than it was mental hometown, a state of mind. Similar to how I'm not an actual fisherman, I'm barely able to bait and weight a line, but I grew up around fishing. It's hard not to, living anywhere with the 'Island' suffix.

I guess it goes without saying that *Jaws*, the film, hit home for me.

I wasn't raised on the eastern tip of Long Island, the bourgeois Montauk wineries and Hamptons mansions that most people who aren't from NY (or the States) associate with the Island. We were in the middle section: a firmly suburban area, home to middle- and working-class families dotted with strip malls and fast food, bookended by the ultra-rich to the east and New York's Five Boroughs to the west.

Which is to say: not what most people would picture as a maritime, beach-going upbringing.

But there's no place on Long Island where you're not twenty minutes away from the water, the Sound to the north and the Atlantic Ocean to the south. That and my uncle was a fisherman and he owns a boat.

With my child's sense of scale, I remembered thinking that the small all-purpose fishing boat was a similar size to the *Orca*, but I did have the perspective to realize that my uncle is no Quint. He possesses way less of a fondness for drinking songs and way more of one for *Star Trek*. All the series. Even *Enterprise*.

But I used to love going out on that boat. Not because I particularly liked fishing but because I liked *Jaws*. Fishing trips were nothing more than extended *Jaws* role-playing sessions.

Those trips usually consisted of catching a few flounders and the occasional sea robin (which scared the hell out of me) with lines I didn't bait myself, staying out on the water until my insubstantial tolerance/interest in fishing was spent. Which isn't to say that we didn't make memories. There was one time where I almost dropped my entire pole into the water after feeling a tug, reeling in, and looking down into the murk to see an enormous spider crab working its way up my line, looking like it had a taste for little boy blood, but anecdotes like that are few and far between.

Under the best-case scenarios my father didn't get seasick and those trips

TAUT LINES: EXTRAORDINARY TRUE FISHING STORIES

out on my uncle's boat would be capped off by watching *Jaws* on Laserdisc, when we returned to shore. (Yeah, the boating *Star Trek* uncle was also the Laserdisc uncle, how cool can one dude get?)

As an adult I still love *Jaws*. Still think it's one of the best movies of all time. And even though I've now grown up and gotten my geography straightened out, even gone to the real Amity, visiting shooting locations on the Vineyard (and karate-ing a few fence posts), I still consider myself an Amity Islander.

But with all that love also came a lot of knowledge and growing up. I've seen a lot more of the world (and A LOT more movies) and I've matured to the point where I can acknowledge that *Jaws* and its impact on cinema and culture was detrimental in many ways.

Wait, what?

If you learn about *Jaws* in a university film studies class, it's very likely that you learn about it in the context of a history lesson. In that context your professor's lecture takes on tones of doomsaying. You're at film school now, and the first things most professors will try to do is challenge your assumptions, and that usually means taking your favorite movies to task. Most academics will admit that *Jaws* is impeccably made, but few will put it alongside Murnau and De Sica when they're teaching you about capital-A Art. After all, as they'll tell you if you didn't already know: *Jaws* was the first summer blockbuster.

The fact that it was an almost instant cultural phenomenon upon release is easy to take for granted, forty years after its debut. But in 1975 movies weren't released like they are now, nationwide blitzkriegs that have a film on 4,000 screens on the same day. Back then movies rolled out, prints rode the highways and byways of America and got to your screen ... eventually. *Jaws* and its generation scared to go in the water was the first step in the direction of complete, inescapable media saturation for new-release films. Spielberg's buddy George Lucas finished the job of making big movies the norm two years later in 1977. *Jaws'* before-then-historic box office records didn't last long in a post-*Star Wars* world.

So there's that kind of impact and legacy. With a direct historical line able to be drawn between the massive, culture-subsuming ad campaigns of summer tent poles and holiday season spectacles, your *Transformers* and your *Avengers*, and Spielberg's little fish movie. And in retrospect it's fun to mythologize the problems the film faced getting to the screen (a tight shooting schedule and last-minute rewrites necessitated by an un-co-operative mechanical shark), but those are quaint footnotes in a history that's nothing but a success story.

If you're a film professor, then maybe you take umbrage with the way the movie changed the cinema landscape, but if it hadn't been *Jaws* that was the first blockbuster, it would have been another movie. The business was always moving in that direction.

Besides, I don't really feel that way. I'm a populist, and *Jaws* is a great film, and lots of great, smaller films still manage to get made in the current model.

Jaws has another, darker legacy, though. One you may learn about in marine biology classes, but would seem wildly out of place in a freshman 'Understanding Film' course. I'm guessing that most ecologists point to *Jaws* as a kind of smear campaign against sharks, and look at Quint, Ahab for the baby-boomer generation, as a slanderous arbiter of destruction. I can't speak to that, though, because the last time I took a biology class I was fifteen and putting pins in earthworms.

I *can* say that I've seen Rene Cardona Jr.'s *Tintorera: Killer Shark* (1977) projected in 35 mm and it was a revolting experience.

And not revolting in the sense that most trash cinema is revolting. You can trust me on this, I'm not only an Amity Islander: I'm a connoisseur of this stuff. I've seen more than a few exploitation pictures. The quasi-softcore *Tintorera*'s attitude towards women is just about par for the grindhouse course, maybe even a little more liberal than its contemporaries because the film ends up having a pronounced 'free love' streak.

No, what's revolting in *Tintorera* – and what sets it apart from every other aquatic horror film that followed in *Jaws*' wake, a sub-genre so large that it's virtually its own genre, full-stop – is the abundance of on-screen violence towards animals.

If there's ever been a film less likely to be endorsed by the ASPCA, and carry the 'No animals were harmed in the making of this film' tag, it's this Mexican/English co-production. *The Adventures of Milo and Otis* may carry the urban legend stigma of animal abuse, but (and I may not be remembering this right) neither Milo nor Otis is spear-gunned on-screen. And say what you will about Italian cannibal films like *Cannibal Holocaust*, there are alternate 'humane' cuts to prove that the animal cruelty can be excised from the films at almost no detriment to the run time or story.

If you tried to cut the numerous shark shootings (yes, with handgun ammunition), spear-gunnings and sea turtle slaughter out of *Tintorera*, you'd be left with forty minutes of Hugo Stiglitz's bare-assed seduction of his various female co-stars. One of whom is the wonderful Susan George of *Dirty Mary*

Crazy Larry and *Straw Dogs* fame, but I struggle to recommend the movie even for George completists. It would probably be more into the wheelhouse of 'mondo' documentary aficionados, and even they would probably find it tiresome.

The *Jaws* DNA in *Tintorera* is so diluted that it's hard to even classify the film as a horror movie, outside of a few bloody shark attacks by the film's titular tiger shark. But there's a good argument to be made that it is the theory of *Jaws* being catastrophically detrimental to the way society views sharks put into living, bleeding action.

Quint may be the most well-known nemesis of shark kind, but at least there's an honor code there and a sense of wonder for the animals that nearly killed him during the war. No one would deny that Quint is a fisherman, and an aspirational one, I imagine, if I were a fisherman. But the shark hunters in *Tintorera* are – close to literally at times – shooting fish in a barrel, with a callousness that only becomes subtext when you consider the intended audience's attitude towards sharks.

It's not so much that these fishing practices existed, but that producers of this film thought that people wanted to see them. A quick Google search brings up the case of a Florida man (always a Florida man) who uploaded YouTube videos of himself shooting various protected species of sharks with a rifle. He didn't get in any trouble for it, either, because upon following up authorities determined that he was in international waters while doing it.

I mentioned I saw this movie projected, but it's not something I sought out and this wasn't some classy repertory screening. No, *Tintorera* played as part of a twenty-four-hour horror movie marathon in Philadelphia. Each year the event sells out within hours of tickets going on sale, and that's with the organizers, Exhumed Films, keeping all eight or nine titles secret. The audience never knows what it's in for until the title card pops up on screen and for the most part we enjoy that element of surprise.

To say *Tintorera* (which was, I think, the third or fourth movie of the night) let the air out of the room would be an understatement. Because not only is it hard to watch the animal killings, easy to wince at the romance, but the movie also has a languorous pace, the more sexually explicit international cut clocking in at over two hours. Although, in the programmer's defense, it was perfectly positioned to get people out of the theater and into the lobby for some refreshments and a bathroom break, so maybe its inclusion was intentional.

Tintorera and its shark-hate makes me ashamed to be an Amity Islander and a coulda-been fisherman.

Sure, it was made for a less discerning market. In America, at least, it played the grindhouse circuit and was therefore meant to shock and titillate drunks and the 'trench coat' crowd, which it probably did with aplomb. But like the tiger shark that pops up as a false-flag in *Jaws* ('They caught *a* shark, not *the* shark,' as Richard Dreyfuss's Hooper says, ruining a fine dinner party), *Tintorera* is a pale pretender.

But it's a pretender that I was reminded of a few months ago when I was at a private party at the Adventure Aquarium in Camden, New Jersey. It was a corporate function and I was there as my girlfriend's guest.

One of her co-workers and I stood staring into the aquarium's largest tank, its centerpiece.

'They're really beautiful,' I said, indicating the sharks behind the foot-thick glass. In the low-light of the after-hours event the toothy sand sharks and bottom-dwelling nurses were even more ghostly than usual. They were graceful and slow, in a roomy enclosure and with three decades of buffer safety separating them from the menace of B-movie actor Hugo Stiglitz.

'I hate them,' the co-worker said in response. 'I can't even look,' she continued. And she was dead serious, she was looking down at the balled cocktail napkin in her hand.

It's completely possible that this young woman had never even seen *Jaws*. But I have to wonder whether her reaction is Amity Island's fault.

Are my connections between this incident, *Jaws*, and its subsequent army of cinematic remoras spurious? Maybe, but movies can be and are propaganda, even when they aren't trying. We talk about *The Green Berets* (1968) and *Zero Dark Thirty* (2012) in a similarly morally complex context, but only because they are more politicized and are presented by their creators as less fictionalized.

Joe Dante's *Piranha* (1978) may not be held up as a cinema classic and was only greenlit by Roger Corman to capitalize on Spielberg's film, but the piranhas are all puppets and, today, we don't have a massive over-fishing problem with piranhas. We don't catch them in huge nets, shear off their fins to make soup and toss their twitching cartilaginous bodies into a trough to be ground up (or worse, back into the ocean, just wasted).

But we do that with sharks. And like 'fishing' with rifles, are we really ready to put net fishing in the same category as sport fishing?

Even for me, someone sympathetic, it gets harder to feel sorry for sharks when humming the *ba-dum ba-dum* of John Williams' iconic score. I'm betting it would be just as hard to convince my friend at the aquarium that shark conservation measures need to be taken. Especially not when shark attacks (or nibbles ... or dorsal fin sightings ...) are sensationalized on the news and even the Discovery Channel's educational/exploitational (edusploitation?) 'Shark Week' ends up being hosted by gorehound horror filmmaker Eli Roth, director of *Hostel*, *Cabin Fever* and, if the rumors are true, *Meg*, a giant shark movie, based on a novel, and slated for 2016. History repeating itself?

I don't want to live on a shark-free Amity Island. And this is coming from someone who loves *Jaws* with all I got.

Forced Perspective

DAVID JAMES KEATON

LIKE MOST BOYS, my brother's injuries start in the garage. What begins innocently enough as a refuge from hot summer days with a promise of shade and cool, concrete floors, usually ends up an obstacle course of cuts and contusions. And for one of his most dramatic injuries in our garage, we were barely inside it. Half in, half out, which might be all the proof you need that a garage is the most dangerous place on the planet if just the door can mess you up. If I get time, I'll tell you about when I tried to help someone cut down the swing door on an airplane hangar with a chainsaw, and how the spring unsprung and the spring block exploded, almost cutting me in half. I was in the doorway then, too.

But my brother's garage-door incident started with us getting chased home from the mudpit, this milky, borderline-stagnant pond where we went fishing for bluegill before, after, sometimes during school. It was filthy, but the only place to fish in Millbury, Ohio. And our grandma had made us a deal, a dollar for anything bigger than our hands. So we'd been pulling them out of the pond for her to fry up for our lunches when all the sudden these older kids in a jacked-up 4 x 4 were tearing after us on our bikes. It was after one of us made some smartass comment (hint: it wasn't my brother). They'd slowed down the truck to ask if we'd caught anything, and we'd gotten so good at it, it felt like a trick question, and I said as much. That day, in fact, we'd caught seventeen bluegill total, maybe ten of them too small to eat, but they were all crowded in a bucket of pond water until we could make sure. And we were fishing with our fingers, too. I know, all fishing is with some fingers, but we just had fishing line tied to our thumbs, near the knuckle and the bottom of the thumbnail, where it didn't start cutting into our skin as fast. On the ends of our lines were some barbed Eagle Claw hooks before the backlash against barbs. They were the bait-holder-style hooks, with thorns up the sides like a rose stem. We were putting wet balls of Wonder Bread on the hooks, so we didn't have much use for bait-holders, and we mistook those thorns for extra traction on the fish lips. But like I said, it didn't matter what we were using. That pond was shallow and stinky but teeming with bluegill, and snapping turtles, who must have eaten more bluegill than we did. These were the only two creatures we ever saw at the mudpit, but there wasn't any money in the turtles.

So seventeen fish were in the bucket when the chase started. I don't remember what I said, or even when we pulled the fishing line off our thumbs. The next thing I knew, we were just flying down the road with a truck weaving and honking behind us. Since I had the shittier bike with no seat, I learned to pedal much faster than my brother, and I got back to our house first. I skidded into the driveway and glanced back to see my brother taking the last turn onto our street so fast his knees were knocking against his handlebars, his pedals a whirling dervish so dangerous that his feet were hovering up and out of the way. I dismounted with the grace of a gymnast and let my bike hit the wall of the garage, leaving a black streak of rubber across the furnace. In a panic, I remembered we were home alone, and I started pulling down the garage door as fast as I could. Right then, my brother came flying down our driveway at Mach 3, feet unsuccessfully trying to get back onto the blur of pedals to stop himself and *bang!* The garage door caught him in the top of the head and scraped him off his bike as quick and efficient as a boot decapitating a dandelion.

His bicycle, now blind, got one good bite on me, a fender clipping me hard in the shin and slicing off a triangle of meat. My brother was down, I was down, and his bike was running up my chest like a slobbering dog greeting you at the door, its front wheel still spinning in my face. The 4 x 4 rumbled up to the edge of our driveway, and a greasy-faced teen leaned out to survey the scene of me wrestling a bike and my brother splayed out Christ-like in the gravel.

'Oh, shit, he's dead,' he laughed. Then the truck was gone with a roar. My brother woke up before the wheels of his bike stopped spinning, and he ran past me into the house screaming his head off. I don't remember who got in trouble for the crack in the garage door or the dent in the furnace, and nobody noticed the gash in my shin. It should have received a handful of stitches, but everyone was too worried about my brother's possible concussion with a football game coming up on Friday. For days, I dreamed of fishing line around my thumbs, strangling the kids from the 4 x 4 like an assassin with piano wire.

He lost the football game, but there's still a scar on my leg. And for about a week, what I thought about most from that day was the smell of that bike tire an inch from my nose and the tiny nipples of rubber on the tread that I'd never noticed before. Then we went back to the mudpit and saw the bucket where we'd left the bluegills to die, tilted on a broken slab of concrete, water on all sides, and now a year rarely passes where I don't regret not dumping out those fish.

When I dropped her off at her apartment, we sat in my Volkswagen Rabbit while she made some calls on her TV-dinner-sized phone to make sure this show was definitely going down. We called it the Walleye Derp, our name for the Walleye Drop, or Walleye Midnight Madness, a New Year's festival in nearby Port Clinton where fishing tournament trophies were handed out, and where a gigantic, sparkling fiberglass fish was dropped from a crane, similar to the New Year's Eve ceremony in Times Square. Well, as close as they could get to it anyway. So instead of a disco ball dropping at midnight, this fiberglass monstrosity would bust open on the ground and dump out hundreds of pounds of Swedish Fish candy, or so we were told.

My rusted car door shrieked when Jenny opened it to leave, and I watched her take out a penny and drop it into a cracked seam in the metal near the passenger's side window crank. It rattled around inside my car door like a piggy bank, and I laughed.

'What was that for?'

'Remind me to tell you a story later.'

'Oh, OK?' I said, a little worried she was gonna break up with me again, and I watched her walk off, unable to shake the idea that something was wrong. I reached across the passenger's seat and shook the door, trying to rattle the penny loose. Unsuccessful, I didn't get much sleep that night, but we got to the Walleye Derp early. Like so early I was convinced the whole thing was an elaborate prank, but then five hours later, people started setting up the porta-potties along the river, and about an hour after that, a tent was erected for the band, so with toilets and music in place, I knew we were in business. Watching the crowd grow, then queue up to urinate, it felt a bit like a live-action version of the Monty Hall Problem, trying to avoid the goat as I went door to door, finding most locked and occupied. Finally inside one toward the end, the antiseptic smells of cleaners assaulting my nose, I was mesmerized by the voices surrounding me. Maybe I'd never been in one of these porta-johns when there wasn't some noisy concert or festival-type situation, so it's possible I never knew the little mesh half-windows on either side of my head projected all the conversations right down the line, amplified right into my ears like I was a bug crawling around some soup-can telephones during a conference call. I urinated fast, then stood there to listen in. I heard someone on the phone mad about missing the fish drop the year before. Never again, he said.

I looked out the right mesh and saw a conversation happening between two porta-potties on that side, at least four people down the row. The sound was so distinct, I could even hear the echoes of their urine in the plastic pans. Once, Jenny and I had visited C.O.S.I., the now-defunct science center twenty minutes away in Toledo, along the Maumee river, and they had a couple giant plastic satellite dishes about fifty feet apart where you could stand with the curve of the dish behind you and have a quiet conversation. Only our conversation turned into an argument, something about the social responsibility of an artist. I can't remember exactly, except that it echoed in my skull like we were screaming in a bucket.

That night after dozens of men tried to get the most deceptive forced-perspective shots of their tournament-winning walleye, and after the giant fiberglass fish was dropped but never hit the ground, we drove home with Jenny's legs up on my dashboard. She lined her feet up with her previous footprints on my windshield.

'What were you going to tell me about again?' I asked after I leaned over to breathe her in, all the sweat and sun trapped in the baby hairs of her arms.

'What?'

'You said to remind you to tell me something. When you put money in my car door.'

She looked at me, considering, then sighed.

'OK, so, I knew this kid who had this cracked piece on the inside panel of his door, kind of like yours, and it made this slot that was perfect for change, like pennies or whatever. It was a great way to save money, basically. And any time he'd stop at a drive-through and get change back, rather than dropping it into the jar to save cats or orphans, he'd drop it into the hole in his door. But eventually, his door starts making jangling sounds, and rattling real loud when he takes hard turns . . .'

'Then what happened?'

'Nothing. He had a car full of money?' she shrugged, then reached into her pocket for a handful of change. She started feeding the coins into the slot on my door, one after the other, all of them rattling to the bottom.

'Whoa, whoa, wait a minute,' I said. 'Didn't it throw his car off balance?'

'What? Shut up.'

I leaned back in my seat and cracked my neck on the headrest, searching my mind for a story from my past that would impress her, but the accident with the garage-door spring hadn't happened yet, and she was already halfway out the door. And as my brother could tell you, halfway in or out was the most dangerous place to be.

She blew a drip of sweat off her nose and smiled, then dropped her last penny into my car door.

Back in high school, I picked a fight with this dim-witted asshole everyone called 'Squeegee.' He got that nickname back in third grade when the bus driver caught him writing a bunch of profanity on the bus windows with his bad breath and knobby fingers. He was a hero at the time, especially when the driver had the principal meet our bus at the curb and march Squeegee into the building with all the gravity of a *Dead Man Walking* situation. But by the time he got to ninth grade, he was a bully and a monster, and one day Squeegee was taking too long at the water fountain and I said, 'You want to practice sucking on something else and give somebody else a turn?' It wasn't my best joke ever, but at least I remembered it, unlike the crack at the mudpit that knocked my brother out, and there was a line of kids behind us who appreciated it enough to start hooting. So ol' Squeegee leaned in and told me to meet him behind the dug-out at 8.00 that night so he could kick my ass. None of my friends heard Squeegee name the place, but word got out, and they wanted to come and help me out, since everyone hated Squeegee, too. But right before my mouth formed the words to tell them to meet at the dug-out, I got the bright idea to send them to a church parking lot instead. I wanted to take out Squeegee myself, and figured I'd be a legend after that bit of misdirection. So at 8.00 that night, my friends went to the church parking lot while Squeegee beat me half to death behind the dug-out, and for years afterwards, I never lived it down, constantly getting wrong directions from my friends. But I felt like my friends were a little impressed, even though they'd never admit it. But that didn't matter as much as the fact that I was impressed I'd gone through with it. Until my brother told me he'd followed me to the dug-out and watched the whole thing from the bleachers. When I asked why he didn't help me out, he said his seats were too good.

I hated him for a while, but then I'd think about the fish, and how five more bluegill might have been enough for the bucket to tip over on its own. Or five more dollars in change.

I was lucky enough to run into Jenny while I still had scabs from the fight, and I told her about the dug-out and the misdirection, and I watched her tune out completely. I heard myself telling the whole story anyway, going through the motions, but all the while thinking about the bowerbirds we learned about together, in the Australian exhibit at C.O.S.I. How the video showed us the male of the species building this crazy tunnel of sticks, lined by an even more complicated avenue of rocks, with smaller rocks toward the front, and larger rocks toward the back, which he utilized to entice a mate. It was the only creature in the animal kingdom that messed with perspective to trick the female. But what we found most interesting was that this bird seemed to do all this work in order to appear smaller. It perpetuated its species and won the day with a show of weakness. Which is how it should be.

As she walked away, I thought about forced-perspective photos in trophy fishing and how I tried to get Jenny to take a picture of me at the Walleye Drop, my hand in the foreground, pretending to hold the giant fiberglass fish behind me. She wouldn't do it. At the time, she was too disappointed that it wasn't full of candy. Or that it never exploded on the ground.

My brother got hurt a lot more than me, or at least it seemed like it with all the attention. A lot of them were my fault though, and for a while it seemed like I was chipping his teeth every week. It was only twice, but it was the same front tooth. The first accident involved a Nerf football and an Etch-A-Sketch. Remember those? Two dials, silver sand, and an invisible needle that drew on the inside of the glass screen like a *Flintstones* dinosaur toiling inside a tiny television. In case you ever wondered, there are all sorts of things waiting to be discovered when you crack open this amazing toy with a hammer in your father's garage. Like it stops working.

So, my brother was lying on the bed playing with this thing over his head, and I casually threw the Nerf football at him as hard as I could. The

Etch-A-Sketch flew from his hands and bashed him full in the mouth. And after a couple seconds of silent bleeding, he tore screaming down the stairs, lips and mouth gushing. I know I got in trouble for that one, but less because of the tooth and more because I used the toy to scrawl 'Aaaaargh!' on the screen, then tried to convince everyone this was the last thing he wrote on impact.

Accident number two. Days after he got his tooth fixed, with all of us kids jealous of his fang-like shard, we were skating on the neighbor's frozen yard when my brother wiped out trying to skate backwards and busted that same tooth all over again. So now that I think about it, I didn't have much to do with his broken tooth that second time around, because that day I was too busy at the other end of the neighbor's frozen field, on my hands and knees with one skate off my foot and in my hand, chopping at the ice. I was oblivious to my wet sock growing heavier and heavier, soaking up all the snow and mud around my numb foot like a magnet, because I could see this fish just under the ice and I needed to hack my way down to it. For some reason, I thought setting it free into the winter air would save it. Or maybe I was going to rush it home to the toilet for rejuvenation. Either way, I was baffled. How could a fish freeze into someone's backyard? I had to have it.

It was a crappie – I could see the spots – and I did chop it free with my skate, at the cost of half the fish's tail and a series of deep gashes across the top of my own wrist. When I got home to show my mom this miracle, she shoved me out of the way, the long phone cord wrapped around her neck as she screamed into the receiver at my father, telling him what I'd done to my brother 'this time.' I turned to see him sitting at the kitchen table with his hockey stick over one shoulder like a soldier, mouth swimming in blood. I walked past him and ran my wrist and the tail under the faucet and wondered how many fish lived in our yards. How many fish hid in our high grass all summer? The yards in our neighborhood were in a constant state of flooding, and you'd have thought we lived in Vietnam instead of a north-west Ohio suburb, but this field had only been frozen for a week. And it had just snowed the week before that. I started to wonder if any puddle sat long enough, would something be swimming in there when you looked away. After the fish in the field, I didn't feel as guilty about the ones we left behind. And this might have nothing to do with anything, but whenever I put a bucket under a leak in a ceiling, I have no problem leaving it overnight, even in the garage. But I rarely look inside.

Border Water

GRETCHEN LEGLER

CRAIG AND I are on our way to the Rainy River to fish for spring walleyes. The Rainy is a great, wide, slow-moving river that runs from east to west, through forests and farms, at the top of Minnesota, separating the state from Canada. Because it is a border water, you can fish the river in early April, after the ice has gone out, a full month before you can fish inland waters.

'It's hard to imagine,' Craig says, as we drive along the Minnesota side of the river, looking across at the brown grass and farms on the opposite bank, 'that just over there is another country.' On both sides of the river there are brown grass and trees and red barns and silver silos. It looks the same. Over there, Canada, rust-colored grass and trees. Over here, Minnesota, rust-colored grass and trees. It *is* hard to imagine. But it is a different country; a place boys rowed across to in rickety boats to avoid being sent to Vietnam. It is beautiful and open and wild along the river. Behind the trees on the Canadian side there is a railroad track, and occasionally a freight train roars by with the speed trains pick up only in the country.

We have purchased Canadian fishing licenses so that we can fish both sides of the river. We have also purchased three dozen minnows and salted them down. You can use Minnesota minnows on the Canadian side as long as they are dead. If you want to use live minnows on the Canadian side, you must buy them in Canada. But you can't cross the border checkpoint at International Falls or Baudette with live minnows, so, if you want to fish legally with live minnows on the Canadian side, you must launch your boat in Canada, which means you must patronize the Canadian resorts, of which there are none on this stretch of the Rainy.

As Craig drives, I read the fishing regulations. I turn to the fish consumption advisory. It says that on the Rainy River between International Falls and Lake of the Woods no one should eat more than one fish meal per month of any size of any species caught there, especially if you are pregnant or plan to be, ever, or are nursing, or plan to ever, or if you are less than ten years old. For years the Boise Cascade paper mill at International Falls has dumped dioxin, mercury, and other poisons into the river. The large fish in the river taste slightly metallic. Two decades ago, the river was a slime pit of stinking paper pulp, great pods of which would burp open on the water and emit putrid gas. Now, at least, old-timers say, the visible pollution is gone, the water is clean and there are fish here again.

'Why are we coming here if all we're doing is poisoning ourselves?' I ask Craig. But, I know why, of course. We are going to be out on the first open water of the season and to fish. That means sitting still and thinking and maybe reading if I get bored, talking quietly about important things, watching the sky, seeing an eagle fly over, a few mallards whiz upriver, the brown grass on the bank, the current bringing big sticks past.

Craig says, 'Why doesn't someone sue Boise Cascade's ass? I don't know how they can get away with polluting like that.'

This is a trip Craig and I have taken for four years in a row. 'These traditional things are important,' he says. 'It's important to have a history of experience together.'

His eyes are on the road, and I watch his profile: a sharp forehead and nose, cheeks, eyes and lips framed by a closely trimmed gray-black beard, and a sloppy, sweat-stained gray Stetson. He looks very young to me, and slightly naive; like a Boy Scout still. I agree with him about the importance of ritual. We fish rainbow trout in the fall at Benjamin Lake for two weekends. We walk the logging trails around Blackduck for grouse. Then there is the season for ducks and geese near Thief Lake. Then we hunt deer in the woods of northern Minnesota to fill our freezer for the winter. When it snows we ski, and when the lakes freeze we fish through the ice for crappies. In the spring comes the Rainy River, then walking in the woods for morel mushrooms, then summer walleye fishing on big, smooth lakes. Our year together is spent in these ways. It is what we do.

But I am uneasy about the trip to the Rainy this time. For one thing, it is always difficult, physically demanding. To load and unload a boat, walk up and down the steep, slippery hill from the river to camp in heavy boots, all is wearing on my body. I get tired. I worry that I am becoming soft and weak. The weather is always unpredictable. One year as Craig and I bobbed in the current, jerking our minnow-baited jigs up and down, snow fell and ice chunks floated past us. Another year it was so warm we fished in shirtsleeves. This year the weather is in the middle. Sunny but cold. But still there is the physical work of it. Hauling. Endless hauling.

But I know my unease has less to do with this, and more to do with the first year we came here. The fishing was so good that year that the river was a solid mass of boats, gunnel to gunnel, bow touching bow, stern to stern. It was sunny, and everyone was having a wonderful time, lifting huge fish from the muddy water, smiling, laughing, weighing the fish, some putting the big ones back, but others keeping stringers of seven-pound fish, whole stringers of fish that would not even taste good, fish that would taste like metal.

At the boat ramp, men milled around, laughing and smoking cigarettes and drinking beer and pop. They were drunken, overloaded, dangerous. The wives and girlfriends of the fishermen stood with poodles on leashes, holding children by the hand, taking pictures of the great catches of fish. The fish-cleaning house was packed, and there was a line outside. The garbage cans in the fish house were overflowing with guts and the orange eggs of the huge spawning female walleyes. Fish heads with shining black eyes flowed out onto the ground. Flies buzzed around. It was a carnival of greed. Hundreds of people appropriating walleye flesh as if it were a right.

I was as giddy as all the rest with our success. Every cast brought in another huge green and gold fish, tugging at my line, twisting and spinning in the water, curved gracefully in the landing net, all muscle. We didn't keep them all, only the small ones. And we only kept our limit: twelve. But we were there.

We camp this year, as always, at Franz Jevne State Park on the river. It is not much of a park: a few dirt pull-outs and two outhouses. The roads are winding and muddy, and the park is dark. Our small camp is in the middle of tall evergreens. I feel vaguely gloomy. Surrounded. It is dim and cool, early evening, and the men around us in other camps are lighting lanterns, starting campfires, firing up cooking stoves. I smell fish and onions and wood smoke.

I see shadows moving behind the canvas walls of tents. I hear muffled, rough voices. I am the only woman here.

In the women's outhouse I sit down to pee and look at the wall in front of me. There is a crude drawing in thick black marker of a woman's vulva, a hairless mound, lips open wide, folds of flesh deep inside. The rest of the body is absent. There is no head, no face, no eyes, no mouth, no arms or legs. Just this one piece, open and dripping, as if it were cut off with a cleaver and set apart. I imagine it wrapped up in white butcher paper, the kind we'll use to wrap the walleye we catch here. 'I want to fill your pussy with a lode of hot come,' the writing above this picture says. Cold air is blowing up from the pit below me, hitting my warm skin. My muscles shrink. On another wall is an erect penis, huge and hairless, drawn in the same black marker. The head on the penis looks to me strangely like the head of a walleye with its gills spread wide. There is no body attached to the penis either, just a straight vertical line from which the organ springs. 'I want to fuck your wet pussy. Let's meet' is scrawled next to it.

I am suddenly terrified and sickened. I hear a threat: I want to rape you; I want to dissect you. I can't pee anymore. The muscles of my stomach and thighs have pulled into themselves protectively, huddling. Between my legs now feels like a faraway cold world, not a part of me. I yank up my long underwear and wool pants, getting shirt tails tucked into the wrong places, and leave with my zipper still down, happy to be outside. As I walk back to our camp I look over my shoulder and left and right into the woods. I wonder if it was that man, or that one, or that one, who wrote this violence on the wall. I am out of breath and still afraid when I tell Craig all of this. I tell him it makes me want to run and it freezes me in place. My voice is wavering. He tells me it is in the men's outhouse, too: a picture of another naked, dripping vulva and the words, 'This is my girlfriend's pussy.' I ask Craig, 'How would you feel if in the men's john a woman had written 'I want to cut your dick off' or 'This is my boyfriend's cock'?' I want to know if this would scare him, too. He says, 'I'd watch out.'

We are anchored in the current, our jigs bouncing on the bottom of the river. The river is wide and powerful and brown. It smells like cold steel. Craig wonders aloud why in all this water the poison and its smell do not dissipate. We are not catching many fish, but some. Crowded around us are men in boats. This is a good spot, on the Canadian side of the river, and the boats push together here. There are no other women on the water. Only men with other men. Some are drinking Diet Coke and munching on crackers as they wait for fish to bite. Others are swigging beer, cracking jokes, laughing. Cigar and cigarette smoke wafts up into the air. I feel as if Craig and I are being watched. A man and a woman in a boat. We watch ourselves being watched. Craig feels this, too. He says, 'All these guys are out here to get away from their wives.'

One of Craig's newspaper colleagues asked him once, in a voice that pleaded with Craig to come clean, to tell the truth, to join the club: 'Do you really enjoy fishing with your wife?' Every time Craig remembers this he laughs. He repeats it sometimes when we are making love in the tall grass beside a trout stream, or when we are stretched out naked together under the covers in our van. He leans over now and asks, smiling, 'Do you really think I can have any fun fishing with my wife?'

We are dressed in heavy wool pants and sweaters and big felt-lined boots. Craig asks me, when I am dressed up like this, if I think anyone can tell I am a woman. The sweater and down jacket hide my breasts. My long blonde hair is under a hat, my face is buried in wool, no one can see my earrings. What would be the thing that would make them know I was not a man among men? What is the line I would have to cross for them to know surely that I was different from them?

'Only when I speak,' I say. 'Or maybe when you lean over in the boat and kiss me. Then maybe they would think I was a woman. But I wouldn't necessarily have to be.'

Until recently it never occurred to me to wonder why I was the only woman I ever knew who walked in the woods with a shotgun looking for grouse, or sat in a duck blind or a goose blind, or crouched up in a tree with a rifle waiting for deer, or went fishing on the Rainy River. It never occurred to me to wonder because I never felt alone, before now.

I used to hate being a woman. When I was very young, I believed I was a boy. I raced boxcars made from orange crates, played football with the neighbor boys and let them experiment with my body, the parts of which seemed uninteresting to me and not valuable. I was with them, watching myself in the light in their eyes, looking at me. I was flattered in high school when someone said to me, 'I like you. You're just like a guy.' The words I liked best to hear were: rangy, tough, smart, cynical. My father made jokes about women's libbers burning bras. I laughed, too. Throughout college I never knew what it was like to touch a woman, to kiss a woman, to have a woman as a friend. All my friends were men. I am thirty years old now, and I feel alone. I am not a man. Knowing this is like an earthquake. Just now all the lies are starting to unfold. I don't blend in as well or as easily as I used to. I refuse to stay on either side of the line.

In the boat next to ours is a quiet man with a fixed smile who has been catching all the fish. He is over a drop-off, his jig sinking exactly twenty-one feet. That is where the fish are. I ask him where he is from, my voice echoing across the water. He says he is from Warren, Minnesota. I ask him if he knows the boy I read about in the newspaper who got kicked out of West Point and was suing for his right to go back. The boy was his town's pride: a track star, a member of the choir, an honor student, handsome, full of promise. At West Point, too, he was full of promise. With his beautiful voice, he sang solo at the White House for the President. Then, on a tip from one of the boy's high school chums, the military started digging around in his past. Before they found out what he knew they would, he came forward and told them the truth. 'I'm gay, sir,' he told his commanding officer.

The man in the boat from Warren pushes his baseball cap back on his head and squints at the sun. He says to me, across the water, 'I knew that boy really well. He was a model for the community. A model for all the younger kids.' He is shaking his head. 'It's hard to figure out,' he says. 'Just so darned hard to figure out why he'd go and do such a thing and ruin his future like that.'

'I hope he wins his case against West Point,' I say. There is more I ache to add. I want to yell across to him, 'What's to figure out? He loves men.' But, I say no more and turn away, ashamed of my silence. As I turn away, the man from Warren is still shaking his head. 'It's just so hard to figure out.'

Craig and I came to the Rainy partly to meet and fish with some old friends of mine, Kevin and Brad, whom I met while reporting for the *Grand Forks Herald* in North Dakota. Kevin and Brad have brought their friend John with them. John is the fishing columnist for the paper and also a professor of English. He is originally from Mississippi.

Around the campfire at night, Kevin tells us about his latest assignment. He is organizing a special section on wolves. The people of Roseau, Minnesota, believe they have a wolf problem and want the Minnesota Department of Natural Resources to get rid of some of the animals.

John is slouched by the fire with his feet straight out, taking long drinks from a bottle of root beer schnapps. Brad and Craig are standing, their hands in their pockets, looking down at the flames and coals. Kevin puts a wad of chewing tobacco behind his lower lip. I squat by the fire, hunched over a mug of tea. John passes me the bottle of schnapps, and I hesitate. For me to drink from it would be to mimic his gesture, to join in, but I am so curious to taste it. I take a small sip and make a face.

Kevin says, 'Farmers think the wolf pack is purposely underestimated.'

Craig asks, 'You mean the government is lying about how many wolves there are so the farmers won't get upset?'

'It's more than the wolf they want to kill,' I say. 'It's what the wolf represents.'

'What's that?' Brad says.

'Lust,' I say. They laugh.

'They want control,' Craig says. 'They want control over nature. That's what management is all about. It's for us, not the animals. Just like with this river.' Craig waves his hand toward the water.

'It stinks,' Brad says.

'Literally,' Kevin says.

'Buffalo shit,' John says.

We all look at him and wait.

'Do ya'll know how much the rivers were polluted by buffalo shit? Millions of buffalo shitting in the rivers back before the white man came and after?' He's not laughing.

'Why, our screwing up the earth and killing animals, it's as natural as buffalo shit,' he says. 'We're part of nature, too, hell. If you fuck around with nature – try to clean up the river, protect the wolves – you'll upset the whole balance of time and evolution. Just leave things be.'

There is a long, uncomfortable silence. Then Craig says, 'The world has had millions of years to get used to buffalo shit. But no matter how much buffalo dung there is in a river, it still will never be as bad as dioxin.'

The next day, Sunday, is the day we leave. Craig and I fish from early morning until noon. When it comes time to load the boat and return to St. Paul, one of us has to get out on shore and drive the car to the boat landing. And one of us has to take the boat by water. I want to go by water, to go fast and have the spray fly up around me and the front of the boat rise out of the river.

Craig says, 'You take the boat.' This is what I want to do, but I am afraid. 'Really?' I ask him. 'Really, I can drive it down?' I expect not to be trusted. 'What about rocks?' I ask.

'Watch out for them,' he says, very casually. He has no second thoughts. He does not understand my timidity.

Once, in the spring, a friend and I sat on the steps of Lind Hall at the University of Minnesota and watched a group of boys playing on their skateboards, jumping high in the air, knees pulled up, big, orange high-tops hovering off the ground, their skateboards flipping under them, over and over. Then the boys would land safely. Then, there they would go again, taking a running leap onto a cement bench, turning on top of it and coming off again. Graceful and noisy. My friend said, 'Guys are brought up to think they can do everything.'

I think of this as I pull away from the shore, waving at Craig. I think of my brothers, Austin and Edward, who climb cliffs and fly airplanes. Many women, I think, grow up believing they can't do anything. One of the tasks I believe I never will be able to do is backing the trailer into the water to load or launch the boat. I have tried and nearly every time have ruined something: cranked the trailer around to dangerous angles, smashed a tail light, backed off the edge of the boat ramp, put the van in reverse instead of forward and driven it to the top of the wheel wells into the water. I know that I can do this physical, mechanical task. What I regret is that I do not simply *assume* I can do it. I wish I could launch into it without reserve, full of confidence, free of doubt. Like a man might.

I have learned from Craig that it is not only gender that makes for my insecurity. When we put the boat in at the Rainy River, Craig is always nervous. He believes he is being watched and judged. But, unlike me, he is protected from ridicule. When we bought the van, it came with a bumper sticker, left there by its previous owner. It says, 'Vietnam Veterans of America.' Craig believes this sticker gives him certain privileges and encourages respect in parking lots and at boat ramps. It prevents laughter. I often think he wishes he had earned this bumper sticker rather than bought it. He was training to be a Navy pilot when the war ended and he was sent home. Sometimes when he meets a man his age and picks up a hint or clue, he asks him, shyly, 'Were you in Nam?' Sometimes they say yes and ask him if he was, and he says, almost apologetically, 'No. Almost.'

I drive the boat down the river, watching out for rocks. I must not hit any rocks. If I hit rocks, I will have failed. I see rocks ahead, but also a spot that looks deep. I go for what I think is the deepest water. Spray comes over the bow and sides. I am bobbing along, zooming, my hair flying out behind me, the shore whizzing past. I am doing it all by myself. My image of my self and my self come together here. I am perfect.

Then the prop grinds against submerged rocks, the motor tilts forward and drags across them, gouging the propeller, ripping the metal as easily as cloth. I crush my teeth against one another. Again, the motor tilts forward, the engine rises in pitch and there is a grating and a crunching. Again and again this happens. I cannot see the rocks. I can't see one rock. I have no idea where they are. I feel defeated. I make it to shore, where men line the banks, and park, hitting one last rock. I pull up the motor to see the damage I have done: the prop is frayed, white paint long gone, twisted silver in its place.

I have fucked up. I never should have been trusted with this boat. I despise myself. It is not my place to drive a boat. It is too big a thing for me. Too dangerous, too demanding. Craig arrives at the boat landing. I start to cry. He says, 'Don't cry. Don't cry. Don't cry. We needed a new prop anyway.' I expect him to be angry. Instead Craig says, 'You need to learn to do this. We should have you practice. You should always drive the boat and back up the trailer, light the stove and the lantern.'

I always expect anger and sometimes feel cheated and lost when I don't get it. I expect anger now, with Craig, because that is what I learned to expect from my father. That is the way my father would have reacted if I had failed in this way in front of him.

I learned many early lessons from my father and have carried them with me into womanhood. For my father there is no middle ground between success and complete failure. I learned from him to expect and strive for perfection and to truly trust no one but myself. 'If you want it done right, do it yourself,' he always said. For my scientist father the world of nature, the world of personal relations and desire, the world of chance and fate, resembles a machine of sorts. Oil it, clean it, take care of it and it will run for you; you can prevent any problem from occurring. As long as you know a thing thoroughly, as long as you have control over it, as long as you command it, it can never surprise you. All of this I learned as a child, each lesson hardening into a code I would adhere to, mostly unwittingly, much of my adult life. Craig is not like my father. Instead of anger from him I get the opposite – laughter!

* * *

It has become tradition with us that while Craig puts the cover on the boat, tucks the life jackets away, winds up the stringer, I clean the fish. I take our collection of walleyes to the fish house and see that inside the screen door five men are working, slicing open the walleyes with long fillet knives, talking about their fishing day. 'Is there room for another person in here?' I ask. I ask this because they are watching me stand outside the door, stringer in hand, wondering with their eyes what I am doing here. I feel unnatural and self-conscious. Perhaps they think of their own wives, or kids, at home and wonder why I am not there, too. One man, the oldest, the one with gray hair and pink ears, says, 'It's kind of cozy in here.' I say that I will wait. I am waiting, watching them slice through the fish, peeling off an entire side of the body, then slipping the knife between the skin and the white flesh and separating the two with one or two strokes. It is remarkable to me how easy it is to slice apart a walleye – carving a breathing thing down to two essential fillets that bear no resemblance to the fish alive. The only way for me to do this is to ignore that what I've got is a fish, something that hours ago was swimming, alive. From behind me comes a man with a stringer of fish he can barely hold up. He barrels around me, steps into the fish house and throws his fish on the counter. He is in. I am still outside.

I pick up my fish and march away. Craig sees me.

'Wouldn't they let you in?'

I say, 'There's no room for a goddamned girl in that fish house.'

I throw down the stringer, the knife, the cutting board, the jug of water, the plastic bags and my orange cleaning tub, fall to my knees on the ground and start slashing at my fish. One, two, three. One, two, three. Three strokes and the fillet comes off clean and smooth. I am angry. I am saying to myself, 'I can do this better than any of those bastards. Better than any of them.' I feel defiant and confident, proud and suddenly cruel. When I do this, I realize, I am leaping across the line between the fish's life and mine, across lines that divide life into death. And I can do it as well as any. I can move as easily as anyone across this space.

Craig wants to take a new route home. I would never dare. I simply take the freeway, the safe and easy route. He chooses a curvy line that runs through the Nett Lake Indian Reservation. We wind, bump and take twice as long, but Craig likes these roads where you cannot see where you are going. There is one right angle after another.

I am exhausted and sad, but feel safe again. 'I should give up and stay home,' I say. 'The worse it gets the more I see I don't have a place out here.' I am looking out the window at the forest bumping past, thinking of the river, the outhouse, the fish house.

Around a sharp corner, a white and brown blur rises from the middle of the road. We see a hawk with a mouse in its claws, a wisp of a tail, four tiny feet hanging down, a little package being carried head forward into the sky by a graceful flapping bird that goes up and up and up and over the tops of the pines. Craig slows down and we both duck our heads and peer out the windows so that we can watch the hawk until it disappears.

Craig sees that I am crying. He asks me, 'What are you afraid of?'

'I am tired and afraid of being the only woman. I am so lonely,' I say.

He is quiet.

'I am afraid of the killing,' I say. 'I'm afraid that I wouldn't know how to live and not murder.' I wipe my nose with the sleeve of my sweater. 'The line is so thin,' I say. 'I'm afraid there is no difference between me and them.'

Craig is quiet again for a long time and then says to me, 'You know, if you don't take your place, then you'll lose it.'

'I'm not sure I want it,' I say. 'Not here. Not like this. Not this place.' In truth, *I am not sure*. Not sure at all. But there has to be a space for me; space for me as a woman out here. There has to be a middle ground. A space between the borderlines. A space where we can all learn to be and live and not murder.

A Defense of Fishermen

GROVER CLEVELAND

B Y WAY OF introduction and explanation, it should be said that there is no intention at this time to deal with those who fish for a livelihood. Those sturdy and hard-working people need no vindication or defense. Our concern is with those who fish because they have an occult and mysterious instinct which leads them to love it, because they court the healthful, invigorating exertion it invites, and because its indulgence brings them in close contact and communion with Nature's best and most elevating manifestations. This sort of fishing is pleasure and not work – sport and not money-grabbing. Therefore it is contemptuously regarded in certain quarters as no better than a waste of time.

Generous fishermen cannot fail to look with pity upon the benighted persons who have no better conception than this of the uses and beneficent objects of rational diversion. In these sad and ominous days of mad fortune-chasing, every patriotic, thoughtful citizen, whether he fishes or not, should lament that we have not among our countrymen more fishermen. There can be no doubt that the promise of industrial peace, of contented labor and of healthful moderation in the pursuit of wealth, in this democratic country of ours, would be infinitely improved if a large share of the time which has been devoted to the concoction of trust and business combinations, had been spent in fishing.

The narrow and ill-conditioned people who snarlingly count all fishermen as belonging to the lazy and good-for-nothing class, and who take satisfaction in describing an angler's outfit as a contrivance with a hook at one end and a fool at the other, have been so thoroughly discredited that no one could wish for their more irredeemable submersion. Statesmen, judges, clergymen, lawyers and doctors, as well as thousands of other outspoken members of the fishing fraternity, have so effectively given the lie to these revilers of an honest and conscientious brotherhood that a large majority have been glad to find refuge in ignominious silence.

Notwithstanding this, weak, piping voices are still occasionally heard accusing fishermen of certain shortcomings and faults. These are so unsubstantial and unimportant that, as against the high place in the world's esteem claimed by those who love to fish, they might well be regarded as non-essentials, or, in a phrase of the day, as mere matters of detail. But, although it may be true that these charges are on the merits unworthy of notice, it cannot be expected that fishermen, proud of the name, will be amiably willing to permit those making such accusations the satisfaction of remaining unchallenged.

The Hangers-on of the Fraternity

At the outset, the fact should be recognized that the community of fishermen constitute a separate class or a sub-race among the inhabitants of the earth. It has sometimes been said that fishermen cannot be manufactured. This is true to the extent that nothing can supply the lack of certain inherent, constitutional and inborn qualities or traits which are absolutely necessary to a fisherman's make-up. Of course there are many who call themselves fishermen and who insist upon their membership in the fraternity who have not in their veins a drop of legitimate fisherman blood. Their self-asserted relationship is nevertheless sometimes seized upon by malicious or ignorant critics as permitting the assumption that the weaknesses and sins of these pretenders are the weaknesses and sins of genuine fishermen; but in truth these pretenders are only interlopers who have learned a little fish language, who love to fish only 'when they bite,' who whine at bad luck, who betray incredulity when they hear a rousing fish story, and who do or leave undone many other things fatal to good and regular standing. They are like certain whites called squaw-men, who hang about Indian reservations, and gain certain advantages in the tribes by marrying full-blooded Indian women. Surely no just person would for a moment suppose that genuine Indians could be treated fairly by measuring them according to a squaw-man standard. Neither can genuine fishermen be fairly treated by judging them according to the standards presented by squaw-fishermen.

In point of fact, full-blooded fishermen whose title is clear, and whose natural qualifications are undisputed, have ideas, habits of thought and mental tendencies so peculiarly and especially their own, and their beliefs and code of ethics are so exclusively fitted to their needs and surroundings, that an attempt on the part of strangers to speak or write concerning the character or conduct of its approved membership savors of impudent presumption. None but fishermen can properly deal with these delicate matters.

What sense is there in the charge of laziness sometimes made against true fishermen? Laziness has no place in the constitution of a man who starts at sunrise and tramps all day with only a sandwich to eat, floundering through bushes and briers and stumbling over rocks or wading streams in pursuit of the elusive trout. Neither can a fisherman who, with rod in hand, sits in a boat or on a bank all day be called lazy – provided he attends to his fishing and is physically and mentally alert in his occupation. This charge may perhaps be truthfully made against squaw-fishermen who become easily discouraged, who 'tire and faint' early, and lie down under the shade to sleep, or go in swimming, or who gaze about or read a book while their hooks rest baitless on the bottom; but how false and unfair it is to accuse regular, full-blooded fishermen of laziness, based on such performances as these! And yet this is absurdly done by those who cannot tell a reel from a compass, and who by way of familiarizing themselves with their topic leave their beds at eight o'clock in the morning, ride to an office at ten, sit at a desk until three or perhaps five, with an hour's interval for a hearty luncheon, and go home in the proud belief that they have done an active, hard day's work. Fishermen find no fault with what they do in their own affairs, nor with their conception of work; but they do insist that such people have no right to impute laziness to those who fish.

Why Fish Stories Should Be Believed

It is sometimes said that there is such close relationship between mendacity and fishing, that in matters connected with their craft all fishermen are untruthful. It must, of course, be admitted that large stories of fishing adventure are sometimes told by fishermen – and why should this not be so? Beyond all question there is no sphere of human activity so full of strange and wonderful incidents as theirs. Fish are constantly doing the most mysterious and startling things; and no one has yet been wise enough to explain their ways or account for their conduct. The best fishermen do not attempt it; they move and strive in the atmosphere of mystery and uncertainty, constantly aiming to reach results without a clue, and through the cultivation of faculties, non-existent or inoperative in the common mind.

In these circumstances fishermen necessarily see and do wonderful things. If those not members of the brotherhood are unable to assimilate the recital of these wonders, it is because their believing apparatus has not been properly regulated and stimulated. Such disability falls very far short of justifying doubt as to the truth of the narration. The things narrated have been seen and experienced with a fisherman's eyes and perceptions. This is perfectly understood by listening fishermen; and they, to their enjoyment and edification, are permitted by a properly adjusted mental equipment to believe what they hear.

This faculty is one of the safest signs of full-blooded right to membership. If incredulity is intimated by a professional member no injustice will be done if he is at once put under suspicion as a squaw-fisherman. As to non-members who accuse true fishermen of falsehood, it is perfectly clear that they are utterly unfitted to deal with the subject. The only theory fitting the condition leads to the statement that any story of personal experience told by a fisherman is to the fishing apprehension indubitably true; and that since disbelief in other quarters is owing to the lack of this apprehension, the folly of accusing fishermen of habitual untruthfulness is quite apparent.

The Taking of the Leviathan

The position thus taken by the brotherhood requires that they stand solidly together in all circumstances. Tarpon fishing has added greatly to our responsibilities. Even larger fish than these may, with the extension of American possessions, fall within the treatment of American fishermen. As in all past emergencies, we shall be found sufficient in such future exigencies. All will go well if, without a pretense of benevolent assimilation, we still fish as is our wont, and continue our belief in all that our brethren declare they have done or can do. A few thousand years ago the question was impressively asked, 'Canst thou draw out leviathan with a hook?' We must not falter, if, upon its repetition in the future, a brother replies: 'Yes, with a ten-ounce rod;' nor must we be staggered even if another declares he has already landed one of these monsters. If American institutions are found adequate to the new tasks which Destiny has put upon them in the extension of our lands, the American Chapter of the world's fishermen must not fail by their time-honored methods and practices, and by such truthfulness as belongs to the fraternity in the narration of fishing adventure, to subdue any new difficulties presented by the extension of our waters.

Why the Biggest Fish Are Always Lost

Before leaving this branch of our subject, especial reference should be made to one item more conspicuous, perhaps, than any other, among those comprised in the general charge of fishermen's mendacity. It is constantly said that they greatly exaggerate the size of the fish that are lost. This accusation, though most frequently and flippantly made, is in point of fact based upon the most absurd arrogance and a love of slanderous assertion that passes understanding. These are harsh words; but they are abundantly justified.

In the first place, all the presumptions are with the fisherman's contention. It is perfectly plain that large fish are more apt to escape than small ones. Of course their weight and activity, combined with the increased trickiness and resourcefulness of age and experience, greatly increase their ability to tear out the hook, and enhance the danger that their antics will expose a fatal weakness in hook, leader, line or rod. Another presumption which must be regretfully mentioned, arises from the fact that in many cases the encounter with a large fish causes such excitement, and such distraction or perversion of judgment, on the part of the fisherman as leads him to do the wrong thing or fail to do the right thing at the critical instant – thus actually and effectively contributing to an escape which could not and would not have occurred except in favor of a large fish.

Beyond these presumptions we have the deliberate and simple story of the fisherman himself, giving with the utmost sincerity all the details of his misfortune, and indicating the length of the fish he has lost, or giving in pounds his exact weight. Now, why should this statement be discredited? It is made by one who struggled with the escaped fish. Perhaps he saw it. This, however, is not important, for he certainly felt it on his rod, and he knows precisely how his rod behaves in the emergency of every conceivable strain.

The Finny Hypnotist

All true fishermen who listen to his plain, unvarnished tale accept with absolute faith the declared length and weight of the fish that was almost caught; but with every presumption, besides positive statement, against them, carping outsiders who cannot fish, and who love to accuse fishermen of lying, are exposed in an attempt to originate or perpetuate an envious and malicious libel.

The case of our fraternity on this point of absolute and exact truthfulness is capable of such irrefragable demonstration that anything in the way of confession and avoidance ought to be considered inadmissible. And yet, simply for the sake of argument, or by way of curious speculation, it may be interesting to intimate how a variation of a few inches in the exact length or a few ounces in the exact weight of a lost fish, as given by the loser, may be accounted for, without meanly attributing to him intentional falsehood. The theory has been recently started, that a trained hunting dog points a bird in the field solely because the bird's scent creates a hypnotic influence on the dog, which impels him by a sort of suggestion to direct his nose toward the spot from which such scent emanates. If there is anything worth considering in this theory, why may not a struggling fish at the end of a line exert such a hypnotic influence on the intensely excited and receptive nature at the other extremity of the fishing outfit, as to suggest an arbitrary and independent statement of the dimensions of the hypnotizer?

With the accusations already mentioned it would certainly seem that the enmity of those who take pleasure in reviling fishermen and their ways should be satisfied. They have not been content, however, in the demonstration of their evil-mindedness without adding to their indictment against the brotherhood the charge of profanity. Of course, they have not the hardihood to allege that our profanity is of that habitual and low sort which characterizes the coarse and ill-bred, who offend all decent people by constantly interlarding their speech with fearful and irrelevant oaths. They, nevertheless, find sufficient excuse for their accusation in the sudden ejaculations, outwardly resembling profanity, which are occasionally wrung from fishermen in trying crises and in moments of soul-straining unkindness of Fate.

Now, this question of profanity is largely one of intention and deliberation. The man who, intending what he says, coolly indulges in imprecation, is guilty of an offense that admits of no excuse or extenuation; but a fisherman can hardly be called profane who, when overtaken without warning by disaster, and abruptly hurled from the exhilarating heights of delightful anticipation to the depths of dire disappointment, impulsively gives vent to his pent-up emotion by the use of a word which, though found in the list of oaths, is spoken without intentional imprecation, and because nothing else seems to suit the occasion. It is by no means to be admitted that fishing tends even to this semblance of profanity. On the contrary, it imposes a self-restraint and patient forbearance upon its advanced devotees which tend to prevent sudden outbursts of feeling.

It must in frankness be admitted, however, by fishermen of every degree, that when the largest trout of the day, after a long struggle, winds the leader about a snag and escapes, or when a large salmon or bass, apparently fatigued to the point of non-resistance, suddenly, by an unexpected and vicious leap, frees himself from the hook, the fisherman's code of morals will not condemn beyond forgiveness the holder of the straightened rod if he impulsively, but with all the gentility at his command, exclaims: 'Damn that fish!' It is probably better not to speak at all; but if strong words are to be used, perhaps these will serve as well as any that can do justice to the occasion.

Uncle Toby, overcome with tender sympathy, swore with an unctuous, rotund oath, that his sick friend should not die; and we are told that 'the accusing spirit which flew up to Heaven's chancery with the oath blushed as he gave it in; and the recording angel as he wrote it down dropped a tear upon the word and blotted it out forever.'

The defense of the fishing fraternity which has been here attempted is by no means as completely stated as it should be. Nor should the world be allowed to overlook the admirable affirmative qualities which exist among genuine members of the brotherhood, and the useful traits which an indulgence in the gentle art cultivates and fosters. A recital of these, with a description of the personal peculiarities found in the ranks of fishermen, and the influence of these peculiarities on success or failure, are necessary to a thorough vindication of those who worthily illustrate the virtues of our clan.

The Fun of Fishing

BY DR. JAMES A. HENSHALL

ANGLING IS AS old as civilization. We read in the classics that in AD 230 the Macedonians fished the river Astræus with the artificial fly. The first book on angling in the English language was printed at Winchester, England, in 1496. Its author was a woman of noble birth, Dame Juliana Berners, prioress of a nunnery near St. Albans. She gave explicit instructions in the art, with directions for making rods and tackle, and gave the formulas for the tying of artificial flies for each month in spring and summer, many of which are in use to this day under various names.

The love of angling has ever gone hand in hand with the love of Nature. For, should the angler catch no fish, Dame Juliana quaintly says: 'Yet atte leest he hath his holsom walke, and mery at his ease. A swete ayre of the swete savoure of the mede flowers; that makyth hym hungry.'

So, as one of the incentives for an occasional outing is a love of angling, it should be remembered that 'It is not all of fishing to fish,' as George Dawson aptly expressed it. Rather, it is the opportunity that angling affords for a realization and enjoyment of Nature's resources, with the subsequent compensation of renewed health and strength. The cares and anxieties and perplexities of everyday life are forgotten as the angler wades the merry stream and casts his flies on the flashing water. He is wholly obsessed with his pursuit and has unbounded faith in his methods.

And while the eager expectancy of a response to his lures absorbs his every faculty, he enjoys, at the same time, in a subconscious way, the bounties of Nature surrounding and investing him. The voices of the stream are ever in his ears – the lapping and purling of the water as it sparkles on the riffle or whirls in the eddies. He is alive to the song of the birds, the hum of insects, and the whispering of the leaves as the sunlight filters through them.

But it does not follow that one must be a fly fisherman to obtain the full measure of enjoyment of such an outing. Mother Nature is equally kind to all who seek her solitudes. Even the boy angler, with bent pin and earthworm bait, is conscious of her moods and expressions, though he does not realize it at the time; in after years there will suddenly flash on memory's mirror that very scene of his boyhood.

He can scent the pungent odor of the mint that grew on the bank and remember the flash of the butterfly's wing that went sailing by, the rustle and quiver of the leaves overhead, and the cool and grateful sensation as he laved his bare feet in the stream. All this he remembers distinctly, even though he fails to recollect whether it was a minnow or a sunfish that he caught, or how many of them.

But better than an occasional outing is to camp for a week or a month beside a tumbling mountain stream, a brawling river, or a placid lake. The pleasures of angling can then be diversified by sauntering through the woods, climbing the hills, or rowing and sailing on the lake. Everywhere, on every hand, there is always something worthwhile – gathering and studying the wild flowers, observing the characteristics of the trees, collecting insects, or watching the amusing antics of the birds – enough to occupy all one's time during the day.

Then at night one can view with wonder and delight the starry canopy overhead, where the stars shine with more brilliancy and in greater numbers than are seen in the haunts of men. Perhaps then only does the city dweller see the flaming belt of Orion, the big and little dippers, and the Pleiades in the full glory of their surroundings.

Though there are degrees in angling, he of the first degree, the still fisher with alder rod, enjoys the sport with as much genuine love and zest as the master of angling with his slender wand of split bamboo and fairylike flies. Even the fisher with hickory pole and crawfish bait finds sport galore in yanking out a channel catfish. The outdoor environment and the voices of Nature appeal to each one the same. All are brothers of the angle.

The expert fly fisher who offers his silken gage of a Jock Scott fly to the lordly salmon, a polka fly to the gamesome black bass, a coachman to the brook trout, or a gray hackle to the graceful grayling, is, perhaps, to be envied. For, although his address to each fish requires various methods and much modification of his tools and tackle, he is equally at home with all – the fifteen-ounce rod for salmon, the seven-ounce for black bass, the six-ounce for trout, or one of five ounces for grayling. So, also, as to the caliber of his line and leader and the size of his fly hook; each must be commensurate with the size and gameness of his quarry.

In legitimate angling the Atlantic salmon is lord of all. His capture requires the skill and finesse of the finished angler, and the use of the most approved tackle, which is the outcome of the experience of centuries. The wild leap for freedom of the hooked fish, his stubborn resistance, his fierce fighting, his sulking, and his final gaffing have been extolled by eminent and expert fishers for hundreds of years, and recorded by the pens of ready and enthusiastic British writers. At the present day, in America, fortunes are spent yearly in his pursuit, for verily it is an expensive sport which can be had only on leased Canadian rivers and to a limited extent on one or two streams in Maine.

The several species of Pacific salmon do not rise to the artificial fly, more's the pity, and are of no interest to the fly fisher. During the days of '54 – 40 or a fight' an old Scotch official and salmon fisher said: 'Dom the country; the saumon will no rise to the fly; let the Yankees have it.'

On the other hand, the favorite American game fish, the black bass, which now has a local habitation and a name in every State of the Union, as well as in Canada and Mexico, can be fished for without money and without price, so far as the waters are concerned. The largemouth black bass was caught by the first English colonists of Virginia, the Carolinas, and Florida, who bestowed on him the names of 'salmon' and 'trout' as a tribute to his gameness. The early French *voyageurs* knew him intimately and well, while the smallmouth black bass was the favorite game fish of enthusiastic anglers of the Middle West fully a century ago. But it was not until fifty years later, when the black bass was introduced into the waters of the Eastern States, that he came into his own as an acknowledged peer among game fishes.

The life histories of both the largemouth and smallmouth bass are now common knowledge. All over the length and breadth of our land, from Maine to California, wherever there is a lakelet, the largemouth bass may be found sunning himself among the water lilies and bulrushes, while the smallmouth bass rears his spiny crest and flashes his bronze armor in almost every stream from New York to Arkansas. No other game fish is now so eagerly sought by the tens of thousands of anglers of every degree as the black bass, and no other game fish is so accessible on lake, pond, or stream, either by wading or fishing from a boat or from the bank.

In the Eastern States no other game fish is so well known and prized as the brook trout. Perhaps no other is held in such veneration by the veterans of the angling guild, who view with sorrow and regret its passing from many of its native streams. And though it is being replaced with the English brown trout and the Pacific rainbow trout, no other can ever win the same love and affection with which the ruby-studded living arrow of the crystal waters is regarded by the old-timers. They hark back to the days of long ago, when barefooted they trudged along the brookside, their pathway adorned with trailing arbutus, their ears attuned to the song sparrow, but with eyes ever alert for the trout under the bank.

And how this is all lived over again as their children and grandchildren go back to the old home, during the vacation months, and fish the same brooks and gather flowers and health. Or perhaps it is the old pond where the bullpout or even a pickerel may still be found and the water lilies still bloom.

If one cannot visit the haunts of the salmon, black bass, trout, or grayling, there are always other fishes to claim the attention of the true angler, who with the lightest tackle can still enjoy the pleasures of the sport. It is not so much the character and esteem of the fish itself as the spirit with which the angler enters into the game. With a rod of three or four ounces and midge artificial flies, the rock bass, white bass, crappie, perch, bluegill, or even the common sunfish will afford as much real sport, *per se*, as more pretentious fishes. And for camp fare there are no better dainties for the camper with a camper's appetite.

In this country of abundance in both species and numbers of fishes, many real game fishes are apt to be ignored. In England, on the contrary, where there are comparatively few species, thousands of anglers who are debarred from preserved waters, or who cannot afford the expense of salmon or trout fishing, are just as enthusiastic in pursuit of such coarse fish as roach, dace, rudd, bream, or barbel, all members of the minnow family, none of which is equal in gameness to our chub or fallfish. We have a minnow in the streams of the Pacific slope three or four feet long that takes bait freely and rises to the artificial fly, but it is not a game fish and is not much sought. And then there is the carp, which is considered a game fish in England.

If one is not a fly fisher he can still use bait, minnows, crawfish, worms, grubs, and grasshoppers. It makes little difference as to the lure employed, for the chief object is to capture the quarry, and it is all one to the fish whether it succumbs to an artificial fly or to the humble and lowly earthworm.

In saltwater, fishing bait is almost universally used, as shrimps, crabs, clams, sand- and blood-worms. And what a joy it is to the men, women, and children of the cities to leave behind the dusty streets, the stifling heat of brick and mortar, for the seashore, to find relief in fishing, bathing, and beachcombing. Even a single trip on an excursion steamer to the fishing banks affords a day of real pleasure long to be remembered.

During the summer blackfish or tautog, bluefish, striped bass, and weakfish may be taken in most places along the coast of the Middle States. The bluefish, however, is rather uncertain in its advent, and may be scarce or plentiful. Like the coyote, it hunts its prey in company, sometimes in countless numbers, and roams along the coast in quest of schools of small fry, on which it descends like the Assyrians of old, its cohorts, however, gleaming in blue and silver instead of purple and gold. Even the flounder, scup, or cunner are not to be altogether despised should the 'tide-runners' refuse to bite. It is only their familiarity with his bait that breeds the contempt of the fastidious angler.

With his boat rocking gently on the incoming tide, the angler, apart from his fishing, is conscious of the white sails shimmering in the offing, the long streamer of smoke from the funnel of an outgoing steamer, and is not unmindful of the erratic flight of the sea gulls as they scream and hover over the shining water and dash into it occasionally for some tidbit of flotsam. He pauses from his fishing once in a while to admire the beauty of the graceful trophies in his basket – their pearly tints and silvery sheen, their jeweled eyes and shapely fins – while the salt breeze fans his cheek as he 'loafs and invites his soul.' Surely the angler has chosen the better part in the catalogue of outdoor sports.

In the ethics of true sportsmanship there are several things in relation to angling that it may be well to remember: Always kill the fish outright as soon as unhooked; whether using natural or artificial bait never, under any circumstances, employ more than a single hook; and never take more fish than your needs demand. The methods of the fish hog are not for us. Rather let us ponder the advice of good Dame Juliana Berners, as applicable now as four centuries ago:

Also ye shall not be ravenous in takyng of your sayd game as to mooche at one tyme . . . As whanne ye have a suffycyent mese ye sholde covet no more at that tyme. Also ye shall beysye yourselfe to nourysth the game in all that ye maye, and to dystroye all such thynges as ben devourers of it. And all those that done after this rule shall have the blessynge of God and Saynt Peter, whyche he theym graunte, that with his preecyous bloode vs boughte.

Treatise of Fishing with an Angle

DAME JULIANA BERNERS

MODERNIZED BY GARRETT COOK

S OLOMON IN HIS parables said a good spirit makes a flowering age; an age that is fair and long. And since it is so, I ask this question: which are the means and causes to induce a man into a merry spirit? Truly to my best discretion it seems that good sport and honest games can bring a man joy with no need for repentance when they are done. So it follows that good sport and honest games are a cause of good times and long life. And therefore now we will speak of four good sports and honest games that I have chosen. That is, to wit, of hawking, hunting, fishing and fowling. The best, in my opinion is fishing (also called angling) with a rod, a line and a hook and therefore to treat this topic, as best my simple wit will suffice, both for the reason Solomon spoke of and also for the reason that reason makes in this way:

Si tibi deficiant medici, medici tibi fiant
Hec tria – mens laeta, labor, et moderatadieta.

You must understand that I am saying that if a man lacks a doctor or medicine, he will make three things his medicine and he shall never need any other. The first of them is a merry thought. The second is a modest labor. The third is a reasonable diet. First of all, if a man will ever more think merrily and have a glad spirit, he must eschew all contrarian company and all places of debate where he might have felt any melancholy. And if he will have a reasonable labor, he must then give in to his heart's ease and pleasure without study, pensiveness or difficulty, seeking a merry diversion which will lighten his heart and delight his spirit. And if he is to eat a reasonable diet, he must eschew all places of rot, which is a cause of suffering and sickness, and he must eat nourishing and enjoyable meals.

Now, I will describe, as briefly as I can, the sports and games I spoke of in order to find the best of them. The right noble and worthy Duke of York, known lately as a master of the game, has described the joys of hunting, and I would describe them similarly. Hunting is too laborious for my taste, however. The hunter must travel beside his hounds until he is sore and covered in sweat. He blows his horn until his lips blister. And when he seeks to unearth a hare, more often than not it is a hedgehog. Thus he chases, and knows not even what he is chasing. He comes home in the evening beaten by rain, pecked, with torn clothes and wet shoes, exhausted. Some of his hounds are lost and some crippled. Such misfortunes and many others befall the hunter, some so harsh that I dare not report it for fear of displeasing those that love to hunt. Thus, I think that it is not the best sport of the four I mentioned.

I also think the sport of hawking is a laborious and noisome one. Often the falconer will lose his birds as the hunter does his hounds and with them, he will lose not only his sport but his prey. His hawk takes a bow and listen not once. When he would have her fly, she will refuse. With misfeeding she shall have frounce, the rue, the cray and many other sicknesses which will cause them to suffer. Thus it is proven that this is not the most satisfying game of the four.

The sport of fowling seems to be the simplest, for in the winter season, the game hunter does not need to toil, but in the hardest and coldest of the weather, when it is at its most grievous, he will not be able to go for his guineas since it is too cold. He will make many a trap and many a snare, but he will do poorly and come morning he will be immersed in pains. There are many more things I could tell but fear of rebuke leads me to stop. Therefore, it seems to be that hunting, hawking and fowling are so laborious and full of grief that none of them serve to lead a man into a merry spirit and therefore, according to Solomon, a long life.

This therefore proves, that of all sports, fishing with an angle is the best. All other manners of fishing are laborious, often making people frustrated and cold, which many times has been the cause of great infirmities, but the angler will avoid cold, sickness and anger and will lose at most but a line or a hook, which he should have a plentiful supply of if he makes them himself, as I shall teach you to later in this treatise. This loss is not grievous and there will be no other conflicts unless the fish gets away after it's hooked or unless he catches nothing, which is certainly not disastrous. If he fails to catch one fish, he might not fail to catch another fish, if he does as this treatise instructs, unless there are none in the water. Yet, he still gets to take a merry walk, taking in the sweet air and flavor of the flowers in the meadow. He hears the melodious song of the fowl. He sees the young swans, herons, ducks, coots, and many other fowl with their broods, which to me seems better than all the noise of hounds, the blasts of horns, and the cry of birds that the hunters, falconers and fowlers can make. And if the angler should catch a fish, there is no man so merry in spirit as he.

Whoever should seek to best enjoy fishing should be sure to rise early. To rise early is the best for the health of his soul, for it causes him to be holy and to the health of his body for it causes him to be whole. It will also help in increasing one's wealth, as the old proverb says. Whoever rises early shall be holy, healthy and happy. Therefore, here I prove that angling enriches one's spirit greatly. As the parable of Solomon says, this doctrine and activity makes one live to a ripe old age and help you be virtuous, gentle and free. I write this simple treatise so that you may learn the craft of angling so that you may enjoy it and your health and longevity will flourish.

If you wish to be crafty as a fisherman, you must first learn to make your harness, that is, your rod and all your colored lines. After that, you must know how to angle, in what part of the water, how deep and what time, for what kind of fish in what weather, how many impediments there are and most importantly, which baits to use for which fish during which month of the year. Then I shall tell you how to make your baits-bread, how to keep them and most useful, how to make your hooks out of steel.

I will now teach you how to make your rod well. Between Michaelmas and Candlemas, cut a staff nine feet long and thick as an arm, made from hazel, willow or aspen and bake it in a hot oven. Then let it cool and dry for a month. Take it then and tie it with a cord and bind it to a great, square tree. Then take a wire that is even, straight and sharp at one end and heat the sharp end in a charcoal fire and burn the staff, keeping it straight where both ends meet and after that burn it at the edge with a spit for roasting birds and with other spits, each larger than the last, until a hole is tapered correctly. In the same season, take a yard of green hazel, wet it evenly, then let it dry with the staff. When they are dry, put the yard through the hole in the staff halfway down and then take a shoot of black thorn, crab tree, medlar or juniper cut in the same season straight set together so that your crop may enter the same hole. Then shave your staff, put iron rings in the cleanest way possible and a pike at the tail end fastened with a vise so that you can take it in and out of your crop. Then set your crop about a hand's length from the outer end of your staff in such a way that it is as big there as any place above it, then fix your crop at the other end down to the fret with a line of six hairs, double the line, fret it fast in the top with a bow and fasten it to your line. Thus will you make a rod so effectively that you can walk around with it and no man who looks at you could know how good it is. It will be nimble and light enough for you to fish with it at your pleasure.

After you have made your rod, you must learn to color your lines. Here is how. First, you must take from a horse's tail the longest and lightest hair you can find, the rounder that it is, the better. Break it down into six parts and every part should be colored differently; yellow, green, brown, tawny, russet and dark blue. To make the green color, take a small amount of ale and put it into a pan and then put half a pound of alum. Let it boil softly for half an hour. Then, take out your hair and let it dry. Then take a pot of clear water and put it in a pan with two hands full of wax, press it with a tile stone and let it boil softly for an hour. When the froth is yellow, then put your hair in it with half a pound of metallic sulphate beaten in powder and let it boil and then take out the heat and dry it and it will be the finest green that can be had for the water. The more copperas you use, the better it will be, so that it does not turn out a rusty color.

There is another way you can make a brighter green. Let your hair boil in a boiling fat of light grayish blue color but do not add copperas or verdigris.

To make the hair seem yellow, dye it with alum as I have said before, and after that with wax without copperas or verdigris.

There is another way to make yellow and you can do it thus: take some ale and a pestle, stamp three handfuls of walnut leaves and put them together, then put your hair in there until the color is as deep as you would like.

To make a russet hair, take a pint of strong lye and a half pint of soot, a little juice from walnut leaves and a quart of alum. Put them all together in a pan and boil them well, then when it is cold put your hair in until it is as dark as you want it.

To make the brown color take a pound of soot and a quart of ale and seethe with as many walnut leaves as you'd like. Then when they are black, set it from the fire and let it lie still until it is as brown as you need it.

To make another kind of brown you take strong ale and soot, temper them together and put your hair in it for two days and two nights and then it shall be a very good color.

To make a tawny color, take lime and water and put them together, then put the hair in for four or five hours. Then take it out and put it into a tanner sole for one day and then it will be a tawny color.

The sixth part of your hair, you will keep white, for the double hook used for the trout and grayling and for small lines to lie in wait for the roach or the dace.

Once your hairs have been dyed, you will need to know when to use which hair. The green color is best in clear water from April to September. The yellow color can be used in any clear water, from September to November, for it resembles the weeds and grasses that grow in rivers.

The russet color will serve all the winter until the end of April, as well in rivers, pools or lakes.

The brown color serves you in water that is black and dead. The tawny color works best in waters that are heavy or swampy.

Now I will tell you how to make your lines. Take your hair and cut a handful or more off the end. At first, your hair will not be strong or steady. Then turn your top to the tail and divide into three parts. Then knit every part at one end by itself and at the other end, knit all three together. And then put the same end in the part of your instrument that has only one cleft. Set the other end with the wedge four fingers wide from the end. Twine every strand one way and fasten it into the clefts straight. And then set that other end fast with the wedge four fingers in all, shorter than your hair. Then strain it a little and knit it for undoing. The instrument should be made of wood, save for the bolt underneath which should be iron.

So when you have as many links as you think will suffice for the length of a line, then you must knit them together with a water knot, or else a duchess, and when your knot is knit, cut off the short ends a straw from the knot. The line will be fine for any fish.

Understand that the hardest and most subtle craft in making your harness is to make your hooks.

For small fish make your hooks of the smallest quarrel needles you can find and then put the quarrel in a charcoal fire until it is the same color as the fire. Take it out then and let it cool and you will find it ready to file. Then with your knife, make the point sharp. Allay it again, or else it will break as it bends. Then bend it once more in the same way. Larger hooks you make in the same way as you would needles for embroidery or cobbling. They should be as sharp as shoemaker's nails. When the hook is bent, beat the back end and file it smooth for fretting the line. Then put it in the fire and give it some heat. Then suddenly quench it and it will be hard and strong.

When you have made your hooks, then you must set them according to size and strength. You should take a small red thread and if it is for a big hook make sure it is twinned. If it is for small hooks don't twin it, and then thickly fret the line so it will fit a wide straw. Then set there your hook and fret the thread with two parts the same length everything should be fretted at. And when you come to the third part, turn the end of your line on the double fret, and fret it so it is doubled at the other third part, then put your thread in at the whole two or three times, and let it go each time around the length of your hook, then bore the hole and draw it until it is held fast and look that your line lies with the hooks, and not without, then cut off the end of the lines and the thread as close as you can to the fret.

So that you know how many hooks and hairs you should use to catch each fish, I will now tell you. First, for the minnow, you should use just one hair. For the roach, the chub, the bleak, the gudgeon and the ruffe with a line of two hairs, for the dace and a large roach with a line of three hairs. For the perch, the flounder and the bream, with four hairs. For the chub, the bream, the tench, and the eel, with six hairs. For the trout, grayling, barbel or a large chub: with nine hairs. For the trout, with twelve hairs. For the salmon, fifteen. Lastly, for the pike, with a chalk line dyed brown and prepared in a manner I shall describe later.

Your lines must be weighted with lead. And you must know the weight nearest the hook shall be no closer than a foot or more away from it. There is a special manner of weights for the ground line and for the float lying on the ground line. Nine or ten of these small weights should be run together. The float weight will need to be heavy enough so that the first pull will bring it down into the water, and make sure they are round and smooth so they do not stick to weeds or stones.

Then you should make your floats the following way: take a cork that is clean and doesn't have any holes and drill into it with a small iron drill and put a straight pin in there, always note the bigger pin, and the bigger hole. Then shape it large at the middle, small in both ends and sharp at the edge and small at both. Make them smooth on a grinding stone or on a tile stone, and make sure that the float for one hair is no more than a small piece, for two hairs the size of a bean, for twelve hairs as a walnut, and so every line according to its portion.

All manner of lines that are not ground lines must have floats and the ground line must have a float.

Now, I have taught you how to make all your harness. And here, I will tell you how to angle.

Understand that there are six ways of angling. One is at the ground for the trout and other fish. Another is at the ground at an arch or a stang where it ebbs and flows for bleak, roach and dace. The third is with a float for all manner of fish. The fourth is with a minnow for the trout, without a weight or a float. The fifth is dragging the ground line for the roach and dace, with one or two hairs and a fly. The sixth is a doubled hook for the trout or the grayling.

For the first and principal point of angling, keep your eyes on the water to see the fish. You may wish to hide behind a bush so that the fish do not see you. If they do, they will not bite. And make sure you don't let your shadow fall on the water because that is something that will frighten the fish. And if a fish is afraid, he will not bite for very long afterwards. For all manner of fish that feed near the ground, angle for them near the bottom so that your hook will drag or lie on the ground. For the fish that feed above, look for them in the middle of the water, the bigger fish you will find in the deepest part of the water. The third good point is that when the fish bite you must not strike too soon or too late.

You must wait until you think the bait is in the fish's mouth and no longer, and this is for the ground. And for the float, when you see it pulled softly under the water, or is carried softly upon the water, then strike. Make sure you never cast harder than the strength of your line so that it doesn't break. If you are lucky enough to catch a great fish with a small harness, you must lead him in the water and struggle with him until he is drowned and overcome. Then take him as well as you can but make sure you keep your line strong. And as much as you can, keep him always under the rod and hold him straight so that your line can sustain and bear his leaps and plunges with the help of your crop and your hand.

Here I shall tell you where you should angle: you should angle in a pool or at a landing, at every place where the water is suitably deep.

There is no greater choice for fishing in deep water than a pool, for it is a prison to all fish and requires less skill to catch them. But in a river, you should fish in any place where the water is deep and clear by the ground; such as gravel or clay, where there are no weeds, and especially if there is a whirlpool or a covert as a hollow bank, the roots of a tree and long weeds are places where fish will hide themselves. It is also good to fish in deep, stiff streams and valleys of water or in flood gates or mill pits.

And at the bank and where the stream runs nearby and is deep and clear by the ground and in any places where you have seen that fish are feeding.

Now you shall know what time of day to angle. From the beginning of May until September: the biting time is early in the morning from four to eight, in the afternoon from four to eight, you also can but it is not as good as in the morning. If it is a cloudy day with a cold wind, it is better than a clear day. Also, many fish in pools bite best in the morning.

And if you should see the trout or grayling leap, fish for him in the manner I tell you to according to the month listed. And where the water ebbs and flows, the fish will bite in some places at the ebb and at some places at the flow after they have rested behind poles, arches of bridges and other such places.

Here you shall discover what manner of weather you should angle in. As I said before, it is best in a dark cloudy day when the wind blows softly. In the Summer when it is burning hot, it is not the right time. From September to April, on a nice day, it is very good to fish and if the wind in that season has part of the Oriental weather, then it is not, neither is it when the wind is strong or when it snows, rains, hails or storms, or if there is thunder and lightning. If the weather is sweltering, then it is not right to fish.

You shall now learn of the twelve sorts of impediments that cause a man to catch no fish. There are twelve kinds, save for those occurrences that happen naturally. The first is if your harness is not even or well made. The second is if your bait is not of good quality. The third is if you do not angle at the right time. The fourth is that the fish are scared off at the sight of you. The fifth is that the water is very thick, white or red because of any recent flooding. The sixth is if the fish are not swimming because the water is too cold. The seventh is if the weather is hot. The eighth, if it rains. The ninth, if it snows or hails. The tenth, if it storms. The eleventh, if the wind is strong. The twelfth, if the wind is in the East, which is the worst. The fish will not usually bite then. The west and the north wind are good but the south is the best.

And now that I have told you how to make your harness so you should fish with it at all points, you should now learn what baits you should use on every manner of fish in every month of the year, which is all the effect of the craft.

If you do not know these baits well, all of your knowledge of the craft will be without purpose for you cannot bring a fish's mouth to a hook without the knowledge of the right bait for the right type of fish.

Because the salmon is the most stately fish one can catch in fresh water, we shall begin at him. The salmon is a gentle fish for he is not difficult to take. Commonly, he is in the deepest part of the rivers, and often he stays in the middle of it so that a man may not come to him. He is in season from March to Michaelmas, during which seasons you will fish for him with the baits I am about to describe. First, at the beginning and ending of the season, you can catch with a red worm and with the grubs that breed in a dung heap and especially with the sovereign bait that breeds under a dock. He will bite not at the ground line but at the float and then you can take him. It is, however, on rare occasions seen with a grub when he is leaping in the same way a trout or a grayling would be. These are proven baits for catching the salmon.

The trout is a toothy fish and also a fervent biter, so we shall speak next of him. He is in season from March until Michaelmas. He is on clean gravel ground in a stream, so at any time, you can fish for him with a ground line. If he is leaping, you can catch him with a fly, early in the day with a running ground line and later in the day with a float line. In March, you can catch a trout by dangling a minnow without a float, drawing up and down the stream until you feel that he has been held fast. In the same time angle for him with ground lines and, to be most certain, with a red worm. In April take the same baits, or lampreys and also the cankerworm that breeds in big trees, and the red snail. In May take the stone fly and the silk worm and the bait that breeds under a fern leaf. In June, take a red worm, cut off its head and then place a codworm in front of it upon the hook. In July, take the red worm and the codworm together. In August, take a fresh fly, the red worm and bacon fat and bind them together on the hook. In September, take the red worm and the minnow. In October, take the same, for they are special to the trout at all times of the year. From April until September the trout leaps; then catch him with a doubled hook according to the month you find at the end of this treatise.

The grayling is also a delicious fish, which you can catch the same way you would a trout. These are the baits you use: in March and April, you will use a red worm, in May the green worm, the dock canker, and the hawthorn worm. In June, you use the bait that breeds between the tree and the bark of an oak. In July, the bait that breeds on a fern leaf, or take a great red worm and cut off its head, put a codworm in front of it. In August, a red worm and a dock worm and the rest of the year, a red worm.

The barbel is a sweet fish but its meat is perilous for a man's body. It has often been known to cause fever. And if it is eaten raw, it has been seen to cause death. In March and April you can use fresh cheese cut into small pieces on the end of your hook, burn it until it is yellow, bind it to the hook with fletcher's silk. This bait is good all Summer. In May and June, take the hawthorn worm and the red worm. You cut off the head and put a codworm on your hook in front of it. In July, take the red worm, the hawthorn worm and the cheese together. In August, the dock leaf worm will work. For the rest of the year, take the tallow of a sheep, soft cheese, a little honey and grind and stomp them together, then add a little flour, make them into small pallets and you will find this a good bait to angle with at the ground. You must let it sink in the water or else it is not good for this purpose.

The carp is a delicacy, but there are few of them in England, and therefore I write the least of him since he is a difficult fish to take. His mouth is so strong that no weak harness may hold him. Regarding the proper bait for carp, I have little knowledge, so I am loathe to write much. But I know well that the red worm and the minnow are good baits and I have heard from reputable sources and books that this is so.

The chub is a stately fish and his head is a dainty morsel. There is no fish with a body so equipped with scales and because he is a strong biter, there are more baits necessary. In March, the red worm is at the ground and he will eat as much of it as he chooses. In April, the ditch canker that breeds in the tree and the worm that breeds between the rind and tree of an oak will work, as will the red worm and the snail. You can also use frogs, also the stone fly or the red snail. In May, you can use the bait that breeds in the osier leaf and the dock canker together on your hook and the bait that breeds on the fern leaf, the bait that breeds on the oak, or a silk worm and a codworm together. In June, take the cricket and also a red worm with the head cut off and put them on the hook. Also, the bait that breeds on the osier leaf, young frogs with all their feet cut off at the knee, the hawthorn and the codworm together, the grub that breeds on the dunghill, and also grasshoppers and bumblebees. You can also try young bees and hornets and the great brown death fly that breeds in meadow paths or the fly that breeds among anthills. In August take earthworms and until Michaelmas, maggots. After that time, earthworms are best.

The tench is a good fish and heals all manner of other fish if they go to him. He spends most of the year in the mud, moving around but little, and you can only see him moving around in June and July. He is a terrible biter and for most of the year you can catch him with brown bread and the great red worm. And you can also take the black blood in a sheep's heart, flour and honey, mix them into a soft paste, anoint the red worm with it for this fish or another and they will bite much better.

The perch is a delicious fish and quite wholesome. These are his baits: in March, the red worm. In April, the twigs found under cow turds. In May, the hawthorn worm and the codworm. In June, the bait that breeds in an old fallen oak and the large canker worm. In July, the bait that breeds on the osier leaf, the bait that breeds on the dunghill, the codworm and the hawthorn worm. In August, the red worm and maggots, and for the rest of the year, the red worm is the best.

The roach is an easy fish to take and if he is fat, quite delicious. In March, he can be caught with the red worm. In April, the twig under the cow turd. In May, the bait that breeds on the oak leaf. In June, the bait that breeds on the osier leaf. In July, house spiders, the bait that breeds on oak and the nut worm, maggots until Michaelmas and after that, bacon fat.

The dace is an easy fish to take and can often be good meat. In March, his bait is an earthworm. In April, the twigs under the cow turds. In May, the dock canker and the bait under the oak leaf. In June, the codworm, the bait under the osier leaf, and the white grub in the dunghill. In July, take house spiders and the flies that breed in ant hills, the codworm and maggots until Michaelmas. And if the water is clear, you will take fish when others take none. It is commonly seen that their biting is like that of the roach, and so do what you do for a roach.

The bleak is a weak fish but he is wholesome. His bait until Michaelmas is the same as I have written before for the roach and the dace and all Summer, you can fish for him with a housefly, and in the Winter with bacon.

The ruffe is a wholesome fish and you can fish for him with the same bait any time of the year in the same way as I told you to fish for the perch, for they are similar fish and eat similar things, save that the ruffe is smaller and you must have smaller bait for it.

The flounder is a wholesome fish and a subtle biter. Commonly, when he takes his meat, he'll eat it at the ground and you must angle to him with a ground line. He has only one bait, which is the red worm, the best bait for all manner of fish.

The gudgeon is a good, large fish and he bites well at the ground. His baits for all the year are the red worm, the codworm and maggots and you must fish for him with a float, letting your bait be on the bottom or else on the ground.

The minnow, when he shines in the water, is better and though his body is little, he is a ravenous and eager biter and you should angle for him with the same baits as you do for the gudgeon.

The eel is a queasy fish, ravenous and a devourer of broods of fish. The pike is the same. I put them both behind all fish when it comes to angling, for if you find a whole group of eels in blue and black water, put your hook in until it is about a foot deep in the hole and use a large angle with a minnow on it as your bait. The pike is a good fish save that he eats as much of his own kind as he does any other, which makes me less fond of him. To catch him, take a roach or a fresh herring and a wire with a hook on the end of it and put it in at the mouth and then put your line and hook in after and draw the hook into the herring's cheek. Then take a lead weight a yard away from your hook and put a float halfway between it and the hook and cast it into a pit that the pike uses and this is the surest way to catch a pike. There are three ways of taking him in. Take a frog and put it on your hook at the neck between the skin and the body, on the back half and put a float in there, then cast it where the pike frequents and you will have him.

Another way is to take the same bait, put it in asafetida and cast it into the water with a cork and you will not fail to get him. If you wish to have some good sport, then tie the cord to a goose foot and you will have a good time watching whether the goose or the pike will fare better.

Now you know with what baits to angle for each kind of fish. Now I will tell you how to keep and feed your live baits. When they are quick and new they are fine but when they have been in a slough or dead then they will not work. The exceptions to this are three kinds of insect, that is, to wit, hornets, bumblebees and wasps, who you shall bake in bread, dip their heads in blood and let them dry. Also excluded are maggots when they breed greatly, you should feed them with sheep's tallow and with a cake made of flour and honey so that they get fat, cleansed well with sand in a bag of blankets kept hot under your gown or something similarly warm for two or three hours. Then they will be ready to angle with. For frogs, cut off the legs at the knees and for grasshoppers cut the legs and wings off the body.

The following good baits are made to last the year. The first is flour and lean flesh off the hips of a rabbit or cat, virgin wax or sheep's tallow ground in a mortar, then tempered at the fire with purified honey and made up into little balls for baiting the hooks. This is good bait for all manner of freshwater fish.

Another: take the same of sheep suet and cheese and grind them together in a mortar, then take thin flour and temper them together, then add honey and make balls of it. This is especially good for the barbel.

Another for dace and roach and bleak: take wheat and seethe it well and put it in blood all day and night.

For baiting large fish, remember this rule: when you have a big fish, undo the mouth and what you find there make your bait, for it is best.

These are the flies which you can use to catch trout or grayling.

MARCH

The dun fly: the body of dun wool and the feathers of the partridge. Another dun fly: the body of the black feathers of the blackest drake and the jay under the wings and under the tail.

APRIL

The stone fly: the body of black wood and yellow under the feathers and under the tail feathers of the drake. At the beginning of May a good fly: the body of rodded wool and wrapped about with black silk, the feathers of the drake and the red capon's plumage.

MAY

The yellow fly: the body of yellow wool, the plumage of a red rooster's wings and of the yellow drake. The black looper: the body of a black sheep and wrapped about with the head of a peacock's tail and the feathers of a red capon, with a blue head.

JUNE

The dun cut: the body of black wool and a yellow border on either side, the feathers of the buzzard bound on with hemp. The moor fly: the body of dusk wool, the feathers of the blackest male wild drake. The tandy fly at Saint William's Day: the body of tandy and wool and the feathers on either side of the whitest male wild drake.

JULY

The wasp fly: the body of black wool wrapped about with yellow thread. The feathers of the buzzard. The shell fly at Saint Thomas' Day: the body of green wool and wrapped about with the head of the peacock's tail. Feathers of the buzzard.

Here follows the order to be made to all those who wish to understand this treatise and use it for their pleasures.

You can angle and take fish at your pleasure with the knowledge here, but I charge you and request in the name of all noble men that you not fish at a poor man's water without his permission. Nor should you break any man's traps on his property. For after a fish is taken if the trap is laid in common waters, then you should take no fish, for the fish in this trap are his. If you take the fish, then you rob him which is a right shameful deed to any noble man to do what thieves do before they are punished for their evil deeds by hanging. If you do as this treatise shows you, you have no need to take any man's fish since you shall have enough fish of your own. If you decide to labor in this way, it will be a pleasure to you to see the bright shining scaled fishes that you have deceived by your crafty techniques. And also, I ask you to break no man's hedge while going about your sport. Take good heed that in going about this, you open no man's gate without shutting it again. You should also not use this advice out of covetousness or to spare your money but only for your solace and health, and especially the health of your soul. When you propose to fish, you may do so without the need of many others to fish with you. By choosing to fish, you will eschew many vices, such as idleness, which is the principal cause that induces a man to indulge in other vices, as it is well known to do. Also you should not be too ravenous in taking said game, which you might do if you follow all the advice in this treatise but that would ruin your sport and also the sport of other men. When you have enough food that you covet no more, stop fishing and you will help yourself to nourish the game and defend it from all things that would devour it. And all those that do after this rule shall have the blessing of God and Saint Peter, that blessing may He grant who bought us with his precious blood.

The Metaphysics of Fly Fishing

CUTTER STREEBY

Metaphysics: The branch of philosophy that treats of first principles, including being and knowing. A speculation on questions that are unanswerable to scientific observation, analysis, or experiment.

'Many go fishing all their lives without knowing that it is not fish they are after.'
– Henry David Thoreau

I'VE WORKED AT North 40 Outfitters for a year in April. I have known many types of people in my studies and travels and have come to recognize that if a person be consumed by a passion greater than materialism, he or she assumes a certain type of bearing. I've known people consumed by bull fights, by religion, by family, by poetry, by art – there is something in common, something basal in these types of people – maybe it's a certain type of talking or thinking, but everything becomes interrelated to whatever has consumed them, and with that, the outside world assumes the shape of their passion. To the writer, a conversation overheard in passing is a passage in a novel, analogously, to the fly fisherman, a certain texture, a certain material is translated into a piece of a bug, a wing, an eye.

Fly fishing, like every true passion, recasts everything in its image: the weather, the sun, the bugs, the flora around the river, one's children, the water temperature and clarity – all become unified and interrelated flowing naturally into the singular act of 'fly fishing.' The act itself here in quotations represents to practitioners something more, something beyond a simple set of skills.

He is standing waist deep in the Mo below Craig Dam, catching his fifth fish in an hour, 'This isn't how I normally fish – I call this 'production fishing',' he tells me in a humble manner, laughing, 'But it gives Jake something to shoot.'

Fred is nymphing with a 'classified' sow bug – Fred tells me and Jake about the evolution of this secret breed of bug, 'It's all hand done. Hand carved, hand painted, hand roasted – you can't buy this anywhere, and I wouldn't want it to get out there.'

In my head, that Kanye track starts playing: 'No man should have all that powAH...'

Fred's esoteric knowledge comes from decades of fly fishing. He has homemade everything, even a hook-remover tool, 'Someone patented this design,' he tells me laughing. 'Called it, "The Guide's Choice". I bet you it was one of my clients.'

He lands his sixth trout and brings it toward the bank, demonstrating to me the proficiency of his design. 'Like that,' he says, and in less time than it took to read those two words, another trout slips back into the water.

It's not the isolated power of the secret sow bug that moves in Fred, it's a deep understanding and union with nature, with a primordial force like the river – this union allows the advanced practitioner an intuitive kind of knowledge that to an outsider like me seems somewhat mystical. And in choosing not to exercise that power or patent it for personal gain, Fred seems to support Rousseau's proof that man is inherently good when in a state of nature.

Fishing that day was a unique experience because there were three generations of fly fishermen on the water. There is empirical evidence that tendency for art runs in families. Like any art, I would hazard the guess that fly fishing is also familial. It's my further conjecture that the rate of familial fly fisher accretion is greater than that of the converse; more fly fishers are brought into the fold by their families than are lost from the family line.

Joe seems to embody this theory, having learned to fly fish from his dad, who in turn learned from Joe's grandfather. 'I don't remember a time when I didn't fly fish,' he tells me, eyes on the water reading shifts and ripples like some occult translator. 'See there,' he points. 'They'll stack there.'

I don't see.

It's a certain kind of reverence that binds a fly fisherman to the water, a reverence present to different degrees in all practitioners. I asked Fred about this almost imperceptible quality, and, perhaps not surprisingly, he had an extensive answer.

'In the life of a fly fisherman,' he begins, his intonation like some type of collegial orator: 'in the life of a fly fisherman there is a pattern I've observed. In the beginning, for the first few years, the fisherman is learning. He knows he knows nothing, and so is always trying to learn and practice.'

The whole time he is discoursing, he is fishing. 'After about five years, this person thinks they know something,' he mends his drift, 'and so becomes stubborn and closed off to learning new things – they think they have the skills down, and so go out to conquer the fish.' (Here I feel some Buddhist or Christian precept is appropriate; for instance, 'Know thyself.')

'Depending on the type of person,' Fred continues, 'this stage in the life cycle of a fly fisherman can last for years, sometimes ten, fifteen – I've met people who have never gotten past it.' He takes a minute to release another trout, eight in an hour and a half if you are counting.

'Sometimes they get past it faster though, and once past it,' he recasts back near the same seam, 'they realize again they know nothing, and from there they're always learning.'

Aristotle, Shakespeare (via Palingenius – thanks, Wikipedia), and many other artists and philosophers have posited their own 'Stages of Man.'

So, am I saying Fred is a philosophical sage? Ha. Perhaps, but more than that I am saying fly fishing is an art that breeds the same type of self-awareness that philosophy and true artworks attempt to elucidate: a self-awareness that allows for complete experiential knowledge of authentic being (be that human nature, the river . . . or something even more collective, pervasive).

Like a Zen koan – fly fishing asks the question: is it the fly that catches the fish, or fishing that catches the angler?

Another exemplar of the fly-fishing philosophy is Sam, waist deep in water, clearing frozen eyelets. He and Paul started the #N40 Fly Shop on a clearance inventory and twenty feet of peg board. Fast forward from 2006 to 2015 and there are now four full fly shops, a team of handpicked, passionate guys and an entire range of initiatives designed to raise awareness of the art of fly fishing. From destination trips to #PassItOn, Sam and the fly shop guys have been a driving force in spreading the 'word' of the flies.

#PassItOn is a way of paying it forward. It is a program designed to get young fly fishers into the lifestyle that is embodied by the guys at the fly shop.

It is a way to foster passion in a younger generation. The program accepts used gear in exchange for a discount on new gear. That gear is then used to outfit the younger generation and get them out on the water.

I won't get any more expansive or encompassing than I already have – the trip out with these guys solidified for me the fact that it's not only passion that unifies true fly fishermen – it's the act itself, like any art, that allows a person to develop a true awareness of themselves – and in developing that awareness, perhaps another precept is revealed: 'Know thyself.'

I'll leave it here with a few relevant quotes that blend lit, philo and fish:

'Some go to church and think about fishing, others go fishing and think about God.'

> – Tony Blake

'Creeps and idiots cannot conceal themselves for long on a fishing trip.'

> – John Gierach

'The charm of fishing is that it is the pursuit of what is elusive but attainable, a perpetual series of occasions for hope.'

> – John Buchan

Farm Ponds

JOHN GIERACH

I THINK THE FIRST fish I ever caught was a bluegill from a pond on my uncle's farm in Indiana, but I can't be absolutely sure. You'd think that would be something you'd never forget – like any number of other firsts I could mention – but although that memory would be no more than about forty years old now, it has become obscured by subsequent fish, of which, I have to say, there have been quite a few.

I suppose my first fish could just as easily have been a little bullhead from the creek at home, but there's something about that pond I can't get out of my mind.

I remember it as small, so, given the propensity of things from childhood to loom larger than they really were, it must have been tiny – maybe a few acres at most. There were cattails growing at the shallow end and the water near the dike was deep enough to swim in, though I never thought it was all that inviting. There were too many weeds and sticks that seemed to want to grab you, and there was this morbid curiosity I had about what else might be down there. I never did get to be much of a swimmer.

The pond stood out in the open not far from the house; a low, unimpressive disk of water you could see from a long way off. Its banks were grazed-over pasture trampled to mud, and there were no trees for shade. The water was clear, though. I can remember wading in the shallows and watching the crawdads skitter along the bottom in front of me. Usually I'd spot their trails of silt first, then the creatures themselves. Eventually I overcame my fear of the pincers enough to try and catch them by hand, at least the little ones that were around in the spring. It wasn't easy.

There wouldn't have been much in the way of natural structure in the pond. It was set in a shallow draw with a seasonal stream running through it, so the bottom would have been shaped like an elongated bowl. But I think I recall Uncle Leonard sinking some old tires and brush in there for fish habitat. Leonard was a serious fisherman and knew about those things. I don't think they referred to it as 'structure' then. I think they just called it 'old tires and slash.' They didn't call it 'habitat,' either. They just said the fish liked it.

One thing I remember clearly is the electric fence you had to cross to get to the pond. Uncle Leonard – being an advocate of one-trial learning – let me go ahead and touch it so I'd know why I was being told *not* to touch it. Leonard once told me, 'Dogs and kids aren't good with ideas, but they learn well from experience.'

In the beginning at least, I fished the pond with a stick, string and worm, along with my cousins Rod and Shorty (Roger and Norma Jean to company). All we knew about fishing was, if you put a worm on a hook and sank it in the water, a fish might eventually come along and eat it. We didn't understand that exactly where in the water, let alone when, might make a difference.

Mostly we got little sunfish, and not too many of those. I know now that's because we mostly fished in the wrong places and because we usually did it in the middle of the day – at the worst possible time.

Leonard, of course, had the thing wired. He'd go out to the pond by himself and come back in an hour or so with enough big bass for supper. These were fish of a size and kind I'd never gotten myself, even though I'd spent a fair amount of time on the same pond. They also reinforced that suspicion that kept me from wanting to swim: the idea that there were things in the water you might not know about. I was astonished. Clearly, there was more to all this than I'd thought.

Leonard fished in the evenings when it was cool and the light was off the water, or sometimes at night when we kids were getting ready to go to bed. We assumed he went out then because that was when the work was finished.

Sometimes he used worms just like we did, but there were also minnows, crawdads, frogs, grubs, crickets and grasshoppers in evidence from time to time. He said that, yes, the kind of bait could make a difference, but added, 'That ain't all there is to it.'

Right, I could see that.

And sometimes he used these plugs with shiny metal scoops and blades on them and painted eyes and scales. Except for the dangling hooks, they had the bright look of toys. I liked them a lot but, although I could see they were supposed to be frogs or minnows, I couldn't believe a fish would actually mistake them for the real thing. Unless this was some kind of elaborate joke (which was always a possibility), Leonard must be right when he said, 'Fish don't think like we do.'

Eventually Leonard showed me how it was done, or, rather, he let me come along and watch and pick up what I could, provided I could keep quiet and stay more or less out of the way. He'd never lecture, but he'd try to answer whatever questions I felt like asking because the type of question would indicate how much information I was able to absorb. That way I didn't get confused and he didn't have to talk any more than was absolutely necessary.

Actually, Leonard was quite a talker most of the time, but on the water he'd go into a trancelike silence for long periods of time. Adults still tell kids to be quiet so they don't scare the fish, but that's not the real reason. It's just hard to explain to a child that a kind of profound physical and mental stillness is required if you want to catch fish. That's one of those things you have to come to on your own. Anyway, I learned not to chatter, and also to choose my questions well and ask them quietly.

Sometimes Leonard would pay me the supreme compliment of saying 'I don't know' instead of making something up, although he could make up some great stuff when he was in the mood. If anything, I appreciate that even more now than I did then, but it still sticks in my mind as one of the first times an adult was honest with me.

There were some years in there when all I wanted to do in the summer was go see Uncle Leonard. That hung on for a while even after my family moved to Minnesota and there was some distance involved. The trips were fewer and farther between then, but they meant a ride on the Vista Dome Limited from Minneapolis to Chicago, a classy train from the days when people really traveled that way. These were my first long journeys alone, and if anyone asked I didn't say I was going to visit my uncle, I said I was going fishing. I was eleven or twelve years old by then and I felt pretty damned worldly.

I'd always gotten along with Leonard, but when my dad and I eventually got into the normal bad times fathers and sons go through, I got interested in the difference between him and my uncle. It didn't occur to me until years later that the main difference was, one *was* an uncle and the other was a dad – two positions with very singular job descriptions.

I always felt like Leonard was telling me the truth as he saw it, while Dad was making what I now see as the classic mistake of telling me the world *was*, in fact, the way he thought it *should* be. The evidence for his position was not always compelling and there was a time when I thought my father was, if not a liar, then at least a propagandist.

Dad would sometimes tell me what I *would*, by God, do when I got older because that's what everyone did, while Leonard, when he said anything at all, tended to allow that I'd do what I thought was best when the time came.

The only limp advice Leonard ever gave me had to do with a girl I went to high school with whom I wanted to seduce. I don't remember exactly what he said, but it was seriously out of character: some kind of obligatory version of what he knew Dad would have said if I'd have dared to ask him about it, namely, 'Keep it in your pants because everyone your age keeps it in his pants,' even though we both knew everyone didn't. It was an awkward moment for both of us.

I finally realized that Dad was an idealist. I came to respect him for that in time, became something of an idealist myself and saw how that can make you impatient. On the other hand, Leonard once told me he didn't care if a guy was an idealist or a Presbyterian as long as he pulled his own weight. Interestingly enough, both of these guys were good fishermen.

In later years I would come to understand the concept of sport, but a farmer in the Midwest of the 1950s had a somewhat different perspective on recreation. That is, he viewed everything he did as a chore, although he'd admit that some chores were more enjoyable than others. When he picked up his rod, Leonard would usually say something like, 'Well, I guess I better go fishing' in the same tone of voice he'd use for 'I guess I better get that tire changed.'

The job here was to collect supper, and the only fish Leonard ever released ('threw back,' that is) were the ones that were too little to keep. When he got as many as he wanted, he'd quit. To him, fish were a crop that just happened to be fun to harvest, and I think it delighted him to be able to cheat the work ethic that way.

To me, fun was fun, although when it was done in the company of an adult and the gratification wasn't immediate, there did seem to be a deeper meaning to it. There were these big fish in there that you could get if you did everything just right, and doing it right could be different today than it was yesterday. Furthermore, there were days when the adult couldn't figure it out any better than I could, and that gave me my first hint that I was not, in fact, stupid (as

I often felt around grown-ups) but that the world was just a complex place where, as Leonard said, 'Some days you get the elevator and some days you get the shaft.'

Occasionally there were some very large bass. I won't try to guess at their size now because I was young and small then and this was a long time ago, but some of them were big enough to scare me a little, even though I still wanted them badly. The fine balance between those two emotions was delicious, and toothy fish like pike and big trout still do that to me. The rod, reel and line become not only instruments for catching fish, but also a way to keep some of these things at a safe distance until you can grab them just right.

It was one of those great mysteries that take hold of you early in life, and so I grew up to be one of those who, for better or worse, take their fishing seriously. Consequently, I got into fly-fishing, an area where considerations of sport come before those of practicality. I believe I stopped short of becoming a snob, though, and I think I owe that to farm ponds. These little puddles filled with panfish and surrounded by cows teach you early on that fishing is not necessarily a fine art.

Farm ponds are a standard fixture in rural America, as ordinary and necessary as barns and barbed wire. You need water for the stock, so you dam a creek or dike up a swale to make a pond. In drier country you might have to sink a well and erect a windmill, or capture irrigation water. There's a science to this, not to mention volumes of water law. You have to know about drainages, soils and dike construction, and you have to be sure you actually have the rights to the water in the first place.

Here in the West, wars were fought over that kind of thing. They're still being fought, for that matter, but now people use lawyers instead of rifles, which makes it even nastier.

Once you had your pond, you naturally tossed some fish in it: probably bluegills and largemouth bass – the two most common warm-water farm pond fish in the US – although other combinations have been known to work, too, and in cooler water you could stock trout. You did this because you were a farmer or a rancher and so you were in favor of self-sufficiency and against waste. This seems to be a genetic predisposition. There's something in the collective rural American consciousness that abhors a fishless body of water.

Some other things would probably arrive on their own in time: things like frogs, the eggs of which might be carried in stuck to the legs of herons. These birds might have dropped by the first year to see what was up and found a largely sterile body of water, although if they came back the next spring there'd be fresh tadpoles to eat.

Many of the aquatic insects would arrive under their own power, while cattail seeds, and maybe the seeds of some trees as well, came via the wind. No one knows where the bullheads came from, but they were always there. Someone once said the entire earth is covered with dormant bullhead eggs that hatch as soon as they get wet.

It's a case of what John Cole calls 'natural persistence.' We humans try to control things, but, for better or worse, the natural process moves in as soon as your back is turned to show you you're not entirely in charge.

Anyway, the dike was built, the water pooled and the organisms that liked it showed up in their own good time. To each new arrival, the place became irreplaceable overnight, as if it had been there for a hundred thousand years. And as long as a pond held water year-round, it would gradually soften at the edges and begin to go wild. A three-generations-old farm pond – one that has attracted cottonwood trees, ducks, muskrats, and such – can be almost indistinguishable from a small, natural lake.

If you happen to enjoy fishing, a dock may have sprouted just as naturally, and sooner or later you'd probably barter yourself into a small boat of some kind. Not a bass boat or anything like that – you'd want a good, workable fish pond and a boat to match, but this was not what you'd call a big-ticket operation. All you needed was some old wooden scow that would stay afloat for a couple hours in the evening.

When the boat finally waterlogged and sank, you might have gotten a new one and left the old wreck on the bottom, planning to dispose of it properly when you got around to it. But there'd be lots of more important things to do, and in time the gunwales would become a faint outline down there in the weeds and muck. Given enough neglect the boat would finally dissolve altogether, saving you a couple hours of muddy work.

If you were like the farmers I remember from my childhood, you wouldn't take the pond too seriously or get too fancy about it, but you'd probably manage it some in an effort to grow the biggest, healthiest fish possible. You might even go to the trouble of calling the County Extension Agent for advice and then buying some fish from a hatchery. Then again, that would cost money, so maybe you'd just catch a few bucketfuls of fish in another pond and haul them in, figuring if they took they'd be free, and if they didn't you wouldn't have wasted any money. Money was precious, but work was just work. There was an endless supply of it.

You'd fish the pond yourself when you had time, for kicks, a good free meal or both. Your kids, and maybe a young nephew, would catch their first fish there, and if you were a nice guy, you might let the occasional stranger fish it as well, if he asked nicely and looked OK.

That's how most of us come to farm ponds as adults: we ask around or just knock on strange doors and humbly ask to fish. It doesn't always work, but if we're polite and don't look like mass murderers, it works often enough.

Maybe you spotted the pond while driving through farm country on your way somewhere else. There may have been fish rising in it, or maybe it just seemed right somehow. A good pond can have a certain look to it, although it's hard to describe exactly what that entails. Vegetation, shade and flooded trees are all good signs, but beyond that there's this kind of beckoning green warmth about it, like the collective auras of fifty largemouth bass hovering over the water. Whatever it is, it's sometimes possible to spot it in a split second at a thousand yards from the window of a speeding automobile.

I've known fishermen to do considerable research on farm ponds and private reservoirs, consulting county maps, aerial photos and tax records. Often people who go to that kind of trouble are looking for something to lease, but not always. Some of them are just hunting for something that's great because it's obscure, and they understand you can't see every farm pond in America from a public road.

Of course there are fishermen who won't look at a farm pond twice, probably because they're sometimes not very pretty as bodies of water go. These would be the same guys who go somewhere exotic, catch lots of huge fish in some lush wilderness, and then claim they're spoiled for anything less; people who have forgotten that, although fishing *can* be an adventure, it is basically just an ordinary, everyday aspect of a good life.

To me, it's the very homeliness of farm ponds that makes them so tantalizing. Some ponds are so well camouflaged that no one pays much attention to them, and so, when the conditions are right, populations of virtually wild fish can just percolate in there, growing larger and larger and not getting especially smart. In this way, a seedy little farm pond is more of a natural setting than a highly regulated catch-and-release trout stream.

If you stay in one part of the country long enough, you might be able to develop a modest network of farm ponds that you can get on. You'll end up with some good, easy-going fishing close to home, and in private moments you can congratulate yourself for being cagey and connected in the finest tradition of the local fisherman. It'll help if you're not too shy about asking, and if you can accept rejection gracefully. It's a cardinal rule of farm ponds that if the man says no, then no it is, and he doesn't even have to explain why.

Now and then money will change hands (and I don't think money is dirty in this context), though often the exchange is something more personal, like some cleaned fish, or a six-pack.

This all fits in nicely with my personal vision of what a fisherman should be. He can be classy if he likes, but beneath that he's funky, rural, practical and not unacquainted with hard work. By that I mean, he may not actually *do* hard work, but at least he knows it when he sees it, which, in turn, means he knows enough to close the gates behind him without being told.

And, most of all, he's not entirely blinded by the scenery and the trappings. Sure, he can have a weakness for trout and big, pretty rivers, but if it's cows and chickens wandering around the banks of the pond (rather than, say, mule deer and blue grouse), then so be it. If the fish don't care, why should he?

My friends and I will usually show up at a farm pond all decked out for high sport with neoprene waders, belly boats, fly rods, cameras: the whole thing. We remember when it was different, but this is just how we do it now. We have become fly fishermen.

Between us we carry fly patterns that imitate just about any warm-water food organism you can name, plus those goofy things that have what pass for anatomical features, but that nonetheless look like nothing nature has ever produced on this planet. After all, fish don't think like we do.

Sometimes we'll take the temperature of the water, someone usually knows what the barometer is doing at the moment and there may be talk of water chemistry, aquatic vegetation, moon phase, photo-periods as they relate to spawning and feeding activity, insect migration patterns and so on.

Now and then the owner of the pond will be impressed. More likely he'll be amused and a little puzzled, wondering how we got it into our heads that anything, let alone fishing, was that complicated.

Acknowledgements

Special thanks to the following people who made this book possible: Duncan Proudfoot, Clive Hebard and everyone at Constable & Robinson for believing in *Taut Lines*; Henry Hughes, Frank Amato, Jeff VanderMeer, Ross E. Lockhart, John Skipp, Rose O'Keefe, and Carlton Mellick III for their invaluable assistance and inspiration; the Mellon Foundation, Rhodes University, Paul Wessels, Robert Berold, and Stacy Hardy for cultivating the seed of *Taut Lines*; the ghosts of Richard Brautigan and Caspar Whitney for unwittingly hovering over my shoulder; and Kirsten, my wife and biggest catch, for the ceaseless love and companionship.

Publication Acknowledgements

'They've All Got That Old Jitterbug Spirit: An Interview with Bill Dance.' Originally published in *ManArchy Magazine*, 2013. Reprinted by permission.

'The Man in the Fish Tote' by Tele Aadsen: © 2012 by Tele Aadsen. Originally published at www.teleaadsen.com. Reprinted by permission of the author.

'Why I Fish' by Kim Barnes: © 2012 by Kim Barnes. Originally published in *Astream: American Writers on Fly Fishing*. Reprinted by permission of the author.

'Treatise of Fishing with an Angle' by Dame Juliana Berners. Originally published in *The Book of St. Albans*, 1496.

'Fish' by Judith Barrington: © 1989 by Judith Barrington. Originally published in *History and Geography* and republished in *Uncommon Waters*. Reprinted by permission of the author.

'The Holy Anglers' by Charles Bradford. Originally published in *The Determined Angler and the Brook Trout*, 1900.

'A New Hand at the Rod' by C.R.C. Originally published in *Outing Magazine*, 1890.

'Magic Hooks' by Brian Allen Carr: © 2016 by Brian Allen Carr. Original to this anthology.

'Chum Some of This: *Jaws* and its Legacy' by Adam Cesare: © 2016 by Adam Cesare. Original to this anthology.

'The Ethics of Skipping School' by Eric J. Chambers: © 2014 by Eric J. Chambers. Originally published in *Tidal Grace*. Reprinted by permission of the publisher.

'Buoy 10: Salmon Fishing in the Half Pipe' by Bill Monroe: © 2008, 2010, 2011, 2012, 2013, 2014, 2015, 2016 by Bill Monroe. Originally published in *The Oregonian* in altered form. Reprinted by permission of the author.

'Trout in Africa: A British Legacy' by Bill Monroe: © 2014 Bill Monroe. Originally published in *The Oregonian*. Reprinted by permission of the author.

'I Used to be a Fisherman' by Weston Ochse: © 2013 by Weston Ochse. Originally published in *Living Dangerously* in altered form. Reprinted by permission of the author.

'Right There' by J. David Osborne: © 2016 by J. David Osborne. Original to this anthology.

'Fishing with a Worm' by Bliss Perry. Originally published in *The Atlantic*, 1904.

'Trophies' by Cameron Pierce: © 2015 by Cameron Pierce. Originally published in *Our Love Will Go the Way of the Salmon*. Reprinted by permission of the author.

'Fishing the Ancient Headwaters' by James Prosek: © 1999 by James Prosek. Originally published in *Audubon Magazine*. Reprinted by permission of the author.

'Garfish' by Jason Rizos: © 2016 by Jason Rizos. Original to this anthology.

'The Fishes of Our Boyhood' by Ed. W. Sandys. Originally published in *The Norfolk Virginian*, 1897.

'The Metaphysics of Fly Fishing' by Cutter Streeby: © 2015 by Cutter Streeby. Originally published in *North 40 Fly Shop Magazine*. Reprinted by permission of the author.

'Big Fish in an Enormous Pond' by Jeremy Wade: © 1998 by Jeremy Wade. Originally published in *Sunday Telegraph*. Reprinted by permission of the author.

'Observations of the Bream' and 'Observations of the Carp' by Izaak Walton. Originally published in *The Compleat Angler*, 1653.

'Without a Backward Cast: Notes of an Angler' by Katharine Weber: © 1991 by Katharine Weber. Originally published in *Uncommon Waters*. Reprinted by permission of the author.

'Bats, Bushes, and Barbless Hooks' by Eric Witchey: © 2016 by Eric Witchey. Original to this anthology.

About the Editor

Cameron Pierce is the Wonderland Book Award-winning author of fifteen books, including the critically acclaimed collections *The Incoming Tide* and *Our Love Will Go the Way of the Salmon*. In 2015, he was the Mellon writer-in-residence at Rhodes University in Grahamstown, South Africa. His work has appeared in *Gray's Sporting Journal*, *Flyfishing & Tying Journal*, *The Barcelona Review*, *Vol. I Brooklyn*, *The Big Click*, and many other publications. He lives with his wife and daughter in Astoria, Oregon.

A List of Fish Illustrations

 Bluegill

 Black Crappie

 Steelhead

 Brook Trout

 Rainbow Trout

 Yellow Perch

Index

S

salmon 6, 68, 73–5, 287, 290
    Atlantic 26, 72, 278
    Chinook 1, 12, 63–6, 214–16,
      219, 220–1
    coho 213–14, 215
    fishing in Scotland 230–2,
      233
    fishing in the Columbia River
      210–21
    Pacific 26, 278
Salmon River, Oregon 11–12,
    14–15
Sandys, Ed. W. 148–58
Schoeffmann, Johannes 25–6,
    27–8
Schramm, Dorothy 14
Scotland 230–3, 234
Scott, Ray 129
sea fishing *see* ocean/ sea fishing
Sea Isle, Galveston 118–21
sea lions 221
Sea of Galilee, Israel 86–7
sea robins 245
seals 215
seasons and bait for fish, Juliana
    Berners on 290–5
seines 152
self-awareness and fly fishing 298,
    299
Serpentine, Canada 73
sharks 1, 2, 244–50

'sheepshead' (freshwater drum)
    152
Shellfish Restoration Project 242
shooting fish 151, 247–8
Shoreham, West Sussex 228
silver bass 154
Slovenia 27
Smith, John 15
Smith River, California 111–12,
    113–14
snakes 22, 182
Soca River, Slovenia 27
social class and fishing 14–16,
    18–19
softmouth trout 29
South Africa 1
spawning 6, 12, 72, 173–6
spearing fish 151, 152, 153
spinners, fishing with 6, 12, 13, 14,
    22, 63, 212
    see also lures, fishing with
spirituality and fishing 2, 16–18,
    19
    see also nature, fishing and
    connecting with
St. Wolfgang, Austria 84
steelheads 3, 6, 18, 108, 110–17
    see also rainbow trout
Streeby, Cutter 296–9
sturgeon 1, 48, 68, 129, 176
suckerfish 153
sunfish 68, 155, 301

Y
Yaquina River, Oregon 66
yellow perch 155

Z
zooids 122–3